Piercing the Corporate Veil in Latin American Jurisprudence

This book is a comparative law study exploring the piercing of the corporate veil in Latin America within the context of the Anglo-American method.

The piercing of the corporate veil is a remedy applied, in exceptional circumstances, to prevent and punish an inappropriate use of the corporate personality. The application of this remedy and the issues it involves have been widely researched in Anglo-American jurisdictions and, until recently, little attention has been given to this subject in Latin America. This region has been through internal political conflicts that undermined economic development. However, the rise of democratic governments has created the political stability necessary for investment and economic development meaning that the corporate personality is now more commonly used in Latin America. Consequently, corporate personality issues have become a subject of study in this region.

Drawing on case studies from Mexico, Colombia, Brazil and Argentina, *Piercing the Corporate Veil in Latin American Jurisprudence* examines the ingenuity of Latin American jurisdictions to deal with corporate personality issues and compares this method with the Anglo-American framework. Focusing in particular on the influence of two key factors – legal tradition and the uniqueness of each legal system – the author highlights both similarities and differences in the way in which the piercing of the corporate veil is applied in Latin American and Anglo-American jurisdictions.

This book will be of great interest to scholars of company and comparative law, and business studies in general.

José Maria Lezcano Navarro is a Panamanian *Licenciado* (lawyer) who graduated from the University of Panama in 2007. He has an LLM in International Commercial Law awarded by the University of Westminster in 2009, and his PhD was awarded by City University London in 2014.

Routledge research in corporate law

Available titles in this series include:

Corporate Social Responsibility, Human Rights and the Law
Multinational Corporations in Developing Countries
Olufemi Amao

The Political Determinants of Corporate Governance in China
Chenxia Shi

The Enlightened Shareholder Value Principle and Corporate Governance
Andrew Keay

Progressive Corporate Governance for the 21st Century
Lorraine Talbot

Rethinking Corporate Governance
The Law and Economics of Control Powers
Alessio Pacces

Shareholder Primacy and Corporate Governance
Legal Aspects, Practices and Future Directions
Shuangge Wen

Understanding Institutional Shareholder Activism
A Comparative Study of the UK and China
Bo Gong

Directors' Decisions and the Law
Promoting Success
Alice Belcher

Rethinking Corporate Governance in Financial Institutions
Demetra Arsalidou

Board Accountability in Corporate Governance
Andrew Keay

Piercing the Corporate Veil in Latin American Jurisprudence
A comparison with the Anglo-American method
Jose Maria Lezcano Navarro

Forthcoming titles in this series include:

The Changing Nature of Corporate Social Responsibility
CSR and Development – The Case of Mauritius
Renginee Pillay

Legal Approaches and Corporate Social Responsibility
Towards a Llewellyn's law-jobs approach
Adaeze Okoye

Behavioural Risks in Corporate Governance
Regulatory Intervention as a Risk Management Mechanism
Ngozi Vivian Okoye

Piercing the Corporate Veil in Latin American Jurisprudence
A comparison with the Anglo-American method

José Maria Lezcano Navarro

LONDON AND NEW YORK

First published 2016 by Routledge

2 Park Square, Milton Park, Abingdon, Oxfordshire OX14 4RN
711 Third Avenue, New York, NY 10017

*Routledge is an imprint of the Taylor & Francis Group,
an informa business*

First issued in paperback 2018

Copyright © 2016 José Maria Lezcano Navarro

The right of José Maria Lezcano Navarro to be identified as author of
this work has been asserted by him in accordance with sections 77 and
78 of the Copyright, Designs and Patents Act 1988.

All rights reserved. No part of this book may be reprinted or
reproduced or utilised in any form or by any electronic, mechanical,
or other means, now known or hereafter invented, including
photocopying and recording, or in any information storage or
retrieval system, without permission in writing from the publishers.

Notice:
Product or corporate names may be trademarks or registered trademarks,
and are used only for identification and explanation without intent to infringe.

British Library Cataloguing in Publication Data
A catalogue record for this book is available from the British Library

Library of Congress Cataloguing-in-Publication Data
Lezcano Navarro, José Maria, author.
  Piercing the corporate veil in Latin American jurisprudence : a
comparison with the Anglo-American method / José Maria Lezcano
Navarro.
    pages cm. — (Routledge research in corporate law)
  Includes bibliographical references and index.
  1. Corporate veil—Latin America. 2. Corporate veil—United
States. 3. Corporate veil—Great Britain. 4. Corporate governance—
Law and legislation—Latin America. 5. Corporate governance—Law
and legislation—United States. 6. Corporate governance—Law and
legislation—Great Britain. 7. Corporations—Corrupt practices.
8. Commercial crimes. I. Title.
  K1315.L49 2016
  346′.066—dc23
  2015030162

ISBN: 978-1-138-84085-0 (hbk)
ISBN: 978-1-138-61452-9 (pbk)

Typeset in Sabon
by ApexCovantage, LLC

Contents

Introduction   xi

I General aspects regarding the piercing of the corporate veil   1
   1. Concept and rationale of piercing the corporate veil 2
   2. Origins of the doctrine of piercing the corporate veil 4
   3. Piercing the corporate veil in the context of private law
      and public law 8
   4. Pro-social policy and capitalist policy 11
   5. Piercing of the corporate veil, in the context of public
      companies 12
   6. Derivations of piercing the corporate veil 13
      6.1 The reverse piercing of the corporate veil 14
      6.2 The piercing of the corporate veil in the context of
         corporate groups 15
         6.2.1 Regulation and its critics 16
         6.2.2 Rationale to pierce the corporate veil of
            corporate groups 17
         6.2.3 Single economic unit 18
  Personal observation 19

II Piercing the corporate veil in an Anglo-American context   20
   1. Piercing the corporate veil in England 21
      1.1 The case of *Salomon* 21
      1.2 The effects of the *Salomon* precedent 23
         1.2.1 Sham exception 24
         1.2.2 Agency 26
         1.2.3 Single economic unit 28
      1.3 The case of *Adam v Cape Industries* 30
         1.3.1 The facts 31
         1.3.2 The corporate veil point (sham argument) 32
         1.3.3 Single economic unit 33
         1.3.4 The agency argument 33

vi *Contents*

      1.3.5 Reception of *Adams v Cape* decision 34

      1.3.6 The piercing of the corporate veil after *Cape* 35

   1.4 The disregard of the legal entity in the context of English statutory law 38

      1.4.1 Fraudulent and wrongful trading 39

         1.4.1.1 Fraudulent trading 40

         1.4.1.2 Wrongful trading 41

      1.4.2 Abuse of company name (phoenix companies) 43

      1.4.3 Tax law and the English corporate entity 45

Summary 47

2. The doctrine of piercing the corporate veil in the US 48

   2.1 State and federal law 49

   2.2 The doctrines of instrumentality and alter ego 52

      2.2.1 The alter ego doctrine 54

      2.2.2 Instrumentality doctrine 56

   2.3 Reality of the American doctrine 58

      2.3.1 Contract and tort cases 59

      2.3.2 Agency and enterprise liability 61

         2.3.2.1 Agency 62

         2.3.2.2 Single economic unit or enterprise liability 62

         2.3.2.3 The current position of American courts in regard of piercing the corporate veil 64

   2.4 The piercing of the corporate veil in the context of American statutory law 66

      2.4.1 Tax law 66

      2.4.2 Labour law 67

      2.4.3 Environmental law 68

   2.5 The role of the concepts of fraud and negligence in the context of corporate veil issues 69

Summary 73

   2.6 Why does the US appear more willing than England to pierce the corporate veil? 74

      2.6.1 The dilemma between the "sledgehammer approach" and the "backdoor approach" 75

Chapter conclusion 76

III Corporate veil in Latin America; general aspects about Franco-Hispanic civil law that have influenced the development of piercing the corporate veil in Latin America   79

1. The roots of the Latin American civil law tradition 80

2. The corporate personality in the Latin American civil law tradition 81

Contents vii

3. Contrast between the common law and the civil law
tradition; the influence of legal tradition over the piercing
of the corporate veil 82
   3.1 Sources of law 84
   3.2 Role of critical thinking or judicial creativity 85
   3.3 Role of legal concepts and principles 87
Personal observation 88

IV The piercing of the corporate veil in Mexico   89
1. The early manifestation of "*la develación de la sociedad anónima*" 89
   1.1 Other early Mexican statutory exceptions to the corporate entity 91
2. The *ley de la desestimación de la persona jurídica societaria* 92
   2.1 The elements required for the application of this remedy 92
   2.2 Circumstances in which *la desestimación de la persona jurídica societaria* is applied; and the entities subject to this regulation 93
   2.3 Effects of *la desestimación de la persona jurídica societaria* 94
Personal observation 94

V The piercing of the corporate veil in Colombia   96
1. Colombian statutory approach to corporate entity issues 97
   1.1 The *Ley 190 de 1995, Estatuto Anticorrupción* 97
   1.2 The *Ley 222 de 1995* 98
   1.3 The *Ley 1258 de 2008* 101
2. The foundation of the Colombian approach to corporate personality issues 102
3. Controversy between statutory exceptions to the corporate personality and the Colombian constitution 103
Personal observation 105

VI The piercing of the corporate veil in Brazil   107
1. The origins of the Brazilian exception to the corporate personality 108
   1.1 *Lei No 8.078 de 11 de septembro de 1990* 110
   1.2 *Lei No 8.884 de 11 de junho de 1994* 111
   1.3 *Lei No 9.605 de 12 de fevereiro de 1998* 112
2. Brazilian Civil Code 113
Personal observation 114

viii   *Contents*

VII   The piercing of the corporate veil in Argentina   116
　　1. *Inoponibilidad de la persona jurídica* 117
　　2. Sanction derived from the *inoponibilidad de la persona jurídica* 118
　　3. Parameter to apply the *inoponibilidad de la persona jurídica* 119
　　4. Who can summon this remedy? 120
　　5. The occurrence of *ultra vires* 121
　　6. Corporate personality issues in Argentina before the rule of *inoponibilidad de la persona jurídica* 122
　　Personal observation 125

VIII   Comparative study between the Anglo-American and Latin American piercing of the corporate veil   127
　　1. Methodology 127
　　2. Rationale to pierce the corporate veil 128
　　　　2.1 US 129
　　　　2.2 England 129
　　　　2.3 Argentina 130
　　　　2.4 Colombia 131
　　　　2.5 Brazil 132
　　　　2.6 Mexico 132
　　　　2.7 Comparison 133
　　3. Legal concepts and principles 134
　　　　3.1 US 134
　　　　3.2 England 134
　　　　3.3 Latin America 135
　　　　　　3.3.1 Argentina 136
　　　　　　3.3.2 Colombia 136
　　　　　　3.3.3 Brazil 137
　　　　　　3.3.4 Mexico 137
　　　　3.4 Comparison 138
　　4. The means to achieve the objective of a mechanism to deal with corporate personality issues 139
　　　　4.1 Sledgehammer approach 139
　　　　　　4.1.1 US 139
　　　　　　4.1.2 Colombia 139
　　　　　　4.1.3 Mexico 140
　　　　　　4.1.4 Brazil 140
　　　　4.2 Backdoor approach 140
　　　　　　4.2.1 England 140
　　　　　　4.2.2 Argentina 141
　　　　4.3 Overall observation 141
　　Personal observation 141

Conclusion   142

Bibliography   145
Index   158

Introduction

The contemporary corporate entity can be considered a pillar of modern capitalist society. It is so due to its attributes of legal personality and limited liability. On the one hand, legal personality allows the corporate entity to own assets, to contract, to sue and be sued; in other words, these attributes allow the corporate entity to interact with society. However, limited liability establishes that the individuals behind the corporate entity are only liable to the extent of their contributions to the company's assets. The importance of these attributes is in the fact that legal personality reduces management and legal costs, and limited liability motivates investors to participate in ambitious projects. If these attributes were not present, the developments enjoyed throughout the last century would have not been possible.

The existence of the corporate entity as an independent and incorporeal creature has not been free of controversy. Since its conception, members' exemption of liability from corporate acts has been questioned. This has been an issue since there are circumstances where, for example, a creditor may wonder if the debtor is trying to avoid an obligation by using the corporate entity. Moreover, fraud tends to be argued. A disconcerted client may argue that the corporate entity was created with the intention to defraud, something that may not necessarily be true. This issue can be attributed to the fact that the contemporary corporate entity was conceived without considering the impact of its misuse. Therefore, this has given rise to what is legally known as the *piercing of the corporate veil*.

The piercing of the corporate veil is a metaphor created in the US courts in order to describe the separate existence between the corporate entity and its members. This metaphor describes the existence of an imaginary veil between the corporate entity and its members, which can be pierced in exceptional circumstances. The piercing of this imaginary veil has been the base on which US jurisprudence has dealt with corporate personality issues and the exceptional circumstances that have been the occurrence of fraud. The concept of fraud, however, is too wide. Therefore, US jurisprudence has gradually shaped the concept of fraud in accord to the circumstances in which the corporate entity is commonly misused.

xii *Introduction*

The US piercing of the corporate veil has been the subject of interest in other jurisdictions. However, this does not mean that the US method has been copied in other jurisdictions. Rather, the mechanisms to deal with corporate personality issues are something that each jurisdiction has developed in accordance with its internal legal needs. It has to be pointed out that to some extent concepts that are part of the North American approach, such as control and fraud, have been used in many jurisdictions. However, the meaning of control and fraud as well as the parameters to determine its occurrence tend to be developed according to the circumstances that generate corporate personality issues in each jurisdiction. This is owing to the fact that the corporate personality, the concept of control and fraud can be considered as something universal yet are implemented in accordance with the circumstances of each jurisdiction.

Based on the uniqueness of each legal system, in this book it is argued that corporate entity issues are dealt by each jurisdiction individually. This is an argument based on the uniqueness of each jurisdiction, as previously mentioned, and the demand for remedies that do not disturb the legal harmony present in each legal system. In order to develop this argument, a comparative law study is presented in this book.

A comparative law study is the most adequate means to support the argument of this book because it allows one to look beyond the North American doctrine. It has to be pointed out that piercing of the corporate veil tends to be addressed from an Anglo-American perspective. Indeed, whenever corporate entity issues are mentioned, minds immediately focus on the North American doctrine. Consequently, other perspectives are ignored.

Latin American countries, specifically Argentina, Colombia, Brazil and Mexico, have been chosen as subjects of study. This is due to circumstances in which the piercing of the corporate veil has been developed in this region. Firstly, Latin America is a region that has developed its legal framework based on the civil law tradition, due to the colonial influence. For that reason, authorities tend to strictly follow positive law; a fact that contrasts the common law approach where authorities have more freedom to act beyond the scope of positive law. Secondly, Latin American countries are relatively new economies. Thus, corporate entity issues are an occurrence that started around three decades ago. This is attributed to the fact that only countries with dynamic economies have experienced corporate personality issues. For most of the twentieth century, while the US and Europe were experiencing industrialization and the economic boom, and were consequently facing corporate personality issues, Latin American countries were fighting for their independence or were under dictatorial regimes. It was not until the late 1970s that Latin American countries gained political stability and gradually started to develop. Therefore, corporate entity issues can be considered as a novelty in the region. Thirdly, Latin American mechanisms are an example that supports the argument presented in this book. Argentina, Colombia, Brazil and Mexico have been chosen as subjects of study because of their advances in this subject. Argentina is the Latin American jurisdiction that pioneered the use of a remedy that directly deals with corporate personality issues. Colombia has a peculiar type of business association that has a regulation that includes a remedy in case of misuse. Brazil has an exception to the corporate entity in its Civil Code, the pillar of the corporate entity. Finally, Mexico is the only jurisdiction with a statute that systematically addresses the disregard of the corporate entity. Although this statute is not in force, it evidences the willingness of Mexican authorities to deal with issues derived from the corporate entity. Each of the chosen jurisdictions offers a case study that has been briefly developed in this book.

In order to develop this comparative study, a functional comparative approach has been adopted. This method is based on the function a legal mechanism has in a jurisdiction. In our case study, the piercing of the corporate veil is a remedy pioneered by the US. Every company law academic and practitioner is familiar with the US doctrine of piercing the corporate veil – a remedy that aims to punish the misuse of the corporate entity. Thus, in this book, this jurisdiction has been taken as a template from which a comparison can be drawn. The objective is to support the argument on which this book has been structured; the individuality of each jurisdiction when it comes to deal with corporate entity issues. Through this comparative study, the different mechanisms that exist in Latin America are going to be demonstrated. These are mechanisms that are used to achieve a similar result to that achieved by the American doctrine. Therefore, it is demonstrated that Latin American countries have not had the need to borrow the North American mechanism in order to pierce the corporate veil.

This book has been structured in eight chapters. The first chapter is about general aspects of the corporate veil. This chapter aims to provide an insight into the subject of the corporate veil. It addresses things related to the corporate personality such as its origins and the relevance it has gained throughout the years. This chapter also addresses the different variations that the corporate entity has experienced due to the emergence of corporate groups and the evolution of commerce. In addition, the position of the author regarding certain aspects of piercing the corporate veil will be presented. The second chapter focuses on the piercing of the corporate veil in an Anglo-American context. As has been pointed out, the US is the jurisdiction adopted as the template in order to conduct this comparative study. Therefore, this chapter addresses the general aspects of the US approach to corporate personality issues. Furthermore, this chapter addresses corporate personality issues in England. The rationale for the inclusion of England is based on two factors; firstly, England was the pioneer in the use of the contemporary corporate entity for commercial purposes; and, secondly, the case of England feeds this comparative study. Although the US and England follow common law traditions, the difference between the legal systems produces different needs. Consequently, corporate entity issues have been dealt with differently in their jurisdictions. This fact is key to the argument presented in this book, xiv *Introduction*

namely the individuality of each jurisdiction. The third chapter is about the aspects of the Franco-Hispanic civil law tradition on which the Latin American legal framework has been developed. It also regards the influence this legal tradition has had on the way corporate veil issues have been handled throughout this region. In this chapter, basic aspects of civil law tradition will be addressed as well as traditional legal concepts and principles that played an important role in the development of the mechanisms employed to deal with corporate entity issues in Latin American countries. The fourth chapter turns attention to Mexico. A brief historical review of the Mexican corporate entity and its issues is provided and the development of the Mexican statute aimed at systematically applying the disregard of the corporate entity is addressed. In this chapter, the rational for this law proposal will be studied as well as the reasons for it not to be in force. The fifth chapter concerns Colombia. In this chapter, the rationale behind the Colombian exceptions to the corporate entity will be addressed. The complication between these exceptions and the Colombian constitution shall also be discussed. The sixth chapter regards Brazil. This is a relevant case study because its mechanism is supported by an exception to the corporate entity contained in the Brazilian Civil Code. This chapter will address the development of this exception to the corporate entity. The seventh chapter is about Argentina. This is a jurisdiction that pioneered the use of a remedy to deal with corporate personality issues. This, along with the rationale for the mechanism's application, shall be discussed. Chapter VIII develops the comparative study on grounds of the functional comparative approach. In this chapter, the peculiarities of each jurisdiction subject of study is brought to light.

This book has been developed to provide a guide regarding Latin American civil law tradition in the context of corporate entity issues. This book is written for researchers who are interested in corporate personality issues. It provides a refreshingly unique case study.

I General aspects regarding the piercing of the corporate veil

The piercing of the corporate veil appears as a mechanism to deal with the imperfections of the corporate personality. The corporate personality was conceived as a perfect means to achieve high profit at a low risk, but gradually the flaws of this invention started to manifest. Opportunists started to use the corporate personality for their own benefit with no regard of the negative effects their activities may have over third parties. Consequently, the piercing of the corporate veil appeared as one of the means to deal with this complication.

It has to be pointed out that the corporate personality, as we know it today, was developed in England at the end of the nineteenth century due to needs resulting from the industrialization of manufacture.[1] Then, on the other side of the Atlantic Ocean, the US adopted the English business entity in order to accelerate the development of its infrastructure (i.e. railways and ports).[2] As a result, both jurisdictions provided the foundations of the contemporary corporate entity, which was then adopted by jurisdictions in Europe and Latin America and molded in accordance with the commercial needs of each jurisdiction.

The fact that England and the US pioneered the corporate personality also made them the first to experience corporate veil issues and therefore the first jurisdictions to apply a mechanism to deal with the corporate veil. Later, mechanisms to pierce the corporate veil were developed in Europe and Latin America. However, it must be stressed that each developed this remedy in accordance with the needs of its legal framework.

In this first chapter the general aspects of piercing of the corporate veil, derived from the application of this remedy throughout the years, will be addressed. In addition, this chapter presents the arguments of the author

---

1 Rickett, C. & Grantham, R. (1998) 'The Bookmaker's Legacy to Company Law Doctrine'. In: Rickett, C. & Grantham, R. (eds.) *Corporate Personality in the 20th Century*. Oxford, UK: Hart Publishing. Page 2.
2 Beattly, J. (2001) *Colossus: How the Corporation Changed America*. New York: Broadway Books. Page 45.

2 General aspects of piercing the corporate veil

regarding certain aspects of piercing the corporate veil. These arguments shall be supported throughout this book.

1. Concept and rationale of piercing the corporate veil

In this book, piercing the corporate veil is defined as the means to ignore the corporation's legal personality and hold shareholders liable for the acts and obligations of the corporation.

Originally, company law in common law and civil law jurisdictions did not include an exception to the corporate personality and limited liability.[3] The early issues that required ignoring the existence of the corporate veil were addressed through traditional legal concepts and legal devices that could be applied depending on the circumstances of the case. Gradually, approaches[4] to deal with corporate veil issues have been introduced. Nonetheless it has to be pointed out that the legal tradition followed by a country is a factor that has influenced the way an approach to pierce the corporate veil has been developed in each jurisdiction. This premise is developed from the fact that judges in common and civil law jurisdictions have a different degree of freedom when using critical thinking. On the one hand, the common law judge has the ability to act beyond the boundaries of statutory law, which has been useful in dealing with corporate veil issues. Consequently, common law jurisdictions have relied on doctrinal approaches to deal with corporate veil issues. On the other hand, in civil law jurisdictions the piercing of the corporate veil has been addressed in an alternative way due to the limitations of the civil law judge to act beyond a statute. Civil law jurisdictions have relied mainly on statutory exceptions to the corporate personality.

The piercing of the corporate veil has a different basis depending on whether it is applied in a common law or civil law jurisdiction. However,

---

3 It is important to add that unlike legal personality, limited liability usually is not mandatory for all corporations. Limited liability is a concept separate to corporate personality. Consequently, it is possible to deal with liability issues without affecting the integrity of the corporate personality. A common way is to contract around limited liability; for example, a creditor that contracts with a company is actually contracting with the company and not with the shareholders. Therefore, the creditor and the company are the parties of the contracts, not the shareholders, who would be regarded as third parties in this situation. The creditor, however, can seek personal guarantees from shareholders in order to secure his credit. Consequently, if the company defaults, the creditor can recover his credit from the shareholders without affecting the corporate personality. This fact describes a means to deal *ex ante* with liability issues. However, in corporate veil issues, usually no preventative measures have been taken by the plaintiff, thus the lack of a statutory exception to the corporate personality and shareholders limited liability creates a difficult situation.

4 Examples of approaches to deal with corporate personality issues are the American doctrine of instrumentality and the Argentinean *inoponibilidad de la persona juridical*. Each is explained later in this book.

General aspects of piercing the corporate veil 3

there is a factor that common and civil law jurisdictions share – the rationale to apply this remedy: "the prevention and punishment of fraud".[5]

The prevention and punishment of fraud have been the justification for the creation of an exception to the corporate veil. However, in the context of the corporate veil, the definition of fraudulent behavior varies across common and civil law jurisdictions. There is not a concrete definition of what can be seen as fraudulent behavior. Consequently, it can be considered that each jurisdiction uniquely engages itself in determining what can be viewed as fraud in this context.

It should be added that, in both common and civil law jurisdictions, the piercing of the corporate veil has been a controversial subject. The corporate personality has gradually gained relevance due to the socio-economic benefits it produces. Consequently, in common law and civil law jurisdictions, a tendency to preserve the corporate veil has been developed. This tendency has been founded on the fact that if the corporate veil could be easily pierced, there would not be any point in incorporating a company, as every claim against the company would most probably jeopardize the investors' assets.[6] Consequently, investors would be reluctant to participate in risky enterprises and the socio-economic benefits produced by the corporate veil would be lost.[7] Therefore, in most jurisdictions piercing the corporate veil is considered a last resource.[8]

In summary, the piercing of the corporate veil is a remedy used to prevent and punish the fraudulent use of the corporate personality. Furthermore, it is a remedy that each jurisdiction has developed individually and shaped in accordance to the social, political and economic factors of a particular jurisdiction.

---

5 I regard the prevention and punishment of fraud as the rationale for piercing the corporate veil. Certainly, each jurisdiction has a different legal system and needs. However, the concept of corporate personality and all it entails is universal. In common and civil law jurisdictions, the corporate entity is recognized but its existence has been questioned mainly on grounds of fraud. Other issues that do not necessarily involve the occurrence of fraud have also triggered the debate over the corporate personality. Nonetheless, fraud has been the main reason to consider this action. This is an argument that I will discuss throughout this thesis and support with my comparative study.

6 Piercing the corporate veil is a remedy that has countered centuries of legal decisions that clearly state that the corporation is a separate legal entity and its owners are not responsible for debts or judgments against it. This remedy definitely undermines the corporate personality and the benefits it produces. See, Bevans, N. (2007) *Business Organization and Corporate Law*. US: Thomson Delmar Learning. Page 275.

7 The author Joel Moskowitz considers there is fear among small businesses in regard to the dramatic consequences of piercing the corporate veil. This fear is founded on losing all assets due to unlimited liability. This fear prevents investors from engaging in what may be considered risky enterprises. See, Moskowitz, J. (1995) *Environmental liability and Real Property Transactions*. 2nd Edition. New York: Aspen Law & Business. At pages 100–2

8 See, Kraakman, R. & Others (2009) *The Anatomy of Corporate Law; A Comparative and Functional Approach*. Oxford: Oxford University Press. At page 139

4   *General aspects of piercing the corporate veil*

2.   Origins of the doctrine of piercing the corporate veil

The piercing of the corporate veil has its origins in the advent of the modern English joint stock company. The joint stock company is considered a person, an entity with capacity to act in the legal world and to be liable. These attributes generate the imaginary veil that separates the shareholders from the corporate entity. However, the corporate veil and the corporate entity, as we know them today, are not a creation of our times.

The legal entity known as corporation was created in Europe during the Middle Ages but its use was limited to political and religious purposes.[9] The early manifestations of the corporate entity as a commercial device happened during the sixteenth and seventeenth centuries. In this period of history, English and Dutch "chartered companies" received the attribute of legal personality and had their capital constituted in shares.[10] These colonial companies had great success, partly because of their use of the corporate entity. As commercial entities they could trade and act under their names. Investors were attracted by the reputation created by these fictitious entities. To a certain extent, they trusted these colonial companies. This gave room for speculation, which in turn produced financial disasters such as the "South

9   The first form of corporation was not created for the practice of commerce; rather it was created to protect the interests of monasteries and municipalities by the use of the advantages of legal personality, which would not be affected by sickness or death. The attributes of corporate personality helped to avoid complications such as the succession of assets; for example, in the case of a religious institution such as an abbey, if the abbot died the passing of the order's land to the new abbot would discontinue. However, by conferring the legal personality to the abbey, this complication was avoided because as a fictitious entity it was not subject to mortality and was considered a person capable of owning property. Pope Innocent IV (in the twelfth century) was the individual who proposed the "fiction theory" in order to address the legal personality of the corporation. In the fiction theory, Pope Innocent IV addressed the corporation as an entity and gave the following definition:

> "The corporation is a separate and distinct social entity, but its legal personality is a mere fiction conceded by the state or created by law."

Originally the corporate fiction was aimed at religious institutions but later the use of this entity was expanded to public institutions such as municipalities and universities. Consequently, a fiction created with a religious connotation gradually became a tool for political ends. See, Sesarego, C. (1999) '*Naturaleza Tridemensional de la Persona Juridica*' *Revista de la Facultad de Derecho de la Pontificia Universidad Catolica de Peru* (No 15). At pages 2–5. See also, Brunetti, A.(2002) '*Sociedades Mercantiles*. Tomo I' Colombia: *Editorial Juridica Universitataria*. At page 83. See also, Dewey, J.(1926) 'The Historic Background of Corporate Legal Personality' *Yale Law Journal* (Volume XXXV). At pages 665–8.

10   See, Iwai, K. *The Nature of the Business Corporation: Its Legal Structure and Economic Functions*. http://iwai-k.com/NatureofBusinessCorporation.pdf (last visit 30 May 2013). At page 5.

General aspects of piercing the corporate veil 5

Sea Bubble".[11] Although the colonial corporate entity could be considered a cousin of the modern joint stock corporation, it did not open the gates to the corporate era. The colonial companies were imperfect due to their lack of regulation. Moreover, there was restricted access to a charter as the use of chartered companies was limited only to merchants who had political connections.[12] It was not until the nineteenth century with the advent of industrialization that the medieval corporation developed into the modern English joint stock corporation.

To take a medieval institution such as the corporation and mold it into a commercial device was an English initiative. The industrialization of manufacture created the need for large amounts of capital that few entrepreneurs could afford. The creation of partnerships was an initiative taken by entrepreneurs to satisfy the needs of capital. However, this provided a temporary solution. The traditional partnerships lacked legal personality and involved high transaction costs as well as legal expenses.[13] Moreover, partners were exposed to the financial risk of the enterprise.[14] Therefore, the creation of a type of business association with legal personality and limited liability for its members became necessary.

The first English Companies Act was enacted in 1844.[15] It introduced the joint stock corporation as a type of business association with the attributes

---

11 The corporate bodies recognized by common law were applied to business organizations in England and Holland when charters were granted to incorporate trading companies that became joint stock companies. These attracted considerable interest. It seemed suddenly to become a widely held belief that to subscribe to a capital fund was to become rich. Speculative excess quickly followed the formation of early trading companies, disillusioning investors in the Dutch East India Company 1609 as they found their capital locked into a company only publishing its account every ten years, and which insisted on paying its dividends in spices (pepper, mace and nutmeg). A century later in England the South Sea Company after a euphoric rise in its share price discovered it had fanned a boom far beyond its own stocks, and persuaded friends in government to pass the 1720 Bubble Act. When this legislation failed to work, the directors off the South Sea attempted to bring legal proceedings to forfeit the charters of other companies, precipitating a collapse in the market, which burst the speculative bubble, and sunk their own company. The reluctance on part of parliament to grant charters for private incorporation led companies to form essentially as partnerships, with rules deriving from the law of partnership, contract and trust. See, Clarke, T. (2007) *International Corporate Governance, a comparative approach.* London: Routledge. Page 3.
12 *Ibid.*
13 See, Micklethwait, J. and Wooldridge, A. (2003) *The Company: A Short History of a Revolutionary Idea.* US: Modern Library. At pages 39–40.
14 Limited liability is not included in a partnership. In this type of association each partner is jointly and severally liable for the debts and obligations of the partnership while he or she is/was a partner. See, Dignam, A. & Lowry, J. (2006) *Company Law.* 7th Edition. Oxford: Oxford University Press. At page 4.
15 The 1844 Joint Stock Companies Act is the basis of the current UK framework for companies. This Act addressed basic aspects of the joint stock company such as: incorporation by simple registration, provided safeguards against fraud by insisting on full publicity and provided a register of companies to hold the public documents provided by the companies. See, *idem.* At page 17.

6 General aspects of piercing the corporate veil

of legal personality. Shareholders' limited liability was a feature introduced later in 1855 with the Limited Liability Act.[16]

While the joint stock corporation was gaining relevance in England, in continental Europe other types of business association, which also included the attributes of legal personality and limited liability, were being developed. Examples are the French *Société Anonyme* (SA),[17] the German *Gesellschaft mit beschränkter Haftung* (GMBH)[18] and the Spanish *Sociedad Anónima* (SA)[19]. Certainly, the creation of a legal entity that confers limited liability was a breakthrough in countries experiencing the boom of industrialization. However, with the introduction of the joint stock corporation (and comparable types of business associations in other jurisdictions) in the commercial context, abuse of the attributes of legal personality and limited liability also existed.

The idea of piercing the corporate veil originated in the courts of the US.[20] The US is the jurisdiction that has substantially dealt with corporate personality issues.[21] This can be attributed to the relevant role that the

16 The 1855 Act allowed the limited liability of members of a company as long as requirements were fulfilled. This Act established shareholder limited liability in its section 8: "If any execution, sequestration or other process in the nature of execution, either at law or in equity, shall have been issued against the property or effects of the company, and if there cannot be found sufficient whereon to levy or enforce such execution sequestration or other process may be issued against any of the shareholders to the extent of their portions of their shares respectively on the capital of the company . . .".

17 The French *Société Anonyme* was introduced in the French Code of Commerce enacted in 1807. However, the attributes of legal personality and limited liability in addition to capital requirements were established in the *loi de mai de* 1863 and the reforms in 1867.

18 The German *Gesellschaft mit beschränkter Haftung* or limited liability company was introduced in Germany in 1892.

19 In Spain the use of business associations became common during colonial expansion (from sixteenth until seventeenth century). However, the concept of corporate personality and limited liability became subject of interest in 1869 and 1885 when reforms to the Spanish code of commerce were made.

20 A pioneer in the study of this legal phenomenon is the American author Maurice Wormser, who addresses this subject in his paper 'The veil of the corporate entity'. See, Figueroa, D. (2011) *Levantamiento del Velo Corporativo LatinoAmericano; Aspectos Comparados con el Derecho Estado Unidense.* 1st Edition. Chile: Editorial el Jurista.

21 Professor Robert Thompson, in an empirical study about piercing the corporate veil, concluded that piercing of the corporate veil is one of the most litigated issues in company law in the US. In his study, Thompson used a pool of 1,600 cases. He found that in 636 cases the veil had been pierced and that in 947 cases it had not. The 636 cases represent 40 per cent, which can be considered a high figure if it is compared with other jurisdictions in which the veil is not frequently or never pierced. The academic Peter Oh, two decades after Thompson's study, refreshes this subject with a new study based on 2,908 cases. He found that the veil had been pierced in 50 per cent of the cases. Both studies included Federal and State courts. Naturally, they classified the cases in accordance with authority and type. However, for the purposes of this thesis I cite the general figures in order to support the statement regarding the American authorities' acceptance of a remedy such as piercing the corporate veil. See also, Thompson, R. (1991) 'Piercing the Corporate Veil: An Empirical Study' *Cornell Law Review* (Issue 76). See, also, Oh, P. (2001) 'Veil-Piercing' *Texas Law Review* (Volume 89). Page 81; U. of Pittsburgh Legal Studies Research Paper No. 2010–06. Available at SSRN: http://ssrn.com/abstract=1557972 (last visit 8 August 2013).

General aspects of piercing the corporate veil 7

corporate personality (first the chartered company and later the joint stock corporation) has played in the development of the infrastructure of the country.[22] The fact that the corporate personality became common use soon produced circumstances (fraud and tort liability) that triggered the question: to what extent should the veil of incorporation be preserved? The US doctrine of piercing the corporate veil is the result of attempts to answer this question.

Although the idea of piercing the corporate veil originated in the US, its company law has not included a specific rule that allows its application. Rather, the piercing of the corporate veil has been applied through a standard developed from jurisprudence dealing with this issue. This standard requires the occurrence of three elements:

- Control by the shareholders over the company to the point that it cannot be considered an independent legal person
- Wrongful or fraudulent conduct by the part of the shareholders
- Connection between the excessive control over the company and the harm or loss suffered by the claimant

This standard has been addressed under the names of instrumentality and alter ego. However, the fact that corporate entity issues have been managed through a doctrinal approach has been the subject of criticism by a sector of the US academia and judiciary.

The criticism of the mentioned standard has been based on the vagueness of the factors that compose it; for example, there is not a parameter to determine excessive control over a company nor is there a clear definition of what can be considered as fraudulent conduct in this context.[23] Therefore, the piercing of the corporate veil is a remedy that has been applied on a case-by-case basis, a factor that has generated uncertainty.[24] However, despite criticism, the US doctrine of piercing the corporate veil has been a subject of interest for academics and judiciary in other common and civil law jurisdictions.

Currently, the metaphor of piercing the corporate veil has become universal. Moreover, academics and courts in different jurisdictions have used other terms to address the piercing of the corporate veil. In English, it has been addressed as *lifting / peeping behind* the veil, *penetrating* the corporate veil, or *ignoring* the corporate veil. In Spanish, it has been referred to as *levantamiento del velo corporativo, rasgado del velo corporativo, inoponibilidad de la persona juridical*. In Portuguese, it is regarded as *desconsideração da personalidade juridical* or *descortinamiento do véu corporativo*. Nonetheless,

---

22 See, Micklethwait, J. and Wooldridge, A. *Supra note* 13. At pages 57–78.
23 See, Strasser, K. (2005) 'Piercing the Veil in Corporate Groups' *Connecticut Law Review* (Issue 37). At pages 645–6.
24 *Ibid.*

8 *General aspects of piercing the corporate veil*

these different terms in different languages make reference to the same remedy: the disregard of the legal entity in order to hold shareholders liable for the corporation. However, each legal system has individually developed its own method for dealing with corporate veil issues. The piercing of the corporate veil may be triggered by a circumstance that in other jurisdictions may not be regarded as a factor that could trigger the application of this remedy.

3.   Piercing the corporate veil in the context of private law and public law

The piercing of the corporate veil is a subject that has become a "universal" aspect of private law. In this book it is considered that in public law cases there is not a real piercing of the corporate veil. This argument is supported on the rationale of public law, which is to regulate the relations between individuals and the state and also enforce public policies. In corporate veil cases where the state is a party and a public policy is in jeopardy, the concept of corporate personality is likely to be ignored.[25] An example is a case involving the policy aimed at the protection of public interest in free competition. To have free competition provides the consumer with better prices and entrepreneurs will look to improve the quality of their products. If the corporate personality is used to engage in monopolistic practices, it is used in a way whereby it is in detriment to public interest as the policy involved promotes free competition. Monopolies produce a rise in product prices and innovation is limited.[26] Therefore, in order to enforce its policy regarding free competition, the state takes measures such as ignoring the corporate entity in order to sanction the individuals that crafted a scheme aimed at creating a monopoly.

Courts in some jurisdictions have even established that corporate personality is irrelevant in public law cases. In Colombia, for example, the Colombian Supreme Court,[27] in dealing with a *Recurso de Casación Penal*[28] involving an issue of a company used to hide assets that were the

---

25 In Chapters II, III and IV, I emphasise and present cases that support this statement.

26 In contemporary economics, monopoly is treated as a source of inefficiency. Lee, D. & Mckenzie, R. (2008) *In Defense of Monopoly, How Market Power Foster Creative Production.* US: University of Michigan Press. At page 1.

27 The **Supreme Court of Justice** is the Highest Judicial body in civil and penal matters and issues of criminal and civil procedure in Colombia. However, the Supreme Court of Justice is not the highest authority in regard to the interpretation of administrative law, constitutional law and the administration of judiciary. The Supreme Court of Justice consist of 23 magistrates and is divided into five chambers.

28 *Casacion* in the civil law tradition is the only means to contest the decision over an appeal. This has its origins in medieval France and gradually was adopted by other continental

General aspects of piercing the corporate veil 9

result of illicit activities, came to the conclusion that for criminal law proceedings, the veil of incorporation does not have relevance.[29] It can be considered that this statement of the Colombian Supreme Court is one of the bases on which Colombian policymakers later developed the *Estatuto Anticorrupción*. Another example can be found in Panama. In a case involving the use of the corporate entity to obstruct judicial enquires and to hide assets derived from illicit activities, the Panamanian Supreme Court of Justice concluded that the corporate personality is disregarded if it obstructs an investigation on which criminal proceedings depend.[30] Certainly, an academic or judicial authority may make reference to the concept of piercing the corporate veil in areas of public law such as criminal and tax law. However, no real corporate personality dilemma exists in this context since the corporate personality is likely to be ignored when it contradicts a public interest represented in a public policy.

In contrast to public law cases, in private law cases the political state is not a party. The concept of private law makes reference to the area of law that usually deals with the relationships between individuals that are of no direct concern of the state.[31] The modern concept of corporate personality was created mainly for commercial purposes and the piercing of the corporate veil was originally created to address issues that derived from the relationship among private individuals (the corporation and other traders). The dilemma about whether or not to ignore the corporate personality was triggered because the fact that an individual requests the court to ignore the corporate personality demands the judge to omit a policy that is aimed at economic welfare. Common and civil law jurisdictions recognize and tend to preserve the corporate entity as part of a policy aimed at economic development. This fact is justified with the objective of the corporate personality; to encourage investment by diminishing the risks that involve every commercial adventure. This objective is achieved by transferring the risk to creditors and tort victims. Undeniably, a degree of unfairness exists but the corporate entity is part of a development policy

---

jurisdictions. The evolution of the civil law tradition into the contemporary civil law, developed the concept of *casacion*. Currently, in civil law tradition countries this is the only means to contest a final court decision. Each civil law jurisdictions, however, has conditioned the use of this legal resource to specific circumstances. Fabrega, J. (1985) *Casacion Civil*. Panamá: editora jurídica. Page 25.

29 "*El que para efectos comerciales y civiles la persona juridical sea un ente distinto de sus socios, es una verdad que no trasciende el ambito penal . . .*" See, *Corte Supreme de Justicia de Colombia, Sala Penal, auto 7183 del 20 de enero de 1993*.

30 See, *Sentencia, Pleno de la Corte Suprema de Justicia. 29 de enero de 1991*.

31 See, Martin, E. (2006) *A Dictionary of Law*. 6th Edition. Oxford: Oxford University Press.

10 *General aspects of piercing the corporate veil*

that is supposed to benefit economic welfare. On the other hand, it cannot be said that there is not a public interest in an individual's claim to pierce the corporate veil. In this context, the public interest lays in preventing and punishing the wrongful use of the corporate entity. However, to trade using the benefits of the corporate personality tends to produce unfair situations for creditors, victims of tort and in some cases shareholders, which are not necessarily derived from the wrong use of the corporate personality. Therefore, different approaches to deal with corporate veil issues have been developed in order to determine whether the policy supporting the corporate personality should be ignored or not. In other words, the interest of an individual (or a small group) has to be balanced against a public interest represented by the policy that supports the existence of the corporate personality.

The corporate personality has not only been discussed in the context of commercial relationships but also in the context of family and labour law. Family and labour law deal with relationships between private individuals and consequently the first thought would be that these two areas are part of the private law "branch". However, there is a strong public interest that makes the piercing of the corporate veil more likely in these two areas than in commercial law. The public interest lies in the fact that in modern societies, aspects regarding children's and workers' rights have gained relevance. In family law, a common misuse of the corporate entity has been the use of the corporate entity as a means to hide assets that are part of a matrimonial regime in order to avoid the distribution of those assets. In labour law, the corporate veil (in some circumstances) obstructs workers from receiving compensation because the corporate entity has run out of assets and shareholders have had their liability limited to their share in the company.

The jurisdictions studied in this book have adopted a similar position about the corporate personality in family and labour law and they generally ignore the corporate personality in this context. The Latin American jurisdictions addressed in this book are those that have dealt with corporate personality issues in a more substantial manner. Moreover, these jurisdictions have introduced an exception to the corporate personality in private law statutes. In England and the US, the piercing of the corporate veil has also been addressed from a private law perspective. The fact that exceptions have been drafted in the context of private law strengthens my belief that piercing the corporate veil is a private law remedy.

It cannot be denied that in modern common and civil law jurisdictions, in public law statutes such as tax law, bankruptcy law and environmental law, direct exceptions to the corporate personality have been introduced. As previously mentioned, I personally do not see a real dilemma regarding the piercing of the corporate veil in this context. However, the existence of a direct exception in a public statute is, I believe, to "emphasize the priority of a public interest". This book focuses on the piercing of the corporate veil in a private law context for reasons already explained. Nonetheless, some public law statutes (such as tax law, environmental law and bankruptcy law) have been included as they contain exceptions to the corporate personality. The inclusion of these statutes is to provide evidence of my thought regarding the tendency of the state (in civil and common law countries) to ignore the corporate personality when a public interest is at stake.

The function of the state is to protect the public's interest.[32] Consequently, a fiction like the corporate personality created for the interest of a small group of individuals will not be protected by the state if it is used against public interests.

4. Pro-social policy and capitalist policy

From the premise about the private law nature of piercing the corporate veil, two concepts have been crafted in order to address the position of the Latin American jurisdictions studied in this book; "pro-social policy" and "capitalist policy".

On the one hand, the concept of pro-social policy makes reference to jurisdictions that have been open to disregard the corporate entity, especially in areas where there is a strong social interest; for example, jurisdictions where the corporate entity has been disregarded without hesitation in environmental law cases. This books employs the word "social" in order to emphasize the tendency to ignore the corporate personality. On the other hand, the concept of pro-capital policy makes reference to jurisdictions that are less keen to disregard the corporate personality, based on fear of undermining the corporate entity and affecting economic growth. In the jurisdictions with a pro-capital policy, a statute with an exception to the corporate entity may exist but its application may not be common due to the importance given to the economic benefits of the corporate entity.

These two concepts have been crafted for the comparative purposes of this book. The use of these two concepts has its rationale firstly based on the critical implications the piercing of the corporate veil has for an economy that depends on the corporate entity and, secondly, on the damage the preservation of the entity may produce to collectivity in some circumstances. The logical thing to do is to establish a balanced approach. However, the Anglo-American jurisdictions and the Latin American jurisdictions, subject of study, have opted for one of the two extremes. The factors rendering a jurisdiction to be more inclined to adopt a particular route over another will be considered in this book.

---

32 The author regards the protection of public's interest as one of the functions of the state and public policies are a means to perform this duty.

12   *General aspects of piercing the corporate veil*

5.   Piercing of the corporate veil, in the context of public companies

The corporate entity can exist as a private company or public company. A private company is one whose shares do not trade freely in impersonal markets and are owned by a small number of individuals.[33] A public company, on the other hand, is a company whose shares are offered to the public in a capital market.[34] In the US and England, public companies are part of business culture. These countries have gradually developed capital markets in which corporate entities can participate. In Argentina, Colombia, Brazil and Mexico, however, the growth of public companies is quite recent. Latin America is a region that has started to experience economic growth since the late 1980s. Before this period, capital markets were small or non-existent in the region due to political instability, a factor that obviously hinders economic growth. Consequently, public companies are not part of business culture in Latin America. In this region corporate entities are commonly private.[35]

As previously said, the disregard of the legal entity is a remedy aimed at making shareholders liable for the acts of the corporate entity. In order to apply this remedy, the occurrence of fraudulent behavior on part of the shareholders is required. Certainly, the fraudulent shareholder must have a degree of control over the company's management in order to achieve its fraudulent purpose. This degree of control is commonly achieved in privately owned companies in which shareholders tend to have an active role in management. In fact the relevant cases dealing with corporate veil issues (which are presented later in this book) in the US, England, Argentina, Colombia, Brazil and Mexico have involved privately owned companies rather than public companies.

This does not mean that the disregard of the legal entity cannot be applied to companies that go public. However, it is not common. The shareholders of a public company tend to have a passive role regarding management. The daily management of the company is a task performed by hired professionals who constitute the directors' board.[36] Consequently, directors face liability if the company defaults due to negligence, reckless management or fraud.[37] Certainly the corporate entity has personality and assets different to those of the directors but hired directors may not be shareholders. Consequently, they may not reap the benefits of the corporate veil. Corporate governance

---

33 See, Kraakman, R. & Others. *Supra note 39*. At page 2.
34 *Ibid.*
35 See, Reyes, F. (2011) *A new Policy Agenda for Latin America Company Law: Reshaping the Closely-Held Entity Landscape.* University of Tilburg. Available at http://arno.uvt.nl/show.cgi?fid=115302 (last visit 13 June 2013). At page 15.
36 Clarke, T. *Supra note 11*. At pages 33–7.
37 *Ibid.*

General aspects of piercing the corporate veil   13

standards, accountability regulations and insolvency laws are some of the methods used to deal with the directors who are responsible for the performance of the corporate entity.

In summary, it is unlikely that piercing the corporate veil will be applied to companies that go public seeing that the equity market has already established the mechanisms to deal with those responsible for the fraudulent use of the corporate structure. The word "structure" is used because at the level of public companies it is almost impossible to talk about a corporate entity. Companies that go public are not one entity. Instead, they are a group of companies with hundreds of shareholders and stake holders. The managers, rather than shareholders, of public companies have control over a "behemoth", which may cause great damage if it is misused. Thus, there are special mechanisms to prevent and deal with fraud at this level.

The piercing of the corporate veil can be considered a special device that can be more efficient if it is used to deal with less complex structures, which are more susceptible to be manipulated by shareholders, such as private companies.

6.   Derivations of piercing the corporate veil

Certainly, trade has changed throughout the years. The relationship between merchants is not what it was 100 years ago. There are factors such as the development of new communication technologies and means of transport that have obligated trade, and all the aspects relating to it, to change in order to comply with the demands of the changing times. The corporate personality has also changed with the evolution of trade, and in turn so has the piercing of the corporate veil.

The title of this section is "derivations of piercing the corporate veil" because changes in the use of the corporate entity have pushed the judiciary to adapt this remedy to contemporary needs. This book addresses two aspects of contemporary trade that have produced derivations from the original piercing of the corporate veil. The first one is related to the confusion of assets and the misunderstanding of the corporate personality. There are circumstances where shareholders are poorly advised and the corporate veil produces damage rather than a benefit. To find a solution they want the veil of their corporate entity to be pierced. This has been called "reverse piercing of the corporate veil". The second aspect is based on corporate groups. The fact that a corporate entity can own shares of another entity has triggered the dilemma about the liability of a parent company for the obligations of the subsidiary. This has given rise to the creation of the single economic unit method. This is in turn based on the disregard of the veil of the companies' part of the group in order to treat them as a unit.

These derivations of piercing the corporate veil are explained in this section for comparative purposes. In the jurisdictions studied in this book, these derivations are part of the mechanisms used to deal with corporate entity

14 *General aspects of piercing the corporate veil*

issues. Therefore, in this chapter a general explanation is provided. In later chapters, the role these derivations have in the jurisdictions subject of study can be further appreciated.

6.1 *The reverse piercing of the corporate veil*

The occurrence of fraudulent behavior is the original trigger for piercing the corporate veil. However, the scope of this remedy has gradually expanded to cases that do not necessarily have a fraudulent element.

Although the span of this research is in the context of fraud, there are cases involving a compensation claim or tort damages in which the corporate personality has been disregarded without the occurrence of fraudulent behavior. It has to be briefly mentioned that currently the piercing of the corporate veil is not only practised in the context of fraud since from this fact a phenomenon worthy of comment can be derived, "the *reverse* piercing of the corporate veil". In a case involving the reverse piercing of the corporate veil, the affected party would not be a creditor; rather, the shareholders themselves would present the claim. In this type of case, the shareholders would seek to disregard the corporate personality when the corporate entity had become an obstacle for the shareholders to recover compensation from circumstances such as an insurance claim or expropriation by the government.[38]

The reverse piercing of the corporate veil has been controversial in the US, where courts have considered that "shareholders cannot have it both ways".[39] Entrepreneurs, when trading under the corporate form, create a veil that they fiercely protect. They therefore cannot dispose of their veil whenever they see fit, as doing so would affect the integrity of the corporate personality.[40]

In other jurisdictions discussed in this thesis, the reverse piercing of the corporate veil has not been an issue. In the case of England, although English authorities are generally reluctant to ignore the corporate personality, in relevant cases such as *DHN Food Distributors v Tower Hamlets London Borough*[41] and *Smith, Stone & Knight v Birmingham Corporation*[42] judges have considered ignoring the corporate personality in favor of the shareholder owners (the facts of these cases will be presented in the chapter regarding the Piercing of the Corporate Veil in England). As will be later explained, English judges

---

38 The author Michael Gaertner defines the reverse piercing of the corporate veil as an attempt by shareholders, or the corporation itself, to pierce the corporate veil existing between the corporation and its shareholders. See, Gaertner, M. (1989) 'Reverse Piercing the Corporate Veil: Should Corporation Owners have it Both Ways?' *William and Mary Law Review* (Volume 30). At page 667.

39 See, e.g., *In re Beck Indus.*, 479 F.2d 410, 418 (2d Cir.), *cert. denied*, 414 US 858 (1973).

40 See, Gaertner, M. *Supra note* 38. At page 682.

41 *DHN Distributors Ltd v Tower Hamlets London Borough Council* [1976] 1 WLR 852.

42 *Smith, Stone and Knight Ltd v Birmingham Corporation* [1939] BCLC 480.

General aspects of piercing the corporate veil   15

have different opinions regarding this subject. Whilst some judges are strictly in favor of the corporate personality, others may disregard it without considering whether the remedy is in favor of the shareholders or creditors.

In Latin American countries, on the other hand, corporate personality issues are relatively recent. Consequently, in reflections over the dilemma about piercing the corporate veil, the policymakers have not considered whether shareholders can benefit from this remedy. In fact, so far the Latin American jurisprudence has not even established a restriction regarding shareholders using the reverse piercing of the corporate veil. Moreover, the facts point to Latin American jurisdiction not opposing reversing piercing of the corporate veil since some relevant corporate personality cases have been based on ignoring the corporate personality to benefit the shareholders. Some examples shall be provided in later chapters, where the disregard of the corporate personality in each jurisdiction is individually addressed.

In the opinion of the author, the reverse piercing of the corporate veil is a consequence of the changes in trade that have affected the corporate personality. For that reason the development of this variation should not be thwarted. Certainly, the American doctrine offers a logical and weighty argument, "Shareholders cannot dispose of their veil whenever they see fit" because it will undermine the corporate personality. However, like the original remedy, this variation should not be restricted because it is one of the mechanisms to solve one of the many puzzles generated by today's corporate entity.

6.2 The piercing of the corporate veil in the context of corporate groups

A corporate group is not a new company nor has legal personality.[43] It is a concentration of companies that may be the result of different circumstances such as the creation of new companies, international mergers or joint ventures.[44] A corporate group can be defined as two or more companies that operate under a similar directive in order to achieve a common objective.

Each company that is part of the group has a legal personality and independent existence. However, in order to achieve the common objective, the companies forming the group accept to operate under the direction of a parent company that establishes the policies and the strategy that the subsidiaries have to follow.

Currently, when corporate groups operate through a network of subsidiaries organized under the laws of many different states, they are referred to as multinational enterprises.[45] Moreover, nowadays the corporate group is the

---

43 Eisenberg, M. (1993) *Corporate Groups*. Gillooly, M. *The Law Relating to Corporate Groups*. Australia: The Federation Press. At pages 2–7.
44 *Ibid.*
45 Vandekerckhove, K. (2007) *Piercing the Corporate Veil*. The Netherlands: Kluwer Law International. At page 5.

16   General aspects of piercing the corporate veil

dominant form of enterprise organization in the largest worldwide markets.[46] The popularity corporate groups have gained also makes corporate veil issues more common in this context.

6.2.1   Regulation and its critics

Traditional company law has been the subject of criticism because it tends to apply the same rules of a natural person shareholder to the corporate entity in its role as a shareholder.[47] This lack of distinction can be attributed to the fact that in the early days of the joint stock corporation only natural persons had the right to be shareholders. A company was not allowed to own shares of another company.[48] Therefore, company law was developed as a body of law to deal with companies formed by individual investors. Moreover, early cases involving the disregard of the legal entity were based on making a natural person liable for the debts of the company.[49] It was not until the late nineteenth century that companies were allowed to own shares of another company.[50]

The role of a corporate entity as a shareholder tends to differ from the role of the natural person shareholder. On the one hand, the corporate entity is not an individual investor; rather, it is a group of investors that trade under the corporate form. Moreover, a parent company creates, operates and dissolves subsidiaries primarily as part of a business strategy in pursuit of the business goal of the larger enterprise; something the parent and all the subsidiaries are pursuing together. On the other hand, a natural person as a shareholder is an individual investor that seeks to profit from their investment and whose role may be passive or active regarding the companies' management.

---

46 *Ibid.*

47 The author Philip Blumberg considers that limited liability for corporate groups emerged from an historical accident. The author considers that the application of liability to insulate from liability parent corporations as well as ultimate investors apparently occurred unthinkingly as a consequence of the recognition of the separate legal entity of a corporation from its shareholders. He considers there was no consideration over the aspects that involve a parent–subsidiary relationship. See, Blumberg, Ph. (2001) 'Accountability of Multinational Corporations: the Barriers Presented by Concepts of Corporate Juridical Entity' *Hastings International and Comparative Law Review.* (Issue 24). At pages 207–304. See also, Fuentes, C. (2009) *Acercamiento al Concepto de Grupos Empresariales: Concurrencia de Elementos para su Existencia.* Revist@ e-Mercatoria. (Vol. 8, No. 1). Available at SSRN: http:// ssrn.com/abstract=1493764 (last visit 30 May 2013).

48 See, Blumberg Ph., *Ibid.*

49 See, Blumberg Ph., *Ibid.*

50 Corporate groups emerged in the US with the liberalization of state corporation laws. The first state that authorized corporations to acquire and own shares of other corporations was New Jersey in 1889. See, Blumberg, Ph. (1990) 'The Corporate Entity in an Era of Multinational Corporations' *Delaware Journal of Corporate Law.* (Volume 15). At page 325.

General aspects of piercing the corporate veil 17

It is not common to find a jurisdiction with a special regulation for corporate groups. Germany is one of the few jurisdictions that has developed a regulation aimed at corporate groups. It is known as *konzerneck*. Germany is an exceptional case. The Latin American jurisdictions studied in this book do not have a regulation for corporate groups and they have instead used other mechanisms to deal with corporate group issues.

6.2.2 *Rationale to pierce the corporate veil of corporate groups*

As has been mentioned, a corporate group is not a new company with legal personality. Each company that is part of the group is an independent legal entity.[51] The relationship between the parent company and the subsidiary derives from the parent company's role as shareholder of the subsidiary. Consequently, the parent has liability limited only to the extent of its contribution in the corporation assets. The piercing of the corporate veil has been applied to establish a parent company's liability for its subsidiary.

The following parameters are used to determine a parent company's liability: the degree of control of the parent company over the subsidiary, the non-compliance with corporate formalities and the lack of the subsidiary's independent objective. These can be considered as universal parameters.[52] The control of the parent company over the subsidiary varies depending on the type of activity and business strategy; for instance, to hold a parent company liable on grounds of control might be a difficult task. Therefore, this argument must be supplemented with other circumstance such as a lack of compliance with corporate formalities.

In this book, corporate formalities are classified into two types: formalities for incorporation and management formalities. On the one hand, formalities for incorporation are the legal formalities established in company law that must be adhered to in order to create a company. The disregard of the legal entity does not apply in this context because if the legal requirements are not followed, the company would not exist. Management formalities, on the other hand, are the formalities that must be adhered to by the company's managers and shareholders.

---

51 However in the case *DHN Foods Distributor* Lord Denning challenged this notion of corporate groups.
52 An example to support this statement is in the cited English case *Smith, Stone and Knight Ltd v Birmingham Corporation* and the Argentinean Case *Cia. Swift de la Plata Sa S/Quiebra C/Deltec Arg. Y Deltec Internacional*. These two cases happened in different jurisdictions. Moreover, both jurisdictions follow a different legal tradition. However, courts in both countries regarded control of the parent company over the subsidiary, the non-compliance with corporate formalities and the lack of the subsidiary's independent objective in order to decide whether or not to ignore the corporate personality. I used only two examples, but later in Chapters II and III I address cases in other jurisdictions in which this set of factors have been used to deal with corporate groups in this context.

18 *General aspects of piercing the corporate veil*

Management formalities, such as the lack of accountability register and lack of records regarding the board of directors' meetings, may be determinant to piercing the corporate veil in the context of corporate groups.[53] The lack of accountability register may create confusion between the finances of the parent and the subsidiary companies, while the lack of minutes from meetings may give grounds to deduce that the subsidiary has not an essential organ (the director's board) for its legal performance. The lack of compliance with management formalities may create grounds to consider that the subsidiary is not an independent legal person. In addition, as a company the subsidiary has to have a specific objective established in the articles of association. Certainly, this can be regarded as part of the formalities for incorporation. However, although the objective of the subsidiary is established in the articles of incorporation this (in some circumstances) is not followed. In the context of corporate groups, a subsidiary that lacks an objective independent from that of the group cannot be regarded as a legal person. The lack of an independent objective can be considered to have derived from the excessive control of the parent company over the subsidiary. In later chapters, the reader can further appreciate that the courts in the common and civil law jurisdictions subject of this study have considered these factors in order to shape their decision over a parent company's liability case.

6.2.3 *Single economic unit*

The fact that the corporate group is based on multiple legal entities acting as a single unit gives rise to another mechanism to deal with a parent company's liability. This has been addressed as a "single economic unit". The single economic unit is a tool that can be used to ignore the corporate personality. This is based on the fact that a group of companies act as a unit in order to achieve a common objective and consequently should answer as a unit for the obligations of the members of the group. [54]

The single economic unit can be considered as a means to deal with the group structure and may differ from the traditional piercing of the corporate veil. Certainly, by disregarding the legal personality of the companies forming the group, a sole unit is rendered. However, a single economic unit does not depend on the occurrence of factors required as standard; rather, a single economic unit usually occurs for purposes of the interpretation of a statutory rule or contractual clause.[55] Moreover, the application of the single economic unit approach tends to be straightforward because the statutory rule or

---

53 *Idem*, at pages 20–3.

54 See, Cheng, T. *Piercing the Corporate Veil Across the Atlantic: A Comparative Study of the English and the U.S. Corporate Veil Doctrines.* Available at: http://works.bepress.com/thomas_cheng/3 (last visit 30 May 2013). At pages 4–15.

55 See, Vandekerckhove K., *Supra note 74*, at page 5.

General aspects of piercing the corporate veil   19

contract clause may have been drafted without considering the principles on which the structure of the corporate group is founded.[56]

The single economic unit can be considered another of the derivations produced by contemporary trading practices. It deviates from the traditional remedy that requires a test, which is a factor that may give the impression that single economic unit can be applied without control. However, the fact that it requires the support of a statutory rule and a contract clause limits the single economic unit to specific circumstances.

Personal observation

The corporate entity has been the result of economic development. The increase of population, the adoption of new political ideas and the creation of the contemporary concept of state, in addition to the development of new technologies, have created the needs for a means to supply the demands of contemporary society. The corporate entity has been one of the means used to provide a solution to the constant demands of infrastructure and development. However, the use of the corporate entity has not only been positive. This tool, created to aid development, has also been a device used by wrongdoers. The corporate personality can be compared to a "knife" as it is an essential tool for a man's subsistence but it can also be a tool used to harm others. In order to counter the inappropriate use of the corporate entity, the piercing of the corporate veil has been developed. It is a remedy that has been developed in accordance with the needs of each jurisdiction. Moreover, it is a remedy that has also evolved with the commercial uses of the corporate entity, and adapted to these new circumstances. An example is the single economic unit approach, which is developed to deal with the inappropriate use of the corporate group structure. It has to be pointed out that piercing the corporate veil is not widely applied in every jurisdiction because it may affect the modern economic framework that depends on the corporate entity. Nonetheless, it is a remedy that exists as an alternative to the wrongs that can arise through misuse of the corporate entity. The following chapters will address how Anglo-American jurisdictions and Latin American jurisdictions have implemented this remedy, and how these jurisdictions have managed to maintain harmony between this remedy and their framework for corporate entities.

56 *Idem*, at page 6.

II   Piercing the corporate veil in an Anglo-American context

As pointed out in the first chapter, the contemporary business entity is an English ingenuity that was adopted and more extensively developed by the US Seeing that the UK and the US are the first to exercise such entity, they are also the first to experience any problems relating to it.

In order to study the piercing of the corporate veil in Latin America, the origins of this legal phenomenon should be understood. Certainly, in the first chapter the general aspects of this subject were established. However, for comparative purposes this has to be addressed to a greater extent in an Anglo-American context. The rationale of this chapter is based on the need for a template from which to draw a comparison. The US is the jurisdiction that has been adopted as such a template. This jurisdiction has not only dealt more with the corporate personality but it has also developed a doctrinal approach to deal with corporate entity issues. This has been the subject of interest for academics in other jurisdictions.

It has to be mentioned that England has been included as the subject of study in this chapter. Moreover, this chapter begins with the piercing of the corporate veil in England. This jurisdiction has been reluctant to pierce the corporate veil. Furthermore, it has not born heavy influence on the development of the Latin American mechanisms to deal with the corporate personality. However, England has been included to supplement this comparative study because of her role in the development of the contemporary business entity and her tendency to protect the business entity.

This chapter starts with the piercing of the corporate veil in England. The English doctrinal and statutory approaches are explored. Following this, the US piercing of the corporate veil is addressed, where the generalities of this subject and the doctrines of instrumentality and alter-ego are studied. In addition, the role of US federal law regarding the piercing of the corporate veil is analyzed in context. Finally, this chapter closes with a reflection over the factors that have made the US and England take different paths regarding the piercing of the corporate veil.

1. Piercing the corporate veil in England

Disregard of the legal entity has been a controversial subject in English company law. The English judiciary has been characterized for being less willing to pierce the corporate veil than has the US.[1] The perception of England as a jurisdiction willing to preserve the corporate personality can be attributed to the fact that less direct approaches to deal with corporate veil issues have been applied by English courts. However, before addressing the methods used by the English judiciary to deal with corporate veil issues, I will proceed to address the case of *Salomon v Salomon Co. Ltd*,[2] which can be considered the precedent that created the foundation of the current position of the English courts with regard to the piercing of the corporate veil.

1.1 The case of Salomon

English company law authors regard the case of *Salomon v Salomon Co. Ltd* as the landmark in the preservation of the corporate entity's integrity and autonomy.[3] This precedent created the foundations of the current position of the English judiciary in regard to the corporate personality.

This case presented an early, and I dare to say simple, scenario, compared to the modern corporate structures. Mr Aron Salomon was a boot maker, who carried out his business as a sole trader. One day, he decided to enjoy the benefits of limited liability and created a company called "*A Salomon & Co Ltd*", to execute the bootmaking business. The members of the company were his wife, his daughter, four sons and himself. Each subscriber took a £1 share. Mr Salomon sold his boot making business to the company for £39,000. Part of the purchase price was used by Mr Salomon to subscribe for a further 20,000 £1

---

1 See, Cheng, T. *Supra note* 79. At page 3.
2 *Salomon* v *Salomon & Co* [1897] AC 22.
3 The case of *Salomon* has been perceived by academia as a landmark of the corporate personality in England. The author, Susan Barber, states that, "In the study of company law it is essential to understand the essential facts and issues of the case; this is the most fundamental decision of the courts in this field." The author, Eilís Ferran, argues that "An incorporated company is a legal persona separate and distinct from the people who hold shares in it and the people who manage it. This has been a foundation stone of company law in the UK ever since the decision of the House of Lords in *Salomon v Salomon & Co Ltd*." The authors Grantham & Rickett point out that the case of *Salomon* "is credited with having articulated the founding propositions of company law, and it is accordingly treated by judges and academics alike with a reverence bordering on the religious." See, Barber, S. (2003) *Company Law*. 4th Edition. Great Britain: Old Bailey Press. At page 5. See, Ferran, E. (2008) *Principles of Corporate Finance Law*. New York: Oxford University Press. At pages 14–15. See, Grantham, R. & Rickett, C. *Supra note* 29. At page 3.

22   *Piercing corporate veil in Anglo-American context*

shares in the company. However, £10,000 of the purchase price was not paid by the company; rather this was given to Mr Salomon in a series of debentures, which in turn gave Mr Salomon a guarantee for the debt. In other words, he had preference over other creditors in case the company defaulted, which is indeed what happened. The business of *A Salomon & Co Ltd* failed, and the company went into liquidation. As a creditor with preference, Mr Salomon claimed for his credit. However, this payment would have left the company without enough assets to cover debts to other creditors. Consequently, Mr Salomon's claim was challenged by the company's liquidator, who claimed that Mr Salomon should answer for the debts of the company. The plaintiff argued that the company had conducted the business as an agent of Mr Salomon and consequently he was responsible for the debts incurred in the course of the agency. The first instance court decided in favor of the plaintiff. Therefore Mr Salomon appealed. Although *Salomon & Co* was properly incorporated, the Court of Appeal considered this fact not to be relevant.[4] Instead, the Court of Appeal focused on whether the sale of Mr Salomon's business to *Salomon & Co* was valid. Should this transaction be supported to enable Mr Salomon to defeat the creditors and under the debentures appropriate the assets to himself?[5]

Based on the facts of there not being a valuation of stock, account of profits and non-influential members of the company (shareholders were considered as dummies used by Mr Salomon to comply with a statutory requirement), the Court of Appeal decided that *Salomon & Co* was a sham created by Mr Salomon to defeat creditors.[6] Therefore, the remedy provided by the Court of Appeal consisted of two options: (1) Mr Salomon had to indemnify the company against the debts and costs, or (2) the Court declared the sale of the business as invalid, set aside the agreement and debentures and ordered Mr Salomon to repay the money of the sale.[7] Undeniably, both options were aimed at setting aside the corporation's legal personality and made Mr Salomon liable for the debts of the company.

The House of Lords, however, rejected the decisions made by the first instance court and the Court of Appeal. The existence of *Salomon & Co Ltd*'s personality was preserved. Their Lordships held that there was nothing in the Companies Act that prohibited what Mr Salomon had done. Lord Macnaghten, Lord Halsbury and Lord Herschell went on to say:

> "It is not contrary to the true intent and meaning of the Companies Act 1862 for a trader, in order to limit his liability and obtain the preference of a debenture-holder over other creditors, to sell his business to

---

4 See, *Broderip v Salomon* [1895] 2 Ch 323. At page 334.
5 See, Kay LJ comments. *Idem.* At page 347.
6 See, Lindsay LJ comments. *Idem.* At page 337.
7 See, *Idem.* At page 347.

Piercing corporate veil in Anglo-American context 23

a limited company consisting only of himself and six members of his own family, the business being then solvent, all the terms of sale being known to and approved by the shareholders, and all the requirements of the Act being complied with."[8]

The decision made by the House of Lords in the case of *Salomon* most definitely affected the corporate entity.[9] It was established that the mere wish to trade using the corporate entity in order to get the benefits of limited liability is not to be regarded as fraud.[10] The whole purpose of incorporating a business is for its member[s] to avoid incurring further personal liability.[11] To presume the creation of a company as fraudulent would defeat the whole notion of the separate existence of the company and make it impossible for small private companies to function in a different way to partnerships. However, it was clear from the decision regarding *Salomon* that had there been evidence of fraud their Lordships would not have recognized the company as a separate entity.

Additionally, it was clarified in the *Salomon* case that being a controller member of a company does not in itself make the company an agent of that member (although the sole objective of the company is to benefit the member(s)).[12] Consequently, the creditors that accept trading with a corporate entity also accept the risk that, should the company default, they would not reach the shareholders' assets. Therefore, creditors have the obligation to establish adequate protections in order to have a higher probability of recovering their credit in case of default.[13]

1.2 The effects of the Salomon precedent

Based on the precedent of *Salomon*, the English judiciary has established that the only condition to enjoy the benefits of the corporate entity is that the company be properly created by registration. The Companies Act 2006 gives the registrar power to refuse to register a company not created for a lawful purpose. In principle, the English judiciary will not allow the use of the corporate entity for fraudulent purposes. However, the piercing of

---

8 See, *Supra note* 94. At page 1.
9 See, Mayson, French & Ryan (2010) *Company Law*. Oxford: Oxford University Press. At page 124, at paragraph 5.2.2.
10 See, Dine, J. (2009) *Company Law*.7th Edition. Basingstoke: Palgrave Macmillan. At page 24.
11 See Lord Watson comments in *Salomon v Salomon & Co.* [1897] AC 22. At page 35.
12 See, Mayson, French & Ryan. *Supra note* 9. At page 133, at paragraph 5.3.6.1.
13 Lord Watson in his comments held that ". . . in my opinion, a creditor who will not take the trouble to use the means which the statute provides for enabling him to protect himself must bear the consequences of his own negligence." See, *Supra note* 11. At page 40.

24 *Piercing corporate veil in Anglo-American context*

the corporate veil is not common in this jurisdiction. I personally consider that the English approach to corporate personality cases involves an extension of liability rather than piercing the corporate veil. As will be shown throughout this section, the English judiciary has opted for not affecting the integrity of the corporate personality.

Certainly, since the decision on the *Salomon* case English authorities have crafted exceptions to the corporate personality. These main exceptions have been developed under the concepts of "sham", "agency" and "single economic unit". However, although these exceptions are currently valid and applicable, none of them have been widely applied.

1.2.1 Sham exception

The Case *Gilford Motors v Horne*,[14] is an early corporate personality case on which the obligations of a natural person were extended to a corporate entity. It was justified through an argument based on the concept of sham. In this case, the defendant was accused of using a company called "JM Horne & Co Ltd" to avoid the effects of a covenant in order not to compete with his ex-employer. The defendant did not hold shares or a position in the company. Instead, his wife and an employee held shares and were the directors of the company. However, the defendant had a strong influence over the management of the company. Therefore, based on the fact that Mr Horne sought to avoid the covenant through a company (that he indirectly controlled) the court considered the company to be a "mere cloak or sham".[15] It was believed that even if a company was properly incorporated, its legitimacy would be doubted if it were suspected of being a device to conceal an illegitimate purpose. However, the outcome of this case was not the piercing of the corporate veil. Rather the effects of the covenant were extended from Mr Horne to the company JM Horne & Co Ltd, and the integrity of the corporate personality was preserved.

The precedent established in *Gilford Motors v Horne* created the basis for the concept of sham to become an available argument against wrongdoers who sought cover behind the corporate personality. In the case *Jones v Lipman*,[16] the argument of sham established in *Gilford Motors v Horne* was again used to deal with the fraudulent use of corporate personality. In this case, the defendant agreed to sell some land but later decided not to complete the sale. The defendant instead chose to transfer the property to a company, of which he and his lawyer were the shareholders and directors. The court

---

14 See, *Gilford Motor Co v Horne* [1933] Ch 935.
15 See, *Gilford Motor Co v Horne* [1933] Ch 935, Lawerence LJ comments at page 965.
16 See, *Jones v Lipman* [1962] 1 WLR 832.

regarded this company as "the creature of the defendant, a device, a sham".[17] However, rather than piercing the corporate veil, the court decided to make the company a second defendant. Furthermore, both defendants were obligated to complete the agreement between the claimant and the first defendant.

Although the outcome of the cited cases did not result in the piercing of the corporate veil, it can be considered that the relevance of both precedents derived from the fact that the scope of the sham exception was defined. Indeed, from this point the judiciary started to consider that the use of the corporate entity as an instrument to escape contractual obligations is a justification to set aside the corporate personality. However, the concept of sham derived from *Gilford Motors v Horne* can be regarded as an incomplete approach because there is not a systematic procedure or set of factors that help to determine whether or not to pierce the corporate veil. Indeed, from the cases *Gilford Motors v Horne* and *Jones v Lipman* the judiciary did not create a method to properly apply this approach, a fact that can be attributed to the concern regarding the principle established in the case of *Salomon*.

However, despite the lack of a systematic method, case law has made the English judiciary consider the occurrence of facts such as the motive for creating a company. The motive can be determined on there being a criminal component or an intention to defraud. Moreover, the exact moment when a company is brought into being is also considered as it helps to define the intention of the incorporator(s); for example, if a person creates a company and then transfers its assets, which are part of legal proceedings, the legitimacy of this legal entity may be regarded as doubtful and thus be considered a sham.

In more contemporary English corporate personality cases, parties seeking to pierce the corporate veil have continued to make use of the concept of sham. An example is the case *Trustor AB v Smallbone & others*.[18] In this case, Mr Smallbone is a director accused of syphoning funds. He had authority to administer Trustors AB monies and using its power transferred the monies to a company called Introcom. Introcom was a company controlled by Liechtenstein Trust, whose beneficiary was Mr Smallbone. In this case, the claimant argued that the company was a sham used for improper purposes. As to be expected, the English court considered setting aside the corporate personality and holding Mr Smallbone liable. In this case the court held ". . . the court is entitled to pierce the corporate veil and recognize the receipt of the company as that of the individual in control of it if the company was used as a device or façade to conceal the true facts, thereby avoiding

---

17 See, *Jones v Lipman* [1962] 1 WLR 832. Russel J comments at page 836.
18 See, *Trustor AB v Smallbone* [2001] 2 BCLC 436.

26   *Piercing corporate veil in Anglo-American context*

or concealing any liability of those individual(s)".[19] However, although the improper use of the corporate entity was recognized, it was not considered to be sufficient justification to pierce the corporate veil.

The concept of sham can be considered as an appropriate basis from which to develop an argument to deal with the corporate personality when used for improper purposes. Nonetheless, since its early days this approach has been covered by the shadow of the precedent established in the case of *Salomon*. The three cited cases present three different periods of time and it can be appreciated that, although there is an evident improper use of the corporate personality, the English courts have opted for maintaining the integrity of the corporate personality and deal with the issue through alternative means.

1.2.2   Agency

The traditional concept of agency addresses a relationship in which a party (named the *principal*) will draw up a contract with another party (named the *agent*) to act on its behalf (or can be a relationship implied from circumstances).[20] Consequently, the acts and contracts made by the agent will make liable and obligate the principal.[21]

Piercing the corporate veil on grounds of agency is not simple because it clashes with the structure of the corporation. The corporation is a person with rights and liabilities but it is an incorporeal being. Thus, this entity acts in society through its administrative organs, which are formed by directors and staff authorized to act on its behalf. The corporation performs through an agency relationship. Moreover, the corporation is an instrument created to carry out commercial enterprises. This entity does that by having complete independence from its shareholders. Hence, to consider a company as an agent of the members would, indeed, defeat the concept of joint stock corporation. The House of Lords, in the decision over the case of *Salomon*, emphasized this fact by stating that a corporation generally is not an agent of its members.[22]

In the case *Smith, Stone and Knight Ltd v Birmingham Corporation*, Judge Atkinson in his decision relied on the concept of agency.[23] In this case, a

---

19 See. *Idem*. At page 7.

20 See, Harris, J. (2005) 'Lifting the Corporate Veil on the Basis of an Implied Agency: A Re-Evaluation of Smith Stone & Kingth' *Company and Securities Law Journal* (Volume 23). At page 4.

21 See, *ibid*. At page 4.

22 In the analysis of the *Salomon* case Lord Herschel comments "In a popular sense, a company may in every case be said to carry on trading for and on behalf of its shareholders. However, in the point of view of the law, this certainly does not constitute the relationship of principal and agent or render the shareholders liable to indemnify the company against the debts incurred." See, Lord Herschel comments in *Salomon v Salomon & Co.* [1897] AC 22. At page 43.

23 See, *Smith, Stone and Knight Ltd v Birmingham Corporation* [1939] BCLC 480.

company ran a subsidiary on land that was acquired by the local council. The parent company did not receive any compensation from the disturbance of the subsidiary's activities made by the council. The council denied compensation based on the fact that both companies were separate legal entities. The judge considered piercing the corporate veil in order to allow the parent company to claim compensation for disturbance. Thus, in order to justify his decision, Judge Atkinson accepted an argument supported by agency. However, rather than traditional agency, he adapted the concept in accordance with the corporate structure and established a test in order to determine whether there was or was not an agency relationship between the parent company and the subsidiary. This test consisted of answering a set of questions regarding aspects of the parent company and subsidiary relationship, such as ownership, control and benefits.[24] Commentators have addressed this variation of traditional agency as implied agency. The concept of agency in this context is aimed at groups of companies and it has been based mainly on the degree of control that the parent company has over the subsidiary.[25] However, an exception based on control does not necessarily provide a strong case.

Throughout the years, corporate groups have gained more relevance and the elements regarding their structure have been the subject of study by commentators and judiciary. As a result, the dominance of the parent company over the subsidiary(s) has been considered as a normal aspect of a corporate group.[26] This form of business organization is based on a group of entities that agree to act under a common administration to achieve a common purpose. Consequently, a degree of control by the parent company over the subsidiary is necessary and it will vary in accordance with the type of enterprise.[27] In order to make a strong case in proving dominance over a subsidiary, the argument must therefore be accompanied by facts regarding the finances and governance of the subsidiary.

24 The Atkinson test consist is six questions, which are:
  1. Were the profits treated as the profits of the parent company?
  2. Were the individuals conducting the business appointed by the parent?
  3. Was the parent company the head and the brain of the trading venture?
  4. Did the parent company govern the venture and decide what should be done and what capital should be invested in the venture?
  5. Did the parent make the profits by its skill and direction?
  6. Was the parent company in effectual and constant control?
25 The approach developed by Judge Atkinson was originally intended to address a corporate group relationship. See, Harris, J. *Supra note* 20. At page 3.
26 See, Fuentes, C. (2009) *Acercamiento al Concepto de Grupos Empresariales: Concurrencia de Elementos para su Existencia.* Revist@ e-Mercatoria (Vol. 8, No. 1). Available at SSRN: http://ssrn.com/abstract=1493764 (last visit 30 May 2013). At page 5.
27 See, Bainbridge, S. *Abolishing Veil Piercing.* Available at http://papers.ssrn.com/sol3/papers.cfm?abstract_id=236967 (last visit 30 May 2013). At page 71.

28 *Piercing corporate veil in Anglo-American context*

Currently, implied agency does not have the same reception as the sham exception.[28] A factor that may have influenced the current perception of implied agency in the corporate veil context is the origins of this exception as it derived from a case that did not involve a misuse of the corporate entity. Instead, the veil was pierced in favor of the incorporators, something that has not been well perceived by judiciary in any jurisdiction.[29] Moreover, the test developed by Judge Atkinson was based mainly on the degree of control of a parent company over a subsidiary. As has been mentioned, the control of a parent company is an aspect that has been gradually accepted with the evolution of corporate groups. Therefore, whether a company is controlled to a higher or lesser degree is an argument that has weakened in deciding whether or not to pierce the corporate veil.

The sham exception as a means to deal with corporate personality issues has provided a more solid ground than the implied agency. This can be attributed to the fact that the sham exception focuses on the occurrence of fraud rather than control.

1.2.3 *Single economic unit*

In principle, a corporate group is not recognized as a new entity but rather each corporate member remains a separate entity with its own rights and liabilities.[30] The concept of a "single economic unit", however, appears as an exception to this principle. Indeed, it is likely that courts show a degree of willingness to regard the corporate group as one economic unit based on the wording of a particular statute or contract (particularly for tax purposes).[31] An example is *Sepia Logistics Ltd (formerly known as Double Quick Supplyline Ltd) and another v Office of Fair Trading*,[32] where the Office of Fair Trading regarded a group of companies as a single economic unit for

---

28 See, Hargovan, A. & Harris, J. *Piercing the Corporate Veil in Canada: A Comparatice Analysis.* Available at http://papers.ssrn.com/sol3/papers.cfm?abstract_id=980366 (last visit 30 May 2013). At page 5.

29 See, Gaertner, M. (1989) 'Reverse Piercing the Corporate Veil: Should Corporation Owners have it Both Ways?' *William and Mary Law Review* (Volume 30). At page 668.

30 This principle is reaffirmed by the Court of Appeal in the case *The Albazero*: "each company is a group of companies. . . is a separate legal entity possessed of separate legal rights and liabilities so that the rights of a company in a group cannot be exercised by another company in that group even though the ultimate benefit of the exercise of those rights would endure beneficially to the same person or corporate body irrespective of the person of body in whom those rights were vested". See, Mayson, French and Ryan. *Supra note 9.* At page 145.

31 See, Farrar, J. (1998) *Farrar's Company Law.* 4th Edition. London: Butterworths. At page 73.

32 See, *Sepia Logistics Ltd (formerly known as Double Quick Supplyline Ltd) and another v Office of Fair Trading* [2007] CAT 13, (Transcript).

Piercing corporate veil in Anglo-American context   29

purposes of an investigation for anti-competitive practices. However, the concept of a single economic unit as a doctrinal approach to deal with corporate veil issues has not been widely accepted.

A doctrinal approach to deal with corporate veil issues via the single economic unit made its debut in the case *DHN Food Distributors Ltd v Tower Hamlets London Borough Council*.[33] DHN Food Distributors Ltd (DHN) was a holding company that ran its business through two wholly owned subsidiaries. One of the subsidiaries held the title of the land where the warehouse that DHN used to carry out its business was located. The borough council compulsorily acquired the land and refused to pay compensation for disturbance because DHN did not own the land and the subsidiary did not have an interest in the business. In other words, the veil of incorporation created a troublesome situation for the parent company. However, the Court of Appeal agreed to disregard the legal entity and consider the group of companies as a single economic unit in order for the parent company to receive the proper compensation for the disturbance of the business. The decision regarding this case was heavily influenced by the comments of Lord Denning, an English judge who has been known for his tendency to favor disregarding the legal entity.[34] Lord Denning, regarding the *DHN* case, argued that the subsidiaries were strongly influenced and subject to the will of the parent company. In the DHN group, there was only one business and two of the three companies forming part of the group did nothing but own the businesses' fixed assets. Therefore, based on this fact, Lord Denning compared the relationship between the parent and the subsidiaries to that of a partnership in which all the partners participate in a business with a common view of profit. These grounds supported the argument that the group of companies was, in reality, a single economic entity and should be treated as one.

The Court of Appeal's decision in the *DHN* case was exceptional for that time.[35] Two years later, the case *Woolfson v Strathclyde Regional Council* presented similar circumstances to those in the *DHN* case.[36] A company carried out its business on a property owned by another company and Mr Woolfson held the majority of shares in both companies. The council compulsorily acquired the land but there was no compensation. Thus, Mr Woolfson claimed for compensation through an argument supported by the precedent established in the *DHN* case. However, the court did not accept the single economic unit argument. The basis of this precedent was

---

33 See, *DHN Distributors Ltd v Tower Hamlets London Borough Council* [1976] 1 WLR 852.

34 See, Dignam, A. & Lowry, J. (2006). *Company Law*. 7th Edition. Oxford: Oxford University Press. At page 36.

35 See, Mayson, French and Ryan. *Supra note 9*. At page 145.

36 *Woolfson v Strathclyde Regional Council* 1978 SC (HL) 90.

30 *Piercing corporate veil in Anglo-American context*

considered weak.[37] Consequently, the approach proposed in the *DHN* precedent lost relevance because of the arguments presented in the decision of *Woolfson*.[38]

As a doctrinal approach to hold shareholders liable (natural and legal persons), the single economic unit has not been widely applied. This was not properly utlized in the *DHN* judgment and the argument to address the companies as a sole unit was not consistent. Moreover, the fact that this was a compensation case, I consider, affected the development of this approach. As mentioned above, the English judiciary may allow an exception to the corporate personality if this has been used as a sham for fraudulent purposes; for instance, the circumstances of the *DHN* case did not fall within the established ground on which to apply this remedy.

The English single economic unit shares the same origins as implied agency as both are based on cases in which the party seeking to pierce the corporate veil is the shareholder who created the veil and benefitted from it. I personally regard this fact as one of the main causes for the single economic unit's lack of success as a doctrine to address corporate entity issues. However, in spite of this, the single economic unit is still an available remedy to address the disregard of the legal entity in English company law.[39]

1.3 *The case of* Adam v Cape Industries

The modern corporate personality has experienced changes since the decision in the case of *Salomon*. The specific facts of the *Salomon* case concerned a small private company established and run by an individual human trader. However, this circumstance gradually changed with the advent of corporate groups and multinational companies. Indeed, a network of subsidiaries created extra layers of limited liability and encouraged ambitious enterprises. Moreover, subsidiaries established in different countries extended company law issues on an international scenario. The principle established in the case of *Salomon*, however, can be considered as one of the few aspects of English company law that has not changed throughout the years: "the corporate personality will not be disregarded unless this has been used for an unlawful purpose".

---

37 Lord Keith of Kinkel questioned the validity of the precedent in *DHN* and the single economic unit approach. He emphasized the exceptional nature of a remedy such as piercing the corporate veil by making reference to the principle previously established with the concept of sham, ". . . the veil will be upheld unless it was a façade." See, Lord Keith of Kinkel comments in *Woolfson v Strathclyde Regional Council* 1978 SLT 159. At page 161.

38 See, Vandekerckhove, K. (2007) *Piercing the Corporate Veil*. The Netherlands: Kluwer Law International. At page 76.

39 See, *Adams v Cape Industries* [1990] BCC 786.

The case of *Adam v Cape Industries* is a contemporary case that has been the subject of interest among the common law judiciary and academia due to the fact that it involved different legal issues (conflict of law, tort and corporate personality issues in the context of corporate groups). However, for the purposes of this thesis I will focus on the corporate personality issue presented, because in this case the different English approaches to deal with the corporate personality are reviewed.

In order to explain the influence of this case on the current English position with regard to the corporate personality, the facts of the case will be briefly addressed. How the English court regarded each of the arguments based on the existing methods to deal with the corporate veil will then be explained.

1.3.1 The facts

Cape Industries (Cape) was a company created in England. It was the parent company of a group of companies and together they were dedicated to the extraction and marketing of asbestos.[40] During the twentieth century, Cape developed a profitable business. By 1953, Cape decided to expand its business to America. Thus, a subsidiary called "North American Asbestos Corporation" (NAAC) was created. It reported high profits during the late 1950s. Meanwhile, early reports of diseases produced by asbestos came to light.

By the 1970s, NAAC and its parent company Cape Industries were sued by the victims of asbestos-related diseases. NAAC arranged a settlement with the victims and paid compensation. However, NAAC exhausted its insurance and to reinsure would have cost more than the business was worth. Therefore, Cape decided to liquidate NAAC as part of a process of reorganization in order to continue the selling of asbestos on the American market. However, new cases against Cape soon materialized, yet Cape Industries refused to appear in American courts. Cape's defence was based on the corporate veil.

The responsibilities of operations previously executed by NAAC were transferred to a company called "Continental Products Corporation" (CPC). CPC was not a subsidiary of Cape. CPC had a relationship with Cape through a company created in Liechtenstein, "Associated Mineral Corporations" (AMC), whose stock was held by a Liechtenstein lawyer who was

---

40 Asbestos is a type of fireproof industrial mineral, which has been catalogued as dangerous. The exposure to this mineral may cause a lung disease (asbestosis) and lung cancer. See, Tweedale, G. & Flynn, L. (2007) *Piercing the Corporate Veil: Caper industries and Multinational Corporate Liability for a Toxic Hazard, 1950–2004.* Published by Oxford University Press on behalf of the Business History Conference. Availabe at http://es.oxfordjournals.org/content/8/2/268.short (last visit 30 May 2013). At page 272.

32 *Piercing corporate veil in Anglo-American context*

instructed by Cape. In other words, AMC was the "middle-man" in the relationship between Cape and CPC.

The plaintiff established proceedings against Cape and obtained a successful judgement in the US courts. Therefore, this judgement was presented in English courts to be enforced against Cape. The plaintiff argued that Cape had continued the asbestos business in the US via CPC. Arguments to make Cape liable were developed on grounds of agency and single economic unit. Furthermore, it was argued that CPC and AMC were part of a sham for Cape to avoid liabilities. However, the English court did not hold Cape liable because the court regarded that Cape had made a legitimate use of the corporate structure.

1.3.2   *The corporate veil point (sham argument)*

The arrangements made by Cape in regard of NAAC, AMC and CPC restructured the whole operation of Cape Industries in the US. Cape industries decided to close its subsidiary (NAAC) in the US to reduce its involvement in the marketing and sale of asbestos. However, it did not cease trading in the US; rather Cape made an agency agreement with another company (CPC), which was a company incorporated in Liechtenstein that AMC managed. During the proceedings the plaintiff sought to prove that this arrangement was made with the intention to constitute a façade for Cape to avoid liabilities towards asbestos victims. Through the sham argument, the plaintiff wanted to trigger the piercing of the corporate veil in order to regard the CPC's presence in the US as the presence of Cape.

The Court of Appeal concluded that AMC was not more than a corporate name, an entity controlled by Cape. Cape held the majority of shares and controlled its management. However, AMC was a company incorporated in Liechtenstein and did not practise any operation in the US. Therefore, although it fell under the scope of sham, it did not help to determine the presence of Cape Industries in the US. On the other hand, CPC was considered an independent legal entity that practised its operations legally. Indeed, there was a connection between CPC and Cape through AMC. However, the Court of Appeal considered that the way Cape restructured its operations was legal.[41] The motives behind the modifications of the group structure were made in order to reduce (future) liability.[42]

The Court of Appeal starts its analysis about the corporate veil point citing the wording of the case *Woolfson v Strathclyde Regional Council*, in which it is said that "it is appropriate to pierce the corporate veil only where special circumstances exist indicating that it is a mere façade concealing the true

---

41 *Supra note* 39. At page 823.
42 *Ibid.*

Piercing corporate veil in Anglo-American context 33

facts".[43] Throughout the analysis of the facts, the court found no special circumstance that could justify this remedy. The Court of Appeal held that "whether or not this is desirable, the right to use a corporate structure in this manner is inherent in our corporate law".[44]

1.3.3 Single economic unit

Cape, NAAC and CPC were separate legal entities. Certainly, Cape and NAAC had a parent–subsidiary relationship and for legal effects Cape was present in the US through NAAC. The restructuring of Cape's operations eliminates its subsidiary NAAC and to trade asbestos CPC was created. The claimant argued that although the companies were separate legal entities, there were special circumstances in which the distinction between companies was ignored and they were regarded as one entity. He cited different precedents such as *DHN Food Distributor Ltd v London Borough of Tower Hamlets* and *Revlon Inc v Cripps & Lee Ltd*,[45] in order to support his argument. However the Court of Appeal rejected the argument based on single economic unit upon the basis of the fact that CPC was not a subsidiary of Cape. CPC had an agency contract with AMC, both different legal entities from Cape.[46]

On the one hand, NAAC was one of Cape's subsidiaries and as such it was subject to Cape's influence over finance and management. The plaintiff argued that Cape was involved in the day-to-day running of NAAC, a factor that undermines the independent existence of a subsidiary. However, the Court of Appeal considered that formalities regarding NAAC's existence were respected, thus the distinction between parent and subsidiary cannot be bridged. On the other hand, regarding CPC, the single economic unit argument was rejected because CPC was not one of Cape's subsidiaries; it was a legal entity independent from Cape.[47]

1.3.4 The agency argument

In this case, agency was one of the plaintiff's arguments to support an action to hold Cape Industries liable and pay compensation to victims affected by asbestos diseases. The plaintiff developed this argument against NAAC and CPC. As is previously mentioned, the former was Cape's subsidiary that was

---

43 *Idem.* At page 516.
44 *Idem.* At page 826.
45 This case involved an issue regarding the ownership of a trademark. For the purpose of determining Revlon Inc as beneficiary of the product, Suisse subsidiary and the parent were regarded as a unit. See, *Revlon Inc v Cripps & Lee Ltd* [1980] FSR 85.
46 *Supra note* 39. At page 823.
47 *Idem.* At page 515.

34   *Piercing corporate veil in Anglo-American context*

liquidated, whilst the latter was an independent company, which continued the operations of the liquidated company.

NAAC as a subsidiary of Cape had its own legal personality, assets and management.[48] The court found that, indeed, NAAC acted in some circumstances as an agent of Cape. NAAC assisted in the marketing of asbestos in the US, it arranged the performance of contracts between US customers and the Cape group, and it had a coordinating role (particularly in arranging delivery). However, NAAC did not have any authority to represent Cape and make it liable for any contract.[49] Thus, the court did not find enough justification to deal with Cape and NAAC as a single entity on grounds of agency.

Regarding CPC, the court considered CPC as a separate and independent entity. Certainly there was a connection created between Cape and CPC through AMC. However, Cape did not hold any shares nor had it any type of direct influence as it had over NAAC. CPC was an independent legal entity with its own business.

1.3.5   *Reception of* Adams v Cape *decision*

The decision over the case of *Cape* has produced different academic opinions. Some of them have been negative, mainly based on the fact that "it constituted an unconscionable denial of human liability for harm caused to other people and therefore the veil should have been lifted on an equitable basis".[50] The decision over *Cape* is also regarded as a precedent that accentuates the conservative position of English courts in regard to the corporate entity.[51] Moreover, it has generated a restrictive approach to corporate personality issues.[52] Indeed, it has considerably narrowed the possible rationale for piercing the corporate veil in England.[53]

Certainly, *Adams v Cape* is a precedent that evidences a degree of unfairness. However, opinions sharing the observations made by the court have also arisen. It has been appreciated that Cape took the necessary steps to "quarantine" the impact of such liability of its business activity.[54] In the case of *Cape* there was not any fraud or intention to harm the claimants. There was only a coherent use of the corporate personality advantages. Moreover, it has to be considered that the corporate personality has evolved and is not

---

48 *Idem* At page 522.
49 *Ibid.*
50 See, Hudson, A. (2012) *Understanding Company Law.* Oxford: Routledge. At page 38.
51 See, Farrar, J. *Supra note* 31. At page 74.
52 See, Dignam, A. & Lowry, J. *Supra note* 34. At page 41.
53 See, Higgs & Goo (2011) *Cases & Materials on Company Law.* 7th Edition. Oxford: Oxford University Press. At page 121.
54 See, Davis, P. & Worthington, S. (2008) *Gower & Davis Principles of Modern Company Law.* 9th Edition. London: Sweet & Maxwell. At page 208, paragraph 2–13.

Piercing corporate veil in Anglo-American context 35

as simple as it was in the days of *Salomon*. Today, the reality is more complex as most large businesses are carried on through the medium of corporate groups of business.[55]

As a personal observation, I cannot deny the occurrence of unfairness. However, I agree with the court's position and the fact that Cape acted legally. I summarize my opinion on the case of *Cape* with the fact that the corporate personality is a tool that when used involves a degree of "collateral damage".

1.3.6 *The piercing of the corporate veil after* Cape

The case of *Cape* definitely refreshed the conservative positions of the English courts with regard to the corporate veil. Prior to the case of *Cape*, the English courts did not pierce the corporate veil, which is a fact that has not changed in the "post-*Cape*" era. English courts have not omitted the option of piercing the corporate veil and have even gone as far as to accept that the veil can be pierced in exceptional circumstances. However, concrete grounds on which to pierce the corporate veil have not yet been developed.

The previously cited precedents of *Gilford Motor v Horne* and *Jones v Lipman* are popular English corporate veil cases in which the corporate personality was not ignored; rather liability was extended. It can certainly be considered that to avoid conflicts with the principle established in the case of *Salomon*, English courts have opted for a less direct approach. An example of this tendency in the period "post-*Cape*" can be found in the case of *Creasy v Breachwood Motors Ltd.*[56] In this case Mr Creasy worked for Welwyn Motors Ltd (Welwyn) as the company's manager. Welwyn conducted its business at premises owned by a company called Breachwood Motors Ltd. (Breachwood). Two individuals owned the shares and were the directors of both companies. It is important to add that both companies were not part of a group; therefore there was not a parent–subsidiary relationship. Mr Creasy was dismissed and he decided to start proceedings for wrongful dismissal. However, before proceedings could be brought against Welwyn, the company ceased trading. Breachwood took over all of Welwyn assets and paid off Welwyn's creditors, with the exception of Mr Creasy's claim. Mr Creasy applied to have Welwyn substituted by Breachwood as the defendant. Breachwood appealed based on the fact that both companies were separate legal entities. Consequently it could not be responsible for the compensation payable to Mr Creasy, which was an obligation of Welwyn. However, the appeal was dismissed. In this case, Richard Southwell QC opined

---

55 See, Lowry, J. & Reisberg, A. (2012) *Pettet's Company Law and Corporate Finance.* Essex: Pearson Education Limited. At page 47.
56 *Creasy v Breachwood Motors Ltd* [1992] BCC 639.

36 Piercing corporate veil in Anglo-American context

that the power of the court to lift the corporate veil exists and should be exercised to achieve justice when necessary.[57] However rather than piercing the corporate veil and holding Welwyn shareholders liable, Breachwood became a defendant.

In the decision in *Creasy v Breachwood Motors Ltd,* the court considered the piercing of the corporate veil. However, this case did not involve a real disregard of the legal entity. In fact, the integrity of the corporate personality was respected. Certainly, the reasoning in this case pointed to piercing the corporate veil yet the influence of the *Salomon* precedent and the reaffirmation of this in the case of *Cape* made the court opt for a less direct approach, extending the proceedings to the other company. It is important to add that even though English courts tend to opt for a less direct approach to avoid conflicts with the corporate personality, the affected party does not always succeed. An example is the decision made in the case *Ord v Belhaven Pubs Ltd,* in which the plaintiff requested to substitute the defendant company for its parent on grounds of the case of *Creasy v Breachwood Motors Ltd,* but the Court of Appeal refused.[58]

A more recent example of the manner in which English courts deal with corporate personality issues is the indirect means used in the 2012 case *Chandler v Cape.*[59] In this case, the plaintiff worked for a subsidiary of Cape plc during the late 1950s and early 1960s. The subsidiary was shut down and 50 years later the plaintiff was diagnosed with asbestosis. The plaintiff started proceedings against the parent company (Cape plc) of the nonexistent subsidiary and the court had to deal with the dilemma regarding the liability

---

57 "The power of the court to lift the corporate veil exists. The problem for a judge of first instance is to decide whether the particular case before the court is one in which that power should be exercised recognising that this is a very strong power which can be exercised to achieve justice where its exercise is necessary for that purpose, but which misused would be likely to cause not inconsiderable injustice." See, the opinion of Richard Southwell QC, *idem* at page 646.

58 In the case *Ord v Belhaven Pubs Ltd,* the plaintiff took a 20-year lease of a public house from the defendant. The defendant was a subsidiary within a group of companies controlled by Ascot Holding plc. The plaintiff alleged serious misrepresentations and breach of warranty and claimed damages in tort and contract. Prior to the, trial the group was restructured and the defendant was left without any substantial assets. Therefore, the plaintiff applied to substitute the defendant company for the parent. The first instance court decided in favor of the plaintiff by considering the restructuring of the group in detriment of the plaintiff's claim unjust. However, the Court of Appeal reversed the first instance decision. Following the precedent established in *Adams v Cape Industries,* the court concluded that the defendant company could not be construed as a mere façade in so far as the transfer of B's assets was undertaken without any intention to harm the plaintiffs. The court held that the motive for the restructuring had been based upon an understandable business decision undertaken as a consequence of decline in the property market. See, case *Ord v Belhaven Pubs Ltd* [1998] BCLC 447.

59 *Chandler v Cape* [2012] EWCA Civ 525.

of the parent company. The court omitted the piercing of the corporate veil because in principle parent companies are not liable for the negligence of the subsidiary. However, liability of Cape plc was established on other grounds. The court regarded the knowledge that Cape plc had over the harsh effects of asbestos as a determining factor. Moreover, the court stressed that Cape plc was liable not because it assumed the liability of the subsidiary but because it owed a duty of care to Mr Chandler.

In the "post-*Cape*" era, no inclination for an approach to pierce the corporate veil has been developed in English company law. However, the piercing of the corporate veil is still constantly debated and opinions about the application of this remedy are never-ending in English courts. The recent decision in the 2013 case *Prest v Petrodel Resources Limited & others*[60] presents a revision of the English cases on this subject. Although this case finished (as have previous cases) without the corporate veil having been pierced and with concurrence to the statement, "the veil can only be pierced in limited circumstances", this case is regarded a breakthrough since it presented a point that is discussed in the first chapter: the relevance of public policy.

Prest v Petrodel Resources Limited & others was a divorce case in which the wife sought to enforce her rights over properties owned by a group of companies of which her ex-husband was the beneficial owner. The issue was whether the court had the power to transfer the properties of the companies to the wife. The question was solved under the Matrimonial Clauses Act 1973. It was emphasized that the Act conferred wide powers to the judge to enforce ancillary relief; to ignore the corporate personality was considered as a faculty of the judge, based on the public interest contained in this Act. However, in this case the veil was not directly pierced. Rather the companies were considered as merely trustees of the husband and consequently the companies were ordered to transfer the assets to the wife. The decision of the Family Court was supported on grounds of the beneficiary ownership of the husband over the companies. Certainly, the companies were properly incorporated and no irregularity existed but the objective of the court was to tackle the concealment tactic.[61] The relevance of this case lies in the fact that concealment tactics that involve the corporate personality have lost relevance in the context of family law.

Since the decision regarding *Cape*, the English courts have continued the tendency to use alternative methods to deal with corporate personality issues. It can be considered that grounds on which an argument to pierce the corporate veil are likely to succeed are limited to cases involving

---

60 *Prest v Petrodel Resources Limited & others* [2012] EWCA Civ 1395.
61 *Idem* at pages 22–9.

38 *Piercing corporate veil in Anglo-American context*

circumstances that affect the interest of the state, such as a corporate entity owned by citizens of an enemy state.[62]

1.4 *The disregard of the legal entity in the context of English statutory law*

The statutory provisions aimed at deterring certain misuses of the corporate entity do not represent a desire of the English judiciary to override the precedent established in *Salomon*. Instead, the statutory bodies in this context are aimed at extending the company's liability to those responsible for the misuse of the corporate personality in determined circumstances.[63] In other words, the corporation's separate personality is not ignored but instead it overrides the principle of limited liability. Certainly, the legal personality may be disregarded if the formalities for incorporation, established in the Companies Act, are not followed. However, when a company is incorporated, all the requirements tend to be followed in order to avoid any future inconvenience.[64]

The current statutory regulation for companies is the Companies Act 2006 which, when dealing with abuses of the corporate personality, is supplemented by the Insolvency Act 1986. Statutory law in this context has been developed as a protection for creditors against losses resulting from negligent and fraudulent management of companies. Indeed, statutory provisions in this context have been developed mainly in the area of insolvency proceedings. Provisions regarding fraudulent and wrongful trading and abuse of the company's name will extend liability to managers when an anomaly is found during the winding up of the company.

---

62 The case *Daimler v Continental Tyre & Rubber Co* [1916] 2 AC 307 involved a company owned by an enemy state. In the case, Continental Tyre Co. sought to enforce a debt owed to them by Daimler. However, the membership of Continental Tyre Co. was comprised of German citizens, a country that at that moment was at war against England. Although Continental Tyre Co. was a UK-registered company, the House of Lords refused to sanction the enforcement of the debt and refused to recognize that this company was an independent entity from its membership. This case is an example of a circumstance where the interest of the state is over the corporate personality and principles that support its existence.

63 Revenue law, Landlord and Tenant Act 1954, Trading with the Enemy Act 1939 and the Insolvency Act 1986, are some of the statutory measures in which the misuse of the corporate entity has been addressed. See, Sealy, L. (2010) *Sealy's Cases and Materials in Company Law.* 9th Edition. Oxford: Oxford University Press. At page 55.

64 There are certain requirements that have lost relevance. An example is the company's membership, due to the recognition of "single man company" in the Companies Act 2006. Prior to the Companies Act 2006, a company was required to have a minimum number of members. In section 24 of the Companies Act 1985 it was established that a person who is a member of a company that does not have the required membership would be held liable together with the company for its debts.

Piercing corporate veil in Anglo-American context   39

These provisions are mainly aimed at directors, who are the ones dealing with the company's management on a daily basis.[65] Shareholders become subject to these rules when they participate or have a strong influence over the board of directors (shadow directors).[66] It is important to add that hired directors do not enjoy the benefits of limited liability, as do shareholders.[67] However, directors cannot be directly sued for the faults of the company. Actions against the company must be addressed against the company; directors will become part of the proceedings when their fraudulent or negligent participation in the company's default has been proven.[68]

1.4.1   Fraudulent and wrongful trading

The concepts of fraudulent and wrongful trading are aimed at controlling directors' behavior and its effects are triggered if an anomaly is found during the liquidation process.[69] Both concepts share a similar objective but have different grounds for their application.

The concept of fraudulent trading was first introduced in section 275 of the Companies Act 1929.[70] The objective of this provision has been to enable the liquidator to seek a contribution to the company's insolvent state from directors whose actions prior to the insolvency proceedings had been fraudulent. The concept of fraudulent trading was expected to provide a basis that would make liable any person who engaged in conduct that would satisfy the definition of fraudulent trading.[71] However, during the 1980s the Cork Committee, which was responsible for reviewing UK insolvency law, considered that the concept of fraudulent trading was inadequate to provide compensation in situations where the person involved was not dishonest but merely reckless or negligent.[72] Thus, in the reforms made to insolvency law,

---

65 See, Sealy, L. *Supra note* 63. At page 53.

66 The concept of shadow director is defined in the Companies Act 2006 section 251: "shadow director means a person in accordance with whose directions or instructions the directors of the company are accustomed to act." See, Mason, French and Ryan. *Supra note* 9. At page 439, paragraph 15.3.3.

67 See, Sealy L. *Supra note* 63. At page 53.

68 See, Davis, P. & Worthington, S. *Supra note* 54. At page 197, paragraph 8–3.

69 See, Dine J. *Supra note* 10. At page 188.

70 See, Mansor, H. (2011) *Solvency, Company Director's Duties and the Problem of Process and Enforcement: A Comparative Study.* The University of Waikato. Available at http://researchcommons.waikato.ac.nz/handle/10289/5851 (last visit 30 May 2013). At page 225.

71 In the case *Re Patrick & Lyon Ltd* [1933] Ch 786 the judiciary defined that "fraud in the context of trading connotes actual dishonesty involving, according to the current notions of fair trading among commercial men, real moral blame." See, *Re Patrick & Lyon Ltd* [1933] Ch 786. At page 790.

72 See, Griffin, S. (2011) *Company Law Fundamental Principles.* 4th Edition. Essex: Pearson Education Limited. At page 341.

40 *Piercing corporate veil in Anglo-American context*

a new provision was introduced whereby civil liability would arise in a much broader context. This has been addressed as wrongful trading.

1.4.1.1 FRAUDULENT TRADING

The provisions concerning fraudulent trading can be regarded as a protection for creditors against fraudulent practices. The directors are, indeed, entrusted with the management and running of the company. Consequently, they are exposed to situations that may motivate opportunistic behavior. Fraudulent trading is currently addressed as a criminal and civil offence.

The Companies Act 2006, section 993 addresses fraudulent trading as a criminal offence that, if the company has been used to achieve a fraudulent purpose, is punished with imprisonment. An example is the case *R v Terrence Freeman*.[73] In this case, the defendant was director of an English company and chief executive officer of a Swiss company, both of which were used to carry out a fraudulent scheme. This consisted of requesting money from investors that was traded using trading platforms and also was promoted as a hedge fund. However, the defendant did not have access to the trading platforms he used to convince investors and the hedge fund was non-existent. The defendant gave false financial statements and did not disclose his criminal record to the investors. For undertaking fraudulent trading and other statutory offences, he was sentenced to seven years' imprisonment.

Fraudulent trading is addressed as a civil liability when, during the course of the company's winding up, it is found out that the business was conducted with an intention to defraud other parties. Different to the criminal offence, the civil offence arises in the context of insolvency proceedings. This issue is currently addressed in section 213 of the Insolvency Act 1986, which also establishes the penalty for this fault. However, because it is a civil offence, there is no imprisonment; rather, liable parties are to make contributions to the company's assets if the company does not have sufficient assets to meet its liabilities.[74] An example is the case *Kevin Ashley Goldfarb (liquidator of Overnight Limited) v Arthur James Higgins, Andreas Charalambous Andreou and Lofti Chareb*.[75] In this case, the liquidator is the company that

---

73 *R v Terrence Freeman* [2011] EWCA Crim 2534.
74 Section 213 of the Act states.
  "(1) If in the course of the winding up of a company it appears that any business of the company has been carried out with intent to defraud creditors of the company or creditors of any other person, or for any fraudulent purpose, the following has effect.
  (2) The court, on the application of the liquidator may declare that any persons who were knowingly parties to the carrying out of the business in the manner above-mentioned are to be liable to make such contributions (if any) to the company's assets as the court thinks proper."
75 *Goldfarb v Higgins & Ors* [2010] EWHC 1587 (Ch).

Piercing corporate veil in Anglo-American context 41

purchased computer parts from Germany. The computer parts were sold at a low price and the only profit that could have been made was from the retention of the Value Added Tax. The company never operated a bank account as all the payments were received and made through an account operated by Mr Higgins. The revenue authorities obtained a default judgment against the company in respect of the VAT due. However, the company's assets were not enough to recover the debt owed. Therefore, the liquidator applied to make the defendants contribute to the company's assets on grounds of the fraudulent trading provision in section 213 of the Insolvency Act 1986.

In order to hold a director liable on grounds of sections 993 or 213, fraudulent intention and behavior must be proved. However, the claimant must be aware that there are other regulations addressing fraud, which in turn may be more suitable to support his claim. In the case *Morphitis v Bernasconi & others,*[76] two former directors of a company in liquidation were accused on grounds of section 213 of carrying on the business of the company with intent to defraud creditors and for other fraudulent purposes and that they were liable to make contribution to the assets of the company. However, although the business was found to be intending to defraud, only one creditor was shown to have been defrauded. Consequently, the court considered that one defrauded party does not fall under the scope of section 213. The court held that a single defrauded person has to develop his/her argument based on the general law of fraud; if one person is defrauded in the course of the company's business, this does not mean the whole business was executed with intent to defraud.

1.4.1.2 WRONGFUL TRADING

Wrongful trading has been addressed in section 214 of the Insolvency Act 1986. Based on this concept, a director or a shadow director will be liable and will have to make a contribution to the company's assets (if the court thinks proper) if the negligent management of the company leads to insolvency. Negligent management has been addressed as wrongful trading because there are cases in which managers keep the company's business afloat even after the accounts or other management information have clearly revealed that the company is in a dire, loss-making position,[77] consequently causing losses to creditors. An example is the case *Liquidator of Idessa (UK) Limited v John Morrison & Christopher Povey.*[78] The liquidator, among

---

76 *Morphitis v Bernasconi* [2003] EWCA Civ 289.
77 See, Davis, P. & Worthington, S. *Supra note 54.* At page 222, at paragraph 9–11.
78 *Liquidator of Idessa (UK) Limited v John Morrison & Christopher Povey* [2011] EWHC 804 (Ch).

42 *Piercing corporate veil in Anglo-American context*

the other claims, considered that the directors should be liable because they had knowledge of the company being on the border of insolvency and they did not take the necessary measures. The court observed facts such as the lack of regular meetings of the board to discuss the financial position of the company, the loss of income from external investors and the expense of financial resources. Based on the lack of measures to prevent the insolvency of the company, the court imposed liability on the directors on grounds of wrongful trading.[79]

In order to support an argument under section 214 concerning wrongful trading, two elements must be proved:

- Knowledge, actual or constructive, that insolvent liquidation was unavoidable
- Failure to take every step to minimize potential loss to creditors

The first point is not aimed at putting pressure on managers. In the case *Earp & another v Stevenson & another*, the court did say that, "directors are not required to be clairvoyants".[80] However, it is considered that a competent director must be aware of the company's finances.[81] Moreover, in a situation of financial difficulties a certain standard of thinking and behavior are expected in order to save the company or at least minimize the loss.[82] Indeed, as long as directors are proven to take measures such as spending cuts and consultations with professional advisors in order to handle the company's financial difficulties, they may be free from liability.[83]

A logical course of action would be to recognize the difficulties of the company and go into voluntary insolvency proceedings. However, although this may mitigate losses to creditors, it is not a guarantee that directors will be free from liability. Certainly, during the winding up of the company some evidence of reckless or negligent management that would put a director within the scope of section 214 may be found. Such an example is the case *Re Farmizer Products Ltd*.[84] In this case, a company went into administration but it was unsuccessful and consequently was placed in voluntary insolvency proceedings. Liquidators claimed that the directors should be liable and contribute to the payment of the company's debts on grounds of section 214. They claimed that the directors were aware of the situation of the company before it went into administration but they continued trading. However, the court did not hold the defendants liable.

---

79 *Idem*. At paragraph 121.
80 *Earp & another v Stevenson & another* [2011] EWHC 1436 (Ch) (transcript). At page 13.
81 *Ibid* .
82 See, Davis, P. & Worthington, S. *Supra note 54*. At page 219 paragraph 9–8.
83 *Ibid*.
84 *Re Farmizer products Ltd* [1995] 2 BCLC 462.

1.4.2 Abuse of company name (phoenix companies)

The abuse of the company's name, known also as "phoenix company", is a situation that results from "the continuance of a failed company by those responsible for that failure, using the vehicle of a new company".[85] This new company trades under the same or similar name, has the same assets as before (acquired for a low price) and exploits its goodwill and business opportunities.[86] Meanwhile, the creditors of the previous insolvent company were left to prove their debts against a valueless shell and the management concealed their earlier failure from the public.[87]

The action of creating a new company that bears the same name and carries the same business may not, in principle, be improper. The lack of success of a company may be for reasons beyond the control of its directors. Moreover, the use of the same assets and trading style of the original company may be the only possibility for the employees to earn their livelihood. An example of this is the case of *Re Lightning Electrical Contractors Ltd*, in which the use of a previous company's name in order to maximize the value of the first company's assets is allowed.[88]

However, the issue arises when the intention of setting a phoenix company is to defraud creditors. The English legislature has addressed this phenomenon through the Insolvency Act 1986. In section 216, the use of the name (or a similar name) by which a company in process of liquidation was known (at least 12 months before the liquidation) is prohibited. Moreover, the directors of the company to whom this restriction applies cannot, for a period of five years thereafter, be director or manager of a company that bears a prohibited name, unless the court so allows. The Insolvency Act sanctions this misconduct in section 217 through the extension of liability to the directors or shadow directors involved in the abuse of the company's name.

The case of *Ricketts v Ad Valorem Factors Ltd* is an example in which the English judiciary addresses the issue of the prohibited name and director's liability.[89] Mr Rickett was the director of the company, Air Component Limited, which went into liquidation. At the time of the company's liquidation, Mr Rickett was also director of another company called Air Equipment Limited, which went into liquidation months later. The creditors of the latter claimed that Mr Rickett should be personally liable for the company's debts on grounds of the prohibited name provision. In the first instance, the court held Mr Rickett liable together with the company for its debts. Therefore,

---

85 See, Davis, P. & Worthington, S. *Supra note 54*. At pages 224–5, paragraph 9–12.
86 *Ibid.*
87 *Ibid.*
88 The case *Re Lightning Electrical Contractors Ltd* [1996] 2 BCLC 302 is cited and commented on by Davis, P. & Worthington, S. *Idem*. At page 225, cite 63.
89 *Ricketts v Ad Valorem Factors Ltd* [2003] EWCA Civ 1706.

44 *Piercing corporate veil in Anglo-American context*

Mr Rickett decided to appeal. The Court of Appeal engaged in studying whether Mr Rickett should be considered as liable on grounds of the prohibited name provision. The names of both companies, as well as the assets that formed the assets of each one, were evaluated in order to determine the association between them and Mr Rickett. The outcome was that Mr Rickett's appeal was dismissed on grounds of section 216(2)(b), which established that similarities of names between the company in liquidation and another company suggested the existence of a relationship between the companies and the manager.[90]

The prohibition in sections 216 and 217 is not absolute. Certainly, this has its exception under the Insolvency Rules 1986. As mentioned in the first paragraph, there are some circumstances in which to trade under the prohibited name may be beneficial. However, the legislature has established some requirements in order to allow the use of a prohibited name. In the Insolvency Rules 1986 rule 4.230 it has been established that the use of the forbidden name will be allowed if the new company has been using the name for at least 12 months and the company has not been dormant.[91] An example of this is the case *ESS Production Ltd v Sully*.[92] In that case, Mr Sully was the principal shareholder of an informal group of companies that used the acronym ESS in their name or trading name. One of the companies went into liquidation. Thus, a solvent company, which was part of the group, bought the assets. The solvent company traded under a name similar to the prohibited name, but creditors knew about it; in fact, the name of the group was well known. Furthermore, it was also a known fact that Mr Sully played an influential role in both companies. The court in the first instance held Mr Sully liable on grounds of section 217(1). However, the defendant appealed, arguing that it complied with the exception to the restrictions over the name established in the Insolvency Rules rule 4.230. The Court of Appeal allowed the appeal of Mr Sully based on the grounds of the Insolvency Rules 1986.

Indeed, the exception to the prohibited name rule exists. However, it is not always possible to be subject to this exception. In the case of *First Independent Factors and Finance Ltd v Churchill and another;*[93] two brothers were

---

90 "It is a name which is similar to the name by which the liquidating company was known and so purposefully suggests an association with that company." *Idem.* At page 6.

91 Rule 4.230 third excepted case: The court's leave under section 216(3) is not required where the company referred to, though known by a prohibited name within the meaning of the section:

  "(a) has been known by that name for the whole of the period of 12 months ending with the day before the liquidating company went into liquidation and

  (b) has not at any time in those 12 months been dormant within the meaning of Section 252(5) of the Companies Act."

92 *ESS Production Ltd v Sully* [2005] EWCA Civ 554.

93 *First Independent Factors and Finance Ltd v Churchill and another* [2006] EWCA Civ 1623 (Transcript: Wordwave International Ltd (A Merrill Communications Company)).

Piercing corporate veil in Anglo-American context 45

directors of a company that went into liquidation. They created a new company with a similar name, which bought the old company's goodwill. The defendants claimed that they knew it was a forbidden name. Therefore, they realized the sale of the business to the new business based on the Insolvency Rules 1986 rule 4.228.[94] Subject to this, providing they gave notice to the previous creditors, they were not personally liable for the company's debts. However, the claimant denied receiving any such notice. Furthermore, the Court of Appeal considered that even if notice were given as claimed, such notice would not have been effective in relieving the appellants from liability under section 217(1). This is because it was a liability that had already arisen by reason of their having acted as directors of the new company *prior to* the giving of the alleged notice.

The provisions against phoenix companies are a result of the need for protection of good faith creditors. However, these rules do not involve piercing of the corporate veil. Instead, these provisions deal with directors and shadow directors who manipulate the corporate entity's assets.

1.4.3 Tax law and the English corporate entity

If there is a conflict between tax law and the corporate entity, it is likely that tax law will prevail.[95] Indeed, my perception of public law as a force stronger than the corporate fiction is evidenced in this area of English law. Certainly, I cannot say that English courts act without considering the circumstances of the case. In England there is a tendency to protect the corporate entity. Consequently a conflict, which is more evident in cases involving corporate groups, exists.[96] I consider that the corporate entity has the opportunity to battle against tax law enforcement in view of the fact that tax provisions are not aimed specifically at the corporate entity; rather these provisions seek to prevent and punish tax evasion. Nonetheless, in this conflict tax law tends to prevail.

An early case that exemplifies the controversy between revenue authorities and corporate groups is *Bartholomay Brewing Company v Wyatt (Surveyor of Taxes)*.[97] In this case, an English corporation had been formed for the purpose of amalgamating three American breweries and carrying on the

---

94 Insolvency Rules 1986, rule 4.228: "(1) Where a company ('the successor company') acquires the whole, or substantially the whole, of the business of an insolvent company, under arrangements made by an insolvency practitioner acting as its liquidator, administrator or administrative receiver, or as supervisor of a voluntary arrangement under Part 1 of the Act, the successor company may, for the purposes of Section 216, give notice under this Rule to the insolvent company's creditors."
95 See, Vandekerchhove, K. *Supra note* 38. At page 484.
96 See, Dignam, A. & Lowry, J. *Supra note* 34. At page 32, at paragraph 3.3.
97 *Bartholomay Brewing Company v Wyatt (Surveyor of Taxes)* [1890–98] 3 TC 224.

46 *Piercing corporate veil in Anglo-American context*

business under one management. The English company, however, faced a local restriction on foreign ownership of real property. Therefore, an American company was created in order to manage the breweries. The English company held the majority of shares in the American subsidiary, but all the commercial operations were carried out in America and managed by the subsidiary. The issue in this case was in determining whether or not the English corporation was carrying on business wholly or partly in England.[98] If so, it would have been taxable for the whole of the profits made (whether remitted to England or not). If not, only the remitted profits would have been taxable. In this case, the court determined that, in principle, shareholders do not manage the company. As an entity independent from its shareholders, a company carries out its own business through its directors and agents. However, although the English company was a shareholder and all the operations and management were carried out in America, the English company was considered to have had a high degree of control over the business decisions. Therefore, on this ground the profits became the subject of taxation.

The cited case took place in the early days of the modern joint stock corporation. Consequently, issues such as place of incorporation and place of business were the subject of analysis in the early days of corporate taxation. However, although corporate taxation has improved and concepts such as a company's residence have been clarified,[99] it has not completely resolved the problem because the use of the corporate group for tax evasion is still a current issue.

Modern tax provisions are aimed at the company's management rather than the corporate entity. As the concept of corporate personality has developed, it has also developed the concept of corporate taxation. Certainly, the structure of the corporate group is complex in that it allows the development

---

98 The issue in this case derived from the fact that in the United Kingdom, income tax was invented before the registered company. In its early days, corporate entity taxation was regulated through the income tax legislation. However, tax law was originally aimed at natural persons, who were subject to taxation as long as they were residents in the UK. As a consequence, this regulation was not suitable for addressing the corporate entity. Indeed, the corporate entity was a new concept and there was no test to determine the residency of a company. Thus, the authorities filled this gap through the "central management and control" test. Through this test, a company's place of residence is determined by identifying the place of management, which was considered the place where the original business was carried out. See, Mason, French and Ryan. *Supra note* 101. At page 647; See, Flannigan, R. (1986) 'Corporations Controlled by Shareholders: Principals, Agents or Servants' *Sask. Law Review* (Volume 51) At page 71.

99 Currently corporate taxation can be regarded as more efficient. An example is the definition of a company's residence: "any corporate body, which is resident in the United Kingdom is subject to corporation tax on its income and chargeable gains, and is not subject to income tax or capital gains tax". See, Income and Corporation Taxes Act 1988, sections 6 and 832(1).

Piercing corporate veil in Anglo-American context   47

of schemes to evade taxes. However, instead of engaging in the "herculean task" of dealing with a group structure, authorities have focused on the management. Managers are the means by which the corporation acts in the real world. Consequently, most of the actions of the company can be attributed to the managers. A recent example is the case *Re Instant Access Properties Ltd; Secretary of State for Business, Innovation and Skills v Gifford and others*.[100] In this case, amongst the charges against the directors was the issue of tax evasion. It was alleged that the defendants, by creating a sham arrangement, which consisted of diverting income to a company incorporated in the British Virgin Islands, had caused or allowed the company to structure its affairs in such a way that the UK tax authority, HMRC, received less money than was properly due.

Certainly, managers tend to be the objective of tax regulation rather than the corporate entity. However, for purposes of the judicial proceedings involving tax evasion, disregard of the legal entity is likely. An example is the case *Re H and others (Restraint Order: Realisable Property)*.[101] In this case, the defendants were the shareholder owners of two family companies used to evade tax duties on a large scale. They were placed under arrest and the corporate personality was disregarded. As a result, the stock in the companies' warehouses and the companies' motor vehicles were treated as available property held by the defendants.

Certainly, in a tax-evasion scheme, managers may not be the brains behind the conduct. However, by establishing measures against managers they become aware of the effects of their (direct and indirect) involvement in a tax-evasion scheme. Thus, this can, to some degree, deter the use of the corporate entity for tax evasion.

Summary

The case of *Salomon* established the basis for the current position of English courts with regard to the corporate personality; i.e., the corporate personality will be preserved as long as it has not been used for fraudulent purposes. However, no clear concept of fraud has been established in this context. Years after the precedent in the case of *Salomon* the judiciary attempted to introduce exceptions based on the concepts of sham, agency or single economic unit. However, the cases in which these concepts were used did not involve the piercing of the corporate veil. Rather, alternative means were used to deal with the corporate personality. Consequently, the English authorities can be considered to have dealt with corporate

---

100 *Re Instant Access Properties Ltd; Secretary of State for Business, Innovation and Skills v Gifford and others* [2011] EWHC 3022 (Ch).
101 *Re H and others (restraint order: realisable property)* [1996] 2 BCLC 500.

48 *Piercing corporate veil in Anglo-American context*

veil issues in a way in which the integrity of the corporate personality is not affected. Moreover, in the case *Adam v Cape Industries,* the English authorities reaffirmed the tendency to preserve the integrity of the corporate personality.

Currently, the piercing of the corporate veil is not a common practice in this jurisdiction. There is no systematic approach to apply this remedy. The grounds on which an argument to pierce the corporate veil is likely to succeed are limited to cases or circumstances that affect the interest of the state. In the context of positive law, rules contained in the Companies Act 2006 and the Insolvency Act 1986 are not aimed at affecting the integrity of the corporate personality. Rather, these rules are aimed at companies' directors and shareholders who have an active role in the management of the company. These statutes are a means to deter and punish the negligent and fraudulent management of the corporate personality. In the context of tax law, there is no direct exception to the corporate personality, but this is likely to be disregarded in this context due to the strong public interest that exists in favor of tax law.

2. The doctrine of piercing the corporate veil in the US

The US is the jurisdiction that can be considered precursor of the doctrine of piercing the corporate veil. Certainly, the fact that the joint stock corporation has been in common use since the early days of the US has also made corporate entity issues common in this jurisdiction. The American author, Maurice Wormser, can be considered a pioneer in the study of this subject. Indeed, he analyzed various situations in which the corporate entity should be ignored. Wormzer generalized that "when the conception of corporate entity is employed to defraud creditors, to evade an existing obligation, to circumvent a statute, to achieve or perpetuate monopoly, or to protect knavery or crime, the courts will draw aside the web of entity, will regard the corporate company as an association of live, up-and-doing, men and women shareholders, and will do justice between real persons".[102]

The analysis made by Wormzer provides the rationale on which the piercing of the corporate veil has been applied in the US courts, which is to prevent and punish the improper use of the corporate entity. However, the formulation of a standardized approach to deal with corporate veil issues has not been an easy task. Company law in the US is a matter left for each state to regulate. Therefore, each state has its own notion about piercing the

---

102 See, Wormser, M. *The Disregard of the Corporate Fiction and Allied Corporation Problems.* At page 40; Cited by Rudorfer, M. (2006) *Piercing the Corporate Veil, A Sound Concept.* New York: New York University. At page 3.

Piercing corporate veil in Anglo-American context   49

corporate veil, which tends to vary from state to state.[103] The uncontrolled piercing of the corporate veil may affect the economic benefits produced by the corporate entity and obstruct the development policies of each state. Consequently, each state has had a strong interest in applying its own laws in the area of piercing the corporate veil.

Nonetheless, in spite of the circumstances the US authorities have managed to create an approach to deal with corporate personality issues. This approach consists of evaluating aspects regarding the degree of control of the shareholders over the company, the occurrence of fraudulent behavior and the existence of a link between the misuse of the corporate entity and the plaintiff's loss or harm. These factors have been arranged under the heading of the doctrine of instrumentality and alter ego. However, before addressing instrumentality and alter ego, the effects of state and federal law over piercing the corporate veil will be explained.

2.1   State and federal law

Each state has evaluated the factors that trigger the piercing of the corporate veil in accordance with their own internal policy. Consequently, some states tend to be more willing than others to apply the piercing of the corporate veil. The different tendencies among the states are demonstrated by Professor Robert Thompson in an empirical study he carried out regarding piercing the corporate veil in the US.[104] Examples of the different tendencies are found in the states of Delaware and New York. In fact, by the time Thompson concluded his study, the state of New York had actually produced more piercing cases than the state of Delaware.[105] On the one hand, the state of Delaware is known as a corporate-friendly jurisdiction and is consequently reluctant to pierce the corporate veil. The position of Delaware authorities regarding the application of this remedy can be attributed to a policy aimed at protecting Delaware corporations. On the other hand, the state of New York has been more open to consider piercing the corporate veil.

---

103 See, Hartman, P. (1982) 'Piercing the Corporate Veil in Federal Courts: Is Circumvention of a Statute Enough' *Pacific Law Journal* (Volume 13). At page 1246.

104 The study made by Professor Thompson was published in 1991. Although it has been more than 20 years since its publication, Thompson's study is still a relevant reference for the study of piercing the corporate veil in the US, because it was the first extensive empirical study in this area. See, Thompson, R. (1991) 'Piercing the Corporate Veil: An Empirical Study' *Cornell Law Review*. Issue 76.

105 By the time Thompson had made his study, he found that the court did not pierce the corporate veil in any of the 11 reported cases decided under Delaware law. The position of Delaware courts on this subject has not changed since Thompson's study. In a relatively recent study made by the authors, Mcpherson & Raja, Delaware courts were found to be still reluctant to pierce the corporate veil. See, *Idem* at page 1052. See also, Mcpherson, R. & Raja, N. (2010) 'Corporate Justice' *Wake Forest Law Review* (Volume 45). At page 949.

50 *Piercing corporate veil in Anglo-American context*

New York is an important centre of commerce and, as in the state of Delaware, the corporate personality does play an important role. However, New York authorities have nonetheless been critical of the concept of corporate personality. This can be attributed to factors such as the influence of Judge Benjamin Cardozo, who questioned the metaphor of the corporate personality in the case *Berkey v Third Ave. Ry. Co.*[106] Although, the veil was not pierced in this case, the comments of Judge Cardozo have markedly shaped New York judges' opinion about whether or not to pierce the corporate veil.

In a corporate veil case involving law from different states, the tendency is to apply the law from the state where the company is incorporated or the law chosen by the parties.[107] However, circumstances tend to differ when piercing the corporate veil involves a federal policy. Federal policies are the results of a need for special regulation regarding the protection of a public interest, which may not be introduced in state company law because it would drive companies out of the state to more hospitable jurisdictions. States in the US compete to provide a friendly environment for incorporation.[108] Consequently, aspects such as the protection of investors, creditors, customers, employees and any circumstance involving a public interest have come from federal legislation.[109]

Federal courts have developed their own approach to deal with corporate veil issues. This has been based on the similar elements considered by the state courts: control over the company and the occurrence of fraudulent conduct.[110] However, federal courts have also included a third point that differentiates the federal approach from the state approach. This third point, regarded by federal courts, is based on the use of the corporation to circumvent a statute or frustrate legislative purpose.[111]

The first chapter of this thesis addressed one of the premises followed in this work, which is based on the non-existence of a real piercing of the corporate veil in the cases where a public interest is in jeopardy. This statement is supported by the prevalence of the public interest over the corporate personality. The fact that the US federal courts have developed an approach to deal with corporate veil issues at federal level does not challenge the statement previously mentioned since the existence of a method to address corporate veil issues at federal level can be considered as a means to emphasise

---

106 *Berkey v Third Ave. Ry. Co* 244 N.Y. 602 (1927).
107 See, Gevurtz, F. (2013) *Piercing, Piercing: An Attempt to Lift the Veil of Confusion Surrounding the Doctrine of Piercing the Corporate Veil.* Available at http://papers.ssrn.com/sol3/papers.cfm?abstract_id=140280 (last visit 30 May 2013). At page 903.
108 See, Cary, W. (1973) 'Federalism and Corporate Law: Reflections Upon Delaware' *The Yale Law Journal* (Volume 83). At page 665.
109 *Idem.* At page 668.
110 See, Hartman, P. *Supra note* 103. At page 1254.
111 *Ibid.*

Piercing corporate veil in Anglo-American context   51

the fact that, in order to pierce the corporate veil, it must have been used in a way that affects public policy.

It is important to point out that the existence of state and federal jurisdictions may produce a conflict of law. This may arise when federal courts have to decide whether to apply federal law or state law. Federal courts have to determine whether federal law is more suitable than state law to deal with a corporate veil issue. The dilemma between both federal and state law in this context derives from the question: which may better serve the interest of public policies?[112]

Indeed, the US courts and academia have questioned the extent to which a state policy regarding the preservation of the corporate veil may frustrate federal regulatory policy. An example of this controversy arises in the case *United States v Bestfoods*.[113] In this case, proceedings were taken against a company due to the pollution caused by its activities. This company was part of a group of companies and the claimants wanted to hold the parent company liable for the damages caused by the subsidiary. However, the Sixth Circuit Court absolved the parent company based on the fact that the parent company could only be held liable if the parent had sole or joint venture operation of the polluting facility. The Sixth Circuit Court applied law from the state of Michigan.[114] Thus, its decision followed notions of separate corporate personality contained in state law. However, the Supreme Court overturned this decision and held the parent company liable by considering the influence of the parent company over the subsidiary on grounds of the concept of operator contained in the Comprehensive Environmental Response, Compensation and Liability Act (CERCLA).[115] The rationale behind the CERCLA has been based on the protection and preservation of public health and the environment, which can be considered as a public

---

112 The author Patricia J. Hartman, engages on the discussion about the role of federal law and state law in cases involving the piercing of the corporate veil. In her article, she establishes a set of factors established on case law and used by federal courts to determine whether to apply federal or state law. These factors include the extent to which:
   1. A federal rule would disrupt commercial relationships predicated on state law.
   2. Application of state law would frustrate specific objectives of the federal programme.
   3. Implementation of a particular rule would cause administrative hardship or would aid in administrative conveniences.
   4. The regulation could lend weight to the application of a uniform rule.
   5. The action in question has a direct effect on financial obligations of the United States.
   6. Substantial interest in the outcome of the litigation exists.
   See, Hartman, P. *Supra note* 103. At pages 1249–50.
113 *United States v Bestfoods* 524 US 51 (1998).
114 *United States v Cordova Chem Co. of Michigan*, 113 F.3d 572, 582 (1997).
115 The concept of operator makes reference to the ownership over the polluting facility. The grounds for the application of this concept in this context will be addressed later in the section regarding piercing of the corporate veil in the US statutory law.

52 *Piercing corporate veil in Anglo-American context*

policy that overrides the concept of corporate personality. The role of CER-CLA in the context of corporate personality issues will be discussed in more detail later in this section.

The plurality of state corporate law, the tendency of each state to create a friendly environment for business and the use of federal law to deal with aspects regarding public interest, have definitely influenced the American doctrine of piercing the corporate veil.

2.2 *The doctrines of instrumentality and alter ego*

The concepts of instrumentality and alter ego are names given to the set of factors that must occur to consider whether or not to ignore the corporate veil. These concepts have developed as different doctrines. The instrumentality doctrine was created to deal with corporate groups and the alter ego doctrine is principally applied in cases where the corporate entity is made up of one or two shareholders.[116] However, although both doctrinal approaches aim at a different objective, they are in essence the same. Both require the occurrence of the same factors in order to evaluate whether or not to ignore the corporate personality: control, fraud and causation.

(1) **Excessive control/lack of separate existence:** This factor consists of the excessive dominance that a shareholder(s) has over the corporate entity, to the point that the separate personality of the corporation and the individual no longer exist. Excessive control is determined through the assessment of the relationship between the corporation and the shareholder. In this assessment, aspects are observed; for example, the influence of the shareholder over the company by the time the plaintiff dealt with the corporation and whether corporate formalities have been followed.[117] The influence of the shareholder is determined in the company's independent decision-making authority.[118] If the corporation has no power to take its decisions, it is likely to be regarded as controlled. With regard to corporate formalities, it has been considered that if a shareholder has not followed the minimum requirements established by law, they should not enjoy the benefits of legal personality and limited liability.

(2) **Fraud and inequitable conduct:** This factor consists of the occurrence of fraudulent or illegal behavior on part of the shareholder controllers of the corporation. The occurrence of actual fraud or the intention to

---

116 See, Rudorfer, M. *Supra note* 102. At pages 4–6.
117 See, Olthoff, M. (1995) 'Beyond the Form-Should the Corporate Veil be Pierced?' *UMKC Law Review* (Volume 64). At pages 313–16.
118 *Ibid.*

Piercing corporate veil in Anglo-American context 53

defraud or the existence of bad faith make piercing the corporate veil likely. The rationale regarding this point is based on the fact that if the acts are treated as those of the corporation alone, an inequitable result will follow.[119]

(3) **Causation:** This factor consists in proving that the misuse of the corporate entity actually caused the claimant's loss.[120] In this thesis, a connection between the uses of the corporate veil for a fraudulent purpose and the loss suffered by the plaintiff as an essential requirement to determine whether or not to pierce the corporate veil is considered. If the piercing of the corporate veil is applied to cases where the corporate entity is not the cause of the loss or harm, this will produce the uncontrolled application of this remedy. As a result, the corporate entity will be undermined.

The courts normally require the occurrence of excessive control over the company and fraud derived thereby in order to pierce the corporate veil. Causation, on the other hand, is not a requirement in some state courts.[121] In fact, there are some cases in which the veil has been pierced based on a circumstance that have had no relation to the harm or loss of the plaintiff. An example is the case of *Sea-Land Services v Pepper Source*.[122] In this case Sea-Land Services (plaintiff) shipped sweet peppers on behalf of "Pepper Source" (defendant). Pepper Source defaulted on the bill. Sea-Land filed a claim against Pepper Source but was unable to collect because Pepper Source had no assets. Therefore, the plaintiff sought to pierce the corporate veil in order to hold the sole shareholder, Gerald Marchese, and other corporations he controlled, personally liable. The court regarded the facts in the light of the precedent *Van Dorn Co. v Future Chem. & Oil Corp*,[123] which can be considered a case in which emphasis was laid on the alter ego approach (explained later). First, with regard to excessive control/lack of separate existence, Marchese was the sole shareholder of the corporation and failed to maintain adequate records of the corporate formalities. Marchese and Pepper Source had the same office and the same expense accounts. Moreover, Pepper Source was not adequately financed for the risks of its business. However, the claimant could not prove the second required circumstance of the alter ego approach, which consisted in proving that the allowance of limited liability would sanction a fraud or promote injustice. Despite the lack of consistent proof to support the second requirement, the Court decided in favor of the plaintiff in the first instance and held the defendant liable.

---

119 *Idem.* At pages 316–18.
120 *Idem.* At pages 318–19.
121 See, Rudofer, M. *Supra note* 102. At pages 9–10.
122 *Sea-Land Services v Pepper Source* 941 F.2d 519 (CA7, 1991).
123 *Van Dorn Co. v Future Chem. & Oil Corp.*, 753 F.2d 565, 569–70 (7th Cir. 1985).

54   *Piercing corporate veil in Anglo-American context*

However, the sentence was remanded because of lack of evidence to support the second requirement. Therefore, an argument supporting the fact that the company was also used to commit tax fraud was presented and the authorities, based on this argument, allowed the disregard of the legal entity.

The decision on *Sea-Land Services v Pepper Source* can be regarded as one against the integrity of the corporate entity. Certainly, Pepper Source did not comply with its obligation and evidently was heavily controlled by Marchese. However, the fraudulent conduct of the defendant must be proved in circumstances related to the case. Tax fraud was far away from affecting the claimant and the fact that the court supported its decision on this factor is one of the reasons for the American doctrine of piercing the corporate veil to be the subject of criticism. Following, I will address the doctrines of instrumentality and alter ego in order to explain its differences and current role in US corporate law.

2.2.1   *The alter ego doctrine*

The piercing of the corporate veil on grounds of alter ego is usually employed in circumstances where the claimant wants to prove that the shareholder(s) has failed to separate his or their affairs from those of the corporation. This approach is likely to be applied when the corporation is made up of one or two shareholders.[124] If the court, based on the proof and circumstances of the case, considers that the separateness of the corporation has ceased, the corporation will be considered as an alter ego of the shareholders. The rationale on which the alter ego doctrine has been founded can be considered as of a punitive nature; if the shareholders themselves ignore the corporate fiction, the court will do so as well in order to protect creditors and society.[125] The circumstances that must occur to trigger the piercing of the corporate veil on grounds of alter ego are:

- a unity of interest and ownership that the separate personalities of the corporation and the individual no longer exists
- if the acts are treated as those of the corporation alone, an inequitable result will follow.

This test on which the alter ego is founded was applied in the case of *Van Dorn Co. v Future Chem. & Oil Corp.* In this case, the claimant sought to recover money owed to him by the defendant company. The claim was based on an allegation of breach of contract and fraud. The

---

124 See, Rudorfer, M. *Supra note 102.* At page 4.
125 Ballantine, H. *Ballantine on Corporations* (rev. ed. 1946). Cited by Rudofer, M. *Idem.*
   At page 5.

Piercing corporate veil in Anglo-American context 55

majority of shares of the defendant company, called Future Chemical, and the other company involved (called Sovereign Oil Company) were owned by one individual who was also the president of both companies. Among other issues analyzed by the court was whether the evidence provided was sufficient to justify piercing the corporate veil. In this case, the court regarded that corporate formalities, such as shareholders' and directors' meetings, were not complied with. Moreover, assets of both companies were intermingled. The court considered that both companies were dominated to the point that their separate existences could not be recognized. In this case the court made reference to the fact that "A corporate entity will be disregarded and the veil of limited liability pierced when two requirements are met: First, there must be such unity of interest and ownership that the separate personalities of the corporation and the individual [or other corporations] no longer exist, and second, circumstances must be such that adherence to the fiction of separate corporate existence would sanction a fraud or promote injustice." [126] The precedent established in the *Van Dorn Co.* case pointed to the fact that unity of interest and fraud are adequate justification to ignore the corporate personality. Moreover, in this precedent the court laid emphasis on the fact that both factors must occur in order to ignore the corporate personality.

The alter ego approach has been applied in more recent cases such as *Semmaterials, L.P. v Alliance Asphalt, Inc.*[127] In this case, the claimant sought to enforce a judgment against the company, Alliance Asphalt Inc. However, the defendant company could not pay the sum requested in the judgment. Therefore, actions were taken against the shareholder controllers. Based on the evidence, the shareholder controllers did not comply with corporate formalities; no shares were issued and shareholders' assets were commingled with corporate funds. Moreover, there was an intention to dissolve the corporation and "rename" the corporation as a new company, engaging in the same type of business as previously (now with a new name). The court decided to consider the defendant company as the alter ego of its controller shareholders and allowed the claimant to enforce its judgment against the shareholders' assets. The court, in this case, considered that preserving the corporate veil would have produced an inequitable result.

The factors that are observed in order to confirm the occurrence of the circumstances required by the test are usually under-capitalization, failure to observe records of corporate formalities, non-payment or overpayment of

---

126 *Van Dorn Co. v Future Chem. & Oil Corp.*, 753 F.2d 565, 569–70 (7th Cir. 1985). At page 570.
127 *Semmaterials, L.P. v Alliance Asphalt, Inc.*, 2008 WL 161797. At page 4.

56 *Piercing corporate veil in Anglo-American context*

dividends or large withdrawals of corporate assets.[128] Some of the courts that have applied this approach are in California and New Jersey.[129]

2.2.2 *Instrumentality doctrine*

The instrumentality doctrine is an approach created to deal with corporate veil issues mainly within the context of corporate groups. Frederick Powell firstly proposed this doctrine in 1931. His objective was to formulate a clear rule for piercing the corporate veil.[130] In the case *Lowendahl v Baltimore & Ohio Railroad,* the approach proposed by Powell was applied and the precedent established became reference for its later application.[131] In this case, two insolvent individuals transferred all their assets to a newly created corporation in exchange for 49 per cent of the shares. The company, *Baltimore & Ohio Railroad,* owned the remaining 51 per cent of the shares. After the claimant, Lowendahl, could not recover his credit from the individuals and the transferee corporation, he sued Baltimore & Ohio Railroad. The claimant argued that the transferee corporation was controlled by Baltimore & Ohio Railroad and requested to pierce the corporate veil to recover from Baltimore & Ohio Railroad. In this case, the court refused to pierce the corporate veil. Firstly, the court considered that the defendant company had no direct relation to the scheme designed by the individuals. Secondly, the court also found that Baltimore & Ohio Railroad did not control the company at the time of the fraudulent transfer. Citing *Powell*, the court established that the party seeking to disregard the corporate entity had to prove:

- The parent controls and dominates the subsidiary to such a degree that the subsidiary is a mere "instrumentality" of its parent.
- Through the domination and control of the subsidiary, the parent is perpetrating a fraud or working an injustice.
- These elements result in an unjust loss or injury to the complainant.

Under the instrumentality doctrine, the complete domination over the corporate entity by its shareholders has to be observed. However, it is important to point out that the ownership of a majority or the complete stock is not

---

128 See, Rudorfer, M. *Supra note 196.* At page 5.

129 See, Blumberg, Ph. (2005) *Blumberg on Corporate Groups.* 2nd Edition. US: Aspen Publishers. At pages 11.01 [A][2], 11–9 to 9.

130 Powell, F. (1931) *Parent and Subsidiary Corporations: Liability of a Parent Corporation for the Obligations of its Subsidiary,* §§ 5, 6. Cited By Blumberg, Ph. (2007) *The Law of Corporate Groups.* US: Aspen Publisher. At page 1.02.1.

131 *Lowendahl v Baltimore & Ohio Railroad* 247 A.D. 144, 287 N.Y.S. 62, aff'd, 272 N.Y. 360, 6 N.E.2d 56 (1936).

Piercing corporate veil in Anglo-American context   57

strong enough proof of dominance. In order to determine whether a company is an instrument of the dominant shareholder(s), factors such as gross under-capitalization or limited decision-making ability of the corporation must occur. In a relationship between a parent company and a subsidiary, dominance is likely to be determined by factors such as same directors and officers working in the parent and the subsidiary, lack of the subsidiary's proper business and complete financing of the subsidiary through parental enterprise.[132]

Following the dominance over the corporate entity, it must also be proven that influence over the company had been used to achieve a wrongful or inequitable result.[133] There is not a clear definition of fraud or wrongful conduct in this context. Consequently, American courts have been liberal in defining the type of behavior that can be considered as wrong in this context, for example: willful breach of contract, asset stripping and even wrongful discharge of an employee.[134]

The third point required by the instrumentality doctrine requires a connection between the dominance and fraud with the injury or loss sustained by the party seeking to pierce the corporate veil. Differing from the alter ego approach, causation is an element that tends to be regarded by the courts that apply the instrumentality doctrine. A recent case where wrongs required by the instrumentality doctrine have been considered is *Fantazia International Corp v CPL Furs New York Inc*.[135] In this case, *Fantazia* entered into a contract with CPL for the distribution and sale of CPL products in exchange for sales commission. However, a dispute arose regarding the sales commission. Thereafter, *Fantazia* started proceedings to recover unpaid commissions and also alleged that CPL was dominated by its parent company to the point that both entities should be regarded as a single economic unit. However, *Fantazia* failed to prove domination of the parent over the subsidiary and whether the relationship between parent and subsidiary was the cause for its loss. In this case, the claimant could not comply with the wrongs established in the instrumentality doctrine: control, fraud and causation. Although, this case did not present a successful claim to pierce the corporate veil, it presented an example of the use of the instrumentality approach to determine whether or not to pierce the corporate veil.

---

132 See, Krendl, C. (1978) 'Piercing the Corporate Veil: Focusing the Inquire' *Denver Law Journal* (Volume 55). At page 5.
133 See, Cheng, T. (2010) 'Form and Substance of the Doctrine of Piercing the Corporate Veil' *Mississippi Law Journal* (Volume 80). At page 505.
134 See, Vandekerckhove, K. *Supra note* 38. At page 81.
135 *Fantazia International Corp v CPL Furs New York Inc*., 67AD 3d 511 – NY Appellate Div., 1st (2009).

58 Piercing corporate veil in Anglo-American context

The instrumentality doctrine is an approach applied mainly in the context of corporate groups and has been applied by courts in New York and Florida.[136]

2.3 Reality of the American doctrine

The American standard to pierce the corporate veil seems simple and easy to apply. Indeed, if the shareholder has complete domination over the corporation used to commit fraud, which proximately caused a plaintiff's injury, the veil will be pierced. However, in practice it is not that simple. In fact, to prove each of these elements is complicated in some circumstances. An example is the case *Walkovsky v Carlton.*[137] In this case, Mr Walkovszky was injured in a taxi accident. The taxi that injured Mr Walkovszky was owned by a company called Seon Cab Corporation. Seon Cab Corporation was part of a group of ten corporations owned solely by Mr Carlton. Each corporation owned only two taxis and carried a lawful minimum insurance of $10,000 per taxi. All the companies operated as a unit and the working capital of the companies was kept to a minimum. Mr Walkovsky received insufficient compensation from Seon Cab Corporation. Therefore, Mr Walkovszky sought to recover the full amount of medical costs as well as compensation for damages. However, even if all the assets of the ten companies were joint, it would not be enough to satisfy the claim. Therefore, he claimed for Mr Carlton to be liable as well. However, the court considered that there was no fraudulent intention from Mr Carlton since he had incorporated and followed that established by the law; i.e., the companies had the minimum insurance and capital which, according to law, is necessary for a company to operate in the state of New York. Unquestionably, Mr Carlton had a high degree of control over the company's part of the group, a factor that makes the piercing of the corporate veil more probable, yet there was no proof of fraudulent intention on the part of Mr Carlton. The fact that he complied with capital requirements established by law was evidence that he operated his companies in a legitimate manner.

As a personal observation, the standard was designed and aimed to deal with the corporate veil in the context of fraud rather than a situation such as the one presented in the *Walkovsky v Carlton* case. Certainly, it may be difficult to prove the occurrence of fraud as in the previously cited case of *Sea-Land Services v Pepper Source.* However, the piercing of the corporate veil in a case involving fraud is more likely than in one that involves tort.

---

136 See, Blumberg, Ph. *Supra note* 130. At § 11.01 [A][2], at 11–5.
137 *Walkovsky v Carlton* 18 N.Y.2d 414 (1966).

2.3.1 Contract and tort cases

The piercing of the corporate veil in the US has been classified in contract and tort cases. This classification derives from the different circumstances presented in both contexts. On the one hand, in a contractual relationship both parties agreed to deal with each other. Therefore, the plaintiff is a voluntary creditor that has chosen to deal with the corporation. The creditor has the opportunity to investigate the company and to choose whether or not to contract. Moreover, the creditor can establish measures to secure its credit, such as higher interest rates or to ask for a personal guarantee from the shareholder. On the other hand, a tort victim is a person who has been harmed by the activities of the company and had no previous relationship with the company. Contrary to a voluntary creditor, a tort victim did not have the opportunity to negotiate and take guarantees to secure proper compensation; rather, a tort victim becomes involved by casualty and there is a probability that the company may not have enough assets to compensate.

Logically, the piercing of the corporate veil should be applied straight away in a case where a person or group of people has been harmed by the activities of a company that do not have enough assets to compensate the victims. However, the reality is that American courts do not frequently pierce the corporate veil in tort cases; rather, the piercing of the corporate veil is likely in a contract case.[138] This has been the subject of criticism by American academia. Some academics have even argued that the corporate veil should be invalid in the context of tort.[139] However, in spite of the criticism, American courts are currently more likely to disregard the corporate personality in contract than in tort cases.

Contract cases can be considered to provide a stronger basis to pierce the corporate veil than do tort cases. Firstly, courts in the US require the occurrence of fraud or inequitable conduct, which is more probable to find in a contract case than in a tort case. An example is in the case *Roofing Ctr. v On Top Roofing, Inc.* The claimant purchased materials that were used for work with customers but the profits were spent on high salaries and extravagant rents. Consequently, creditors were not paid and the court allowed the piercing of the corporate veil.[140] Indeed, a voluntary creditor is more likely to be affected by fraud or reckless behavior, thus demonstrating the use of the

---

138 See, Millon, D. (2006) *Piercing the Corporate Veil, Financial Responsibility and the Limits of Limited Liability.* SSRN eLibrary. Available at http://papers.ssrn.com/sol3/papers.cfm?abstract_id=451520 (last visit 30 May 2013). At pages 1318–25.

139 The commentators Henry Hansmann & Reinier Kraakman are some of the academics in favor creating liability for corporate torts. They propose that limited liability must be abolished, at least as to certain types of creditor claim. See, Hansman & Kraakman (1991) 'Towards Unlimited Liability for Corporate Torts' *Yale Law Journal* (Volume 100) 1879.

140 *Roofing Ctr. v On Top Roofing, Inc.* 807 S.W.2d 545, 547 (Mo. Ct. App. 1991).

60 *Piercing corporate veil in Anglo-American context*

corporate form to undermine the bargaining that has gone on between the company and its creditors. Secondly, due to the different nature of the relationship between the corporate entity and the tort victim, the piercing of the corporate veil tends to be decided on whether or not the corporate formalities were followed by the members of the company.[141] However, corporate formalities are normally followed, therefore complicating the development of an argument to support the application of this remedy. The previously cited case of *Walkovszky v Carlton* is an example. Mr Cartlon undoubtedly created the companies to benefit from the corporate personality and limited liability. However, he complied with the requirements established by the law. Although, the compensation paid by the insurance was small, Mr Carlton complied with the minimum established by the law. To look at corporate formalities to determine whether or not to pierce the corporate veil in the context of tort has been the subject of criticism due to the fact that the veil may be pierced under circumstances that have no relation to the cause that produced the harm or injury.[142]

The existence of the corporate veil cannot be abolished in the context of tort because this will undermine the concept of corporate personality. I support this statement on the basis that corporate personality was created to diminish the exposure to the risk involving a commercial adventure. Financial risks are not only in a contractual context but also in the context of tort. Certainly, it may be unjust for the tort victims in cases such as Union Carbide's Bhopal disaster.[143] However, the corporate personality and the attribute of limited liability were created to protect investors and their assets, as is presented on the case *Cotton v Gaylord Container Corp.*[144] In this case a parent company called Gaylord Container Corporation and its subsidiary Gaylord Chemical Corporation operated next to each other and shared facilities. Nonetheless, each had its own manufacture and sales business independent from each other. Gaylord Container had decided to form Gaylord Chemical as a separate corporation in order to isolate the risk of the separate

---

141 See, Barber, D. (1981) 'Piercing the Corporate Veil' *Williamette Law Review* (Volume 17). At page 381.

142 See, Blumberg, Ph. (1987) *The Law of Corporate Groups. Tort, Contract and other Common law Problems in the Substantive Law of the Parent Subsidiary Corporations.* US: Aspen Publisher. At page 163.

143 "Union Carbide India Limited" (UCIL) was a part of a multinational group of companies. Due to negligence a gas leak produced one of the worst industrial disasters. Legal proceedings were taken by the victims in order to make the holding company "Union Carbide Corporation" (UCC) (which held 51 per cent of UCIL shareholding). However, on 14 January 1987 the US Second Circuit Court of Appeals in Manhattan upheld a decision by the US District Court to send the legal case against UCC to India. It ruled UCIL was a separate and independent legal entity managed and staffed by Indian citizens. See, http://www.ncbi.nlm.nih.gov/pmc/articles/PMC1142333/ (last visit 10 July 2013).

144 *Cotton v Gaylord Container Corp* 691 So. 2d 760, 763 (La. Ct. App. 1997).

Piercing corporate veil in Anglo-American context 61

chemical operation in a separate entity and to protect the rest of its considerable investment in Gaylord Container from any potential creditors of Gaylord Chemical. A chemical disaster happened and the victims sued Gaylord Chemical. Moreover, the claimants sought to include the parent company in the proceedings by requesting to regard both companies as a single business enterprise. The single business enterprise, or single economic unit, is an approach aimed at disregarding the corporate personality and limited liability protection in the context of corporate groups. However, in order to regard a group as a unit it must be proved that the parent company has somehow abused the corporate form. In the argument made by the claimants, there was no allegation that Gaylord Chemical would not be able to pay the damages nor was there an attempt to prove that there was an abuse of the privilege of incorporation. The claimants instead emphasized the business and physical connections between the two plants, their common ownership and the various means by which the two were operated in a co-ordinated manner. The court decided to maintain the separate existence between the parent and subsidiary based on the fact that there was not an occurrence of fraud or wrongdoing or abuse of the corporate form by part of the parent company.

The fact that the piercing of the corporate veil is likely to happen in cases involving an issue derived from a contract evidences that this doctrine has been developed to prevent and punish the unjust enrichment of the shareholders at the expense of the corporation's creditors. In some circumstances, tort victims may not receive proper compensation and shareholders may not be held liable for the harm produced by the activities or products made by the corporation. This is unarguably unfair yet the piercing of the corporate veil was a remedy created without an altruistic purpose.

2.3.2 Agency and enterprise liability

The concepts of agency and enterprise liability are other alternatives that have been considered by the US courts for dealing with corporate veil issues, mainly in the context of corporate groups. The author Kurt Strasser considers these alternatives to the piercing of the corporate veil as "more episodic than systematic".[145] This statement by Strasser is justification for the fact that agency and enterprise liability are used to validate ignoring the corporate entity in a setting where the piercing of the corporate veil was either not available or not requested by the parties. Moreover, the context in which these approaches are applied does not involve the occurrence of a fraudulent

---

145 See, Strasser, K. (2005) 'Piercing the Veil in Corporate Groups'. *Connecticut Law Review*. Issue 37. At pages 645–6.

62 *Piercing corporate veil in Anglo-American context*

or wrongful action as they are based on the excessive control of one company over another.

2.3.2.1 AGENCY

In the US, the concept of agency has been considered as an alternative route to the imposition of liability upon a parent corporation for the acts of its subsidiary.[146] However, it has been complicated to adapt the concept of agency in this context due to the fact that in the parent–subsidiary relationship, agency relationship does not exist. All agency relationships consist of an expressed agreement in which a party called the principal gives authority to another party to act as its agent. All the acts made by the agent under the name of the principal will render the former liable. However, this is not the case for corporate groups. As explained in the first chapter of this thesis, corporate groups are based on a group of companies that act under the direction of one company in order to achieve a common purpose. Each of the companies forming the group is considered an independent entity with its own businesses and liabilities. If a parent company contracts its subsidiary to act as its agent, the former will be held liable for the acts of the latter on grounds of agency. Otherwise, "agency" would not be considered an appropriate means for holding the parent company liable.

In cases where a subsidiary is not solely owned by the parent but has the same directors and is used only to benefit the parent company, it may be argued that the subsidiary is merely an agent of the parent. Moreover, the subsidiary's attachment to the parent gives ground to argue the existence of implied agency. However, American courts have dealt with parent company's liability using the doctrines of instrumentality and alter ego rather than using implied agency.[147] Implied agency in this context is based on control and unfairness, which are the grounds on which instrumentality and alter ego are based.[148]

The US courts do not rely on the concept of agency to deal with corporate veil issues. Notably, an approach based on agency has not been widely accepted in the US.[149]

2.3.2.2 SINGLE ECONOMIC UNIT OR ENTERPRISE LIABILITY

The "single business enterprise" is a concept aimed at dealing with corporate personality issues in the context of corporate groups. The approach

---

146 See, Blumberg, Ph. *Supra note* 130. At page 307.
147 See, Barber, D. (1981). 'Piercing the Corporate Veil' *Williamette Law Review*. Volume 17. At page 401.
148 See, Henn, H (1983). *Laws of Corporations and Other Business Enterprises*. 3rd Edition. US: Student Edition. West Pub. Co. At page 258.
149 See, Barber, D. *Supra note* 147. At page 401.

Piercing corporate veil in Anglo-American context 63

based on this concept does not focus on discussing and questioning separate liability rules for the individual corporate entity and its corporate parent shareholder. Instead, this approach focuses on the business as a whole and aims to determine whether the corporate group should be regarded as a unit. In order to decide whether the group should be considered as a unit, the internal organization and management structure of the enterprise would be taken into consideration rather than the culpability and wrongful conduct involved in the case. Indeed, the approach aimed at regarding a group of companies as a unit can be considered as an alternative to piercing of the corporate veil in the context of tort. The case *In re Oil Spill by the* Amoco Cadiz is an example.[150] The issue in this case derives from a mechanical malfunction of a super tanker called *Amoco Cadiz,* which caused the ship to drift and crash into rocks on the coast of Breton, France. The accident produced an oil spill on the coast of France, causing environmental damage and losses for communities in the coast. Therefore, in the US courts the Republic of France and the affected parties started legal action against the companies forming the group to which the *Amoco Cadiz* belonged. The basis of the claim was the negligent operation and faulty design of the super tanker. The defendant companies claimed exoneration of liability based on the concept of separate corporate personality. The court evaluated facts such as the duty of the subsidiaries to provide proper maintenance in order to maintain the ship seaworthiness and the degree of influence the parent company (Standard Oil Company) had over the subsidiaries involved in the case. In this case, the court found the parent company to be liable together with its subsidiaries:

> "As an integrated multinational corporation which is engaged through a system of subsidiaries in the exploitation, production, refining transportation and sale of petroleum products throughout the world, Standard is responsible for the tortuous acts of its wholly owned subsidiaries and instrumentalities . . . Standard exercised such control over its subsidiaries AIOC and Transport that those entities would be considered mere instrumentalities of Standard Oil Company . . . Standard is therefore liable for its own negligence and the negligence of AIOC and Transport with respect to the design, operation, maintenance, and crew training of the *Amoco Cadiz.*"[151]

In the *Amoco Cadiz* case the concept of enterprise liability was presented as a means to address the liability of the group. However, this concept is not normally applied alone. Enterprise liability is applied together with labour

---

150 *Oil Spill of the Amoco Cadiz off the Coast of France* 35 Fed. R. Evid. Serv. 1204 (1984).
151 *Idem.*

64 *Piercing corporate veil in Anglo-American context*

and environmental regulations. Labour and environmental regulations contain policies that are aimed at protecting interests that are over the concept of corporate personality. By ignoring the legal personality of the companies part of the group and addressing a corporate group as a unit, the liability that exists in cases involving a public interest that has been affected is reinforced.

2.3.2.3 THE CURRENT POSITION OF AMERICAN COURTS IN REGARD OF PIERCING THE CORPORATE VEIL

Throughout this section I have pointed out that some US courts give different weight to a factor that may not be of interest to another state court. In this section, the multiple-jurisdiction factor has been evidenced, which is the reason the piercing of the corporate veil is a complex subject in the US. However, in spite of differences among state courts, American courts share the contention that a strong justification is required in order to ignore the corporate personality.

American courts tend to preserve the corporate personality if there is no strong justification to ignore it. An example is the recent decision in the case of *Complete Transportation, LLC v CPM Colchester, et al LLC*.[152] In this case, the claimant sought to recover his credit from the defendant company, which was an LLC. One core argument used by the claimant was the excessive control the defendant had over the company. In its analysis, the court cited the Connecticut General Statute, in particular a section corresponding "Relations of Members and Managers to Persons Dealing with a Limited Liability Company", and pointed out the liability of members and managers to third parties. In sections 34–133 (Conn. Gen. Stat. § 34–133), it is established that the liability is limited. The court regarded previous case law and cited passages involving the instrumentality doctrine and the requirements for its application. Case law in this area indicated the fact that ". . . disregard the fiction of a separate legal entity, to pierce the shield of immunity afforded by the corporate structure in a situation in which the corporate entity has been so controlled and dominated that justice requires liability to be imposed on the real actor".[153] Based on statements such as this, the court structured its decision and considered that on grounds of instrumentality, the plaintiff could not prove the occurrence of wrong other than the defendant company's inability to pay. Thus, the piercing of the corporate veil was denied.

---

152 This case was decided by the Superior Court of Connecticut in February 2013 and may be subject to further appellate review. *Complete Transportation, LLC v CPM Colchester, et al LLC.* 2013 Conn. Super. Lexis 342.

153 *Angelo Tomasso, Inc. v Armor Construction & Paving, Inc.*, 187 Conn. 544, 552, 447 A.2d 406 (1992).

Another example is the case *Joseph Friend v Remac America, Inc.*[154] In this case the claimant, while working for the defendant, suffered injuries and claimed compensation. However, the defendant company did not pay proper compensation to the claimant. Thus, the claimant requested the piercing of the corporate veil on the two-prong test (control and fraud) and moreover reinforced his claim on the argument of undercapitalization and lack of compliance of corporate formalities. The claimant emphasized the lack of proper insurance coverage to protect employees. However, the court pointed out that the test with which the claimant wanted to justify the piercing of the corporate veil is applicable to contract cases, not to tort cases such as the then present claim. The court in this case said that the shareholders and managers were not liable for the torts of the company. Moreover, the claimant could not prove undercapitalization or lack of compliance with corporate formalities. The claimant alleged undercapitalization based on the fact that the company had not bought enough insurance cover. The court considered the claimant´s claim inadequate and decided not to pierce the corporate veil.

In the case *Jaclinn Pulman v Alpha Media Publishing Inc* the exceptional nature of piercing the corporate veil is also present. In this case the claimant presented her claim in New Jersey courts.[155] The claimant invested in a bungalows project and was told that a company called Maxim owned the bungalows. The claimant trusted the company and felt secure because she had the impression she was investing with a solid company. However, the claimant researched the project and discovered that Maxim was not the owner of the project. Moreover, she lost her money when it was revealed that the bungalows project was a Ponzi scam. The claimant sued a group of companies involved based on the fact that she was fraudulently misrepresented and also requested the piercing of the corporate veil. The New Jersey court required the concurrence of control and the use of the influence over the company to achieve fraud. The claimant alleged that the defendant created a cluster of companies in order to carry out the scam. However, the claimant pleaded the piercing of the corporate veil as a separate cause of action. Consequently, it was denied. The piercing of the corporate veil is not considered as a cause of action in New Jersey courts.

The three cited examples present three different circumstances in which the piercing of the corporate veil is denied. In these three cases, the claimants presented poor justification for piercing the corporate veil. American courts are willing to ignore the corporate personality if it is improperly used. In these cases, the courts evaluated and considered the application of this

---

154 *Joseph Friend v Remac America Inc.*, Civil Action No. 3:12-CV-17.
155 *Jaclinn Pulman v Alpha Media Publishing INC* 2013 US Dist. Lexis 50697.

66 *Piercing corporate veil in Anglo-American context*

remedy. However, to pierce the corporate veil American courts require strong justification.

2.4 *The piercing of the corporate veil in the context of American statutory law*

In the US the piercing of the corporate veil has been developed as a doctrine but not as a statutory rule. As previously mentioned, company law in the US is a matter regulated by each state. Consequently, since the early days of American Company Law, states have competed to develop an environment favorable for the incorporation of companies. Notably, the incorporation of companies represents a profitable business for the state and its inhabitants. Therefore, in order to attract investors, states' corporate laws have been drafted focusing on aspects such as the preservation of the corporate veil.

Currently, there is not a direct exception to the corporate personality in US Company Laws. However, this does not mean that a measure to enforce public policy has not been taken. The author Harry G. Henn comments: "The corporate entity will be recognized, but will not be permitted to be a device to defeat public policy."[156] The statement made by Henn is shared in this thesis. Indeed, in the first chapter it is stated that a public interest protected by a public policy will prevail over the corporate personality. The state has a duty to protect public interests and a statutory rule is a means used by the state to fulfill its duty to protect the public interest. US tax law, labour law and environmental law are areas in which the corporate personality is likely to be ignored by the US authorities in order to enforce a public policy.

2.4.1 *Tax law*

In the context of tax law, for state and federal tax purposes, the corporate entity is usually recognized, although disregarded when used as a tax-evasion device.[157] Originally, tax law was silent in respect of this matter. However, the decision of the US Supreme Court on the case of *Higgings v Smith* shed light on this subject.[158] In this decision it was established that the government might disregard sham corporations whenever that would best serve the purpose of a tax statute and that a taxpayer who has chosen to do business as a corporation must accept any tax disadvantage of that

---

156 See, Henn, H. *Supra note* 148. At page 359 §150.
157 See, Henn, H. *Supra note* 148. At page 372§153.
158 *Higgings v Smith* 308 U.S 473, 60 S.Ct. 355, 84 L.Ed. 406 (1940). Cited by Henn H. *Idem*. At page 373.

form.[159] In other words, the taxpayer will not be permitted to renounce the corporate entity for their benefit.

2.4.2 Labour law

Corporate personality may produce different questions in the context of labour law cases; for example, to what extent should a parent company accept responsibility for their subsidiaries' unfair labour practices? Alternatively, to what extent should a collective bargaining agreement covering the employees of one corporation be extended to cover another nominally separate yet still commonly owned entity? However, although there have been questions and reflections on this subject, the public interest that exists regarding the protection and enforcement of workers' rights tends to prevail over the corporate personality dilemma. The US Federal Courts have assumed the task of formulating a federal common law of labour relations, a fact that has left many aspects of the employment relationship subject to exclusive federal control and furthermore to be entirely immune from state regulation.[160] The National Labour Relations Act (NLRA) is a regulation that deals with collective bargaining agreements, working hours, employment discrimination and wages. The NLRA is one of the most notorious regulations that has been developed and applied in labour cases involving the corporate personality. From the application of the NLRA in corporate personality cases, the concepts of "single economic employer" and "alter ego" have been introduced to American labour law. The former is based on determining whether nominally independent enterprises are sufficiently intertwined and whether they should be considered a single employer for NLRA purposes. The latter seeks to determine whether the existence of a corporate entity is an attempt by the employer to avoid obligations. Both approaches focus on review aspects concerning management and corporate formalities. Moreover, it can be considered that the single economic employer is founded on the approach developed from the concept of a single economic unit previously mentioned. Indeed, the single economic employer transfers liability to the companies forming the group as if they were a whole.

As a personal observation, the application of the NLRA can be considered as an attempt to make the piercing of the corporate veil in labour law cases coherent. The corporate personality cannot be disregarded in every labour controversy because doing so would affect its integrity. Certainly, workers' rights take priority due to the public interest that exists regarding the

---

159 *Ibid.*
160 See, Mcleod, W. (1991–2) 'Shareholder's Liability and Workers' Rights: Piercing the Corporate Veil Under Federal Labor Law' *Hofstra Labor Law* (Volume 91). At page 117.

68 *Piercing corporate veil in Anglo-American context*

enforcement of these rights. However, there must also be a rational justification for the use of this remedy. Therefore, through the application of the rules contained in the NLRA, the US judiciary has introduced the single economic employer and alter ego approach to systematically apply this remedy in this context.

It is worth adding that approaches formulated from the application of the NLRA have been applied together with other labour statutes such as the WARN Act (Workers Adjustment and Retraining Notification)[161] and ERISA (the Employment Retirement Income Security Act).

2.4.3 *Environmental law*

In the US the piercing of the corporate veil in statutory interpretation is best illustrated in the field of environmental law; indeed, during the 1970s concern for the environment started to arise in the mind of the American public.[162] The Comprehensive Environmental Response, the Compensation and Liability Act (CERCLA) was a result of the concern regarding the need for a rule to deal with the release of hazardous substances. The rationale of CERCLA was based on a public policy aimed at the protection of the environment. However, Federal courts in this context do not disregard the legal entity straight away. In CERCLA liability is imposed depending upon four circumstances but for the purposes of this section, only the first one will be addressed. It has been established that the owner and operator of a polluting vessel or facility will be liable for environmental contamination.[163]

The US is known for its strong industry, which has been developed through the use of corporate groups. Many industrial activities involve hazardous practices and, in cases of environmental disasters, parent companies and other subsidiaries part of the group are free of liability thanks to the group's structure. In some circumstances, the affected parties seek to make the parent company liable; thus the concept of "operator" established in CERCLA has been used to support an action against a parent company. The use of the

---

161 The WARN Act of 1988, 29 U.SC. §§ 2101–2109, requires certain employers, inter alia, to provide their employees with 60 days' prior notice before engaging in a plant closing or other large layoff. Since the WARN Act only applies to businesses with 100 or more employees, veil piercing and single enterprise issues arise when affiliated corporations individually fall below the threshold but together aggregate the requisite number. See, Presser, S. (2006) 'The Bolgalusa Explosion, "Single Business Enterprise" "Alter Ego" and other error: Academics, Economics, Democracy and Shareholder Limited Liability. Back Towards a Unitary "Abuse" Theory of Piercing the Corporate Veil' *Northwestern University Law Review* (Volume 100). At page 416.

162 See, Noonan, P. (1990) 'Pierce or not to Pierce? When, is the question. Developing a Federal Rule for Piercing the Corporate Veil Under CERCLA' *Washington University Law Quarterly* (Volume 60). At page 735.

163 Section 107(a)(1) of CERCLA, 42 USC § 9607(a).

concept of operator derives from the fact that subsidiaries operate under the instructions of the parent. However, to address the parent corporation under the concept of operator contained in the Act is complicated because a subsidiary, in principle, operates as an independent entity from its parent and the influence of the parent over the subsidiary is the result of an agreement between both in order to achieve a common purpose. Moreover, in the Act there is not a clear definition of what can be considered as an operator in this context. Therefore, the alter ego doctrine has been employed to supplement the concept of operator in order to enforce the policies contained in CERCLA.[164] The use of the test contained in the alter ego approach can be considered as a better means to determine parent liability for the subsidiary's actions. By evaluating aspects such as compliance with corporate formalities and financial independence, the degree of control of the parent over the subsidiary can be determined thus establishing whether the parent company can be viewed as operator or not.

The previously cited case of *The United States v Bestfoods* is a relevant case in this area. In this case the court dealt with the dilemma about whether the parent company could be considered as an operator for the purposes of CERCLA. Moreover, the court tried to provide a definition of operator in this context. To deal with the concept of corporate groups is complicated but the precedent in *United States v Bestfoods* has provided a reference for contemporary cases; an example being *AMW Materials Testing, Inc v Town Babylon*.[165] In this case a fire produced the release of a hazardous substance kept in a building owned by the defendant. Thus, the claimant sought to hold the defendant liable on grounds of the concept of operator contained in CERCLA and the precedent set by *United States v Bestfoods*.

2.5 The role of the concepts of fraud and negligence in the context of corporate veil issues

Among the imperfections of the US doctrine of piercing the corporate veil, one aspect that should be analysed is the use of the remedy to deal with corporate veil issues derived from damages produced by negligence. In this thesis it is considered that corporate personality issues involving fraud must be handled separately from cases involving negligence. To include the concept of negligence together with fraud is not appropriate because negligence involves an issue where producing loss or harm is unintentional. The issue on mixing the concepts of fraud and negligence lies in the fact that it

---

164 See, Noonan, P. *Supra note* 162. At page 741.
165 *AMW Materials Testing, Inc v Town Babylon*, 584F. 3d 436, Court of Appeals, 2nd Circuit 2009.

70 *Piercing corporate veil in Anglo-American context*

complicates the application of a remedy such as piercing the corporate veil, which was originally created to deal with the fraudulent use of the corporate entity.

If the corporate personality is used to achieve a fraudulent purpose this will be ignored; this is the premise on which the piercing the corporate veil has been built. The application of this remedy in cases in which a fraudulent intention does not exist has contributed to the uncertainty that surrounds this subject. The omission of the original trigger (fraudulent behavior) makes the piercing of the corporate veil void of its original purpose (punishment and prevention of fraud) and renders this remedy unpredictable. Some American academics consider the unpredictability of the doctrine as convenient because it encourages wrongdoers to abstain.[166] However, in this thesis unpredictability is considered a factor that undermines the concept of corporate personality because it gives room for the application of piercing the corporate veil in circumstances that do not necessarily require this remedy.

Currently, the piercing of the corporate veil has been considered as a last resort, due to its unpredictability.[167] As mentioned, the exceptional circumstances are based mainly on the concept of fraud. If this trigger is omitted, it gives room for an uncontrolled and unjustified application of this remedy.

As stated, corporate entity issues derived from fraud and those derived from negligence should not be confused. However, what is negligence in this context? In this book the concept of negligence refers to the harm produced by reckless management and tort damages produced by the practice of dangerous activities. Reckless management produces harm to different parties that have a direct relation with the corporate entity; for example, workers may not get their wages and creditors may not recover their credit because the company ran out of assets due to irresponsible management. The inadequate practice of dangerous activities, on the other hand, generally consists of damages to parties that do not have any relationship with the corporate entity; for example, a chemical disaster that affects a town and pollutes the environment. However, there are also cases in which dangerous activities may affect parties that have a direct relationship with the entity such as the employees, who may be affected if the company does not comply with security requirements.

The objective of the corporate entity is to protect shareholders from these situations. However, to preserve the corporate personality presents a dilemma based on the unfair result that may be produced in some circumstances if the

---

166 See, Bainbridge, S. *Abolishing Veil Piercing.* SSRN eLibrary Available at http://papers. ssrn.com/sol3/papers.cfm?abstract_id=236967 (last visit 30 May 2013). At pages 46–9.
167 See, Bevans, N. (2007) *Business Organization and Corporate Law.* US: Thomson Delmar Learning. At page 275.

Piercing corporate veil in Anglo-American context   71

corporate personality is preserved. This "fairness dilemma" can be considered as the reason for the concept of negligence to be considered when dealing with corporate personality issues. Currently, in the US the piercing of the corporate veil has been requested by affected parties in cases were no fraudulent behavior was seen to have existed; a factor that can be attributed to the mix of the concepts of fraud and negligence when talking about corporate personality issues. However, it is likely that the US courts will deny the piercing of the corporate veil if there is no fraud or an evident inequitable result. Evidence of this can be found in an example such as the case *McCloud v Bettcher Industries Inc.*[168] The claimant in this case worked for a subsidiary and sustained injury while operating a bread machine. Therefore, the claimant sought to pierce the corporate veil to hold the parent company liable together with his employer. However, the court considered that the parent as a shareholder could not be held liable for the torts of its subsidiary. The court maintained that a party seeking to pierce the corporate veil must establish that the owners, through their domination, abused the privilege of doing business in the corporate form, thereby perpetrating a wrong that resulted in injury to the affected party. In this case there was not an abuse of the corporate form. Another example can be found in the case *Smith v Delta*, decided by the New York court.[169] In this case the claimant was injured while working for a company managed by the defendant. The claimant claimed for compensation not only against the employing company but also the defendant company and individual parts of this entity. However the claimant failed to justify on what grounds the corporate veil should be pierced in this case. He did not prove that the defendant failed to adhere to corporate formalities, inadequate capitalization or commingled assets. The court considered that a party seeking to pierce the corporate veil must establish that the owners, through their domination, abused the privilege of doing business in the corporate form by perpetrating a wrong or injustice against the affected party.

In these two examples, the piercing of the corporate veil was denied based on a lack of consistent argument to justify the application of this remedy. The purpose of citing these cases is to show the occurrence of pleas based on a cause that does not involve fraud. To allow and reflect over the piercing of the corporate veil in cases where no fraudulent behavior exists creates uncertainty. Indeed, the fact that a court considers this action without the occurrence of the original trigger creates a perception that this doctrine may be applied whenever it is summoned.

Although the concept of negligence has been considered by the US doctrine, the corporate personality issues in this context have been handled

---

168 *McCloud v Bettcher Industries Inc* 90 AD 3d 1680, NY Appellate Div., 4th Dept 2011.
169 *Smith v Delta Intl, Mach, Corp.*, 2010 NY: Appellate DIV., 2nd Dept 2010.

72 *Piercing corporate veil in Anglo-American context*

in a more practical way in certain areas of law; for example, damages derived from reckless management in the context of public companies. In this context, hired directors rather than shareholders manage modern US companies. These hired directors do not receive the benefits of the corporate personality and limited liability, as do the shareholders. Consequently, authorities do not need to deal with the corporate veil in this situation. For this task, accountability and management regulations have been developed in order to deter and penalise reckless management. An example is the American Sarbanes Oxley Act, a regulation that strengthens accountability controls, increases the oversight role of boards of directors and renders the penalties for fraudulent and negligent activities more severe.[170]

The existence of statutes aimed at dealing with reckless management in the context of public companies evidences the existence of a more practical method to deal with corporate personality cases where no fraudulent behavior exists. In other words, a statutory approach in this context can be considered as more practical. If statutory exceptions were developed in critical areas such as reckless management and environmental law, the piercing of the corporate veil would be a less uncertain subject.

Some civil law jurisdictions have been practical and have handled issues derived from negligence in statutory rules. An example is Brazilian environmental law in which it is established that the corporate entity will be ignored in cases involving damages to the environment. As has been mentioned throughout this thesis, civil law jurisdictions adhere to positive law. Definitely, this is an influential factor for the development of a statutory exception to the corporate personality. However, the existence of an exception to the corporate veil in Brazilian environmental law can be attributed to the need of a rule aimed at helping to enforce public policies in this area of law. The occurrence of negligence is common in environmental disasters. To use this as a remedy for piercing of the corporate veil is not suitable for this sort of circumstance. Consequently, it is appropriate to apply a direct statutory exception in this context.

It is important to add that the development of a rule to deal with the corporate personality in a case that does not involve fraud must be based on the legal framework and legal needs of each jurisdiction. As I emphasise throughout this thesis, economic development has strong influence over the corporate personality and all the aspects that surrounds this concept.

My case study, Panama, is a jurisdiction in which the piercing of the corporate veil has been recent. Panama has developed as a financial service provider. Industrial activity does exist in this country but on a small scale

---

170 Sarbanes–Oxley Act of 2002 (Pub.L. 107–204, 116 Stat. 745, enacted 30 July 2002).

Piercing corporate veil in Anglo-American context 73

in comparison to industrialized countries. Moreover, companies tend to be private rather than public. The existence of more private companies can be attributed to the fact that funding can be gathered from local banks. The existence of a small capital markets with few public companies and little industrial activity makes the occurrence of reckless management and tort damages infrequent issues. As I have mentioned, an approach to piercing the corporate veil must be based on the legal framework and the usage that is given to the corporate entity. In Panama, the joint stock corporation has been developed in an environment that allows the corporate entity to be used in a way that makes the occurrence of fraudulent intention likely. Certainly, it cannot be denied that cases involving loss or harm produced by negligence may arise. For example, reckless management may leave workers without payment. However, Panamanian labour law has already included a mechanism to deal with this issue and does not necessarily involve engaging the corporate veil dilemma. The rule contained in the Article 92 of the Panamanian Labour Code not only allows the setting aside of the corporate personality on grounds of fraud but also on grounds of negligent management causing the company's impossibility to pay its employees.

The piercing of the corporate veil as a remedy based on the prevention and punishment of fraud should have the scope for its application limited to this context. To attempt to pierce the corporate veil in situations that do not involve fraud creates uncertainty because there will be no specific ground for the application of this remedy. Moreover, it contradicts the exceptional nature of this remedy by allowing parties requesting its application whenever they want, a fact that definitely would undermine the concept of corporate personality.

Summary

The US is a jurisdiction that presents a complex legal system. Unquestionably, the plurality of state jurisdictions and a federal jurisdiction have generated different opinions and perspectives about the piercing of the corporate veil. However, despite the doctrines of instrumentality and alter ego being considered as the only systematic approach to deal with corporate veil issues, they present a set of circumstances that have to occur in order to ignore the corporate personality; namely, the main trigger, which is the occurrence of wrongful and fraudulent behavior. Nonetheless, there have been cases involving corporate personality issues that have not necessarily involved the occurrence of fraudulent behavior. Consequently, the American judiciary has also relied on other approaches to deal with corporate entity issues such as agency and the single economic unit. In the context of statutory law there is no direct exception to the corporate personality. However, this can be ignored based on public policies aimed at protecting a public interest.

74 *Piercing corporate veil in Anglo-American context*

2.6 *Why does the US appear more willing than England to pierce the corporate veil?*

The US and England are countries of common law tradition, have strong markets and prosperous economies. The corporate personality has been key in the development of these countries.[171] Consequently, both tend to respect the integrity of the corporate personality. However, when it comes to situations that involve an improper use of the corporate personality, the US has evidenced more willingness to ignore the existence of the corporate personality than England. In fact, the piercing of the corporate veil has been a common issue in US company law. This chapter has addressed the American doctrines of instrumentality and alter ego. Both doctrines are the result of rich case law on piercing the corporate veil.

However, the fact that the US has developed to a greater extent the doctrine of piercing the corporate veil does not mean that the US authorities will pierce the corporate veil whenever this action is requested. The US authorities tend to preserve the integrity of the corporate personality. Nonetheless, it has been perceived that the US is a jurisdiction willing to pierce the corporate veil because a series of factors that make this subject gain more relevance in the US.

The US has a federal government, a fact that in turn makes the US a complex jurisdiction. Company law and all the aspects related to it have been left as a matter for each state to regulate. Consequently, each state has a different opinion about the piercing of the corporate veil. Certainly, the doctrines of instrumentality and alter ego are structured on the same concepts: control, fraud and causation. However, each state has its own perception of each of these concepts. Moreover, when corporate personality issues go beyond state borders, conflicts of laws arise not only between state laws but also between state law and federal law. As a result, the diversity of opinions and constant debates about piercing the corporate veil stimulate the development of this subject. In contrast, England has a more centralized type of government. As a consequence, court decisions tend to have a more uniform effect than in the US. Evidence of this is the English case of *Salomon v Salomon Co.* In England, the precedent established in the *Salomon* case is the foundation of the current position regarding the piercing of the corporate veil, the preservation of the corporate personality. It cannot be denied that among the English judiciary and academia there have been different opinions on this subject. However, the general tendency is to follow the precedent established in the case of *Salomon.*

---

171 See, Micklethwait, J. and Wooldridge, A. *Supra note 43.*

Piercing corporate veil in Anglo-American context   75

In addition, another factor that has to be considered is the perception of the concept of fairness in this context. It can be considered that English authorities tend to be stricter than the US. An example is the previously cited case of *Adams v Cape*. In this case, the US authorities decided to hold Cape Industries liable. However, when English authorities were requested to recognize and enforce this judgment, they refused to do so. Their refusal was based on the lack of a strong justification to ignore the corporate personality. The US authorities tend to consider the piercing of the corporate veil in cases that do not necessarily involve a fraudulent or wrongful conduct. In contrast, English authorities emphasized in the case of *Cape* that the corporate veil should not be pierced merely because it is just to do so.[172]

The US and England share the same legal tradition and the corporate personality has been relevant to their economies. However, the geographical dimension, organization of government and judiciary and the role of the concept of fairness are factors that in this thesis are considered to have had an effect over the piercing of the corporate veil in the US and England. These factors are of special attention because they are precisely what make each of these jurisdictions unique.

2.6.1   The dilemma between the "sledgehammer approach" and the "backdoor approach"

The piercing of the corporate veil is a subject that has been regarded differently in the US and England. As stated in Chapter I, the piercing of the corporate veil is a remedy that each jurisdiction adapts in accordance with its legal needs. The "sledgehammer approach" and the "backdoor approach" are names used in this section to address the different paths that the US and England have taken to pierce the corporate veil. I address both approaches under these headings for the purpose of this section, which is to determine what can be the most suitable position for my case study, Panama. I am not arguing that Panama should copy the American or English approaches; rather my intention is to present my opinion about whether Panama should be active or passive with regard to corporate veil issues (the Panamanian corporate personality and the piercing of the corporate veil is a subject that will be properly addressed in Chapter IV).

On the one hand, the US deals in a straightforward manner with the corporate personality. The doctrines of instrumentality and alter ego are a means to piercing the corporate veil. Hence, it can be considered as a jurisdiction that has used a "sledgehammer approach" because it directly strikes the concept of corporate personality. England, on the other hand, has opted for not attacking the corporate personality but instead looking

---

172 *Adams v Cape Industries* [1990] BCC 786. At pages 544–5.

76 *Piercing corporate veil in Anglo-American context*

for alternative ways in which to deal with corporate veil issues. In this chapter, it was noted that English cases dealing with corporate personality issues did not finish with piercing of the corporate veil. The fact that the integrity of the corporate personality has not been affected makes this a "backdoor approach" because it looks for an alternative, less direct, means to establish liability for the corporation's acts.

These different approaches trigger the following question: which approach provides a more suitable basis for the Panamanian approach? Some may argue that a "backdoor approach" is more convenient for Panama in view of the fact it is a financial service provider and relies on the incorporation of companies. A "backdoor approach" will not worry investors nor undermine the corporate personality; and the same will help to deal with the misuse of the corporate personality. However, in this thesis it has opted for a "sledge-hammer approach".

A "backdoor approach" requires a high degree of judicial creativity in order to find a concept that suits the case and that can be justified. This degree of judicial creativity exists in common law tradition countries such as England but not in civil law tradition countries such as Panama. The "backdoor approach" is less combative yet it can be considered as being surrounded by uncertainty.

As a personal observation, a statutory rule is more compatible with the Panamanian legal framework. Panama is a civil law tradition country and as such it relies on statutory law. The motive behind the inclination for a "sledgehammer approach" is based on its practicality. A statute that directly deals with the corporate personality tends to be based on circumstances that may occur in any case and in any area of law. A statutory approach, however, has a drawback. A statute cannot cover every matter and legal loopholes will come to light with the application of the statutory rule.

Undeniably, a statute that directly allows the piercing of the corporate veil will be subject to criticism because it may be seen as something that will undermine the Panamanian corporate personality. This is a disadvantage that faces the "sledgehammer approach". Nevertheless, in this thesis it is considered the more appropriate approach.

Chapter conclusion

The US and England are the jurisdictions where corporate personality has been used to a greater extent. England is the jurisdiction that pioneered the use of corporate personality as a device for commerce and the US has used this instrument even more extensively. In fact, it can be considered that the modern corporate entity is originally Anglo-American. The piercing of the corporate veil is a phenomenon that derived from the existence and common use of the corporate personality by Anglo-American jurisdictions. Furthermore, whilst being the jurisdictions that pioneered the use of this entity, they were thus the first to experience the dilemma of whether or not to pierce the corporate veil. However, although the US and England share a similar principle rationale for piercing the corporate veil (the punishment and prevention of fraud), this subject has been addressed differently by both jurisdictions.

On the one hand, the English authorities have been reluctant to apply a remedy such as piercing the corporate veil. This position was defined in the case of *Salomon*. Since that decision, approaches based on concepts such as sham, agency and single economic unit have been proposed. However, no systematic approach to apply this remedy has derived from these concepts. The concept of sham has had more acceptance as a means to deal with corporate veil issues. However, in cases where it has been used to support an argument against the corporate personality, the decision has not been the piercing of the corporate veil but rather liability has been extended to the companies or defendants. The precedent of *Salomon* is solid and thus authorities have opted for alternatives that do not affect the integrity of the corporate personality in order to avoid conflict.

In this chapter, it has been pointed out that English authorities have adopted a different approach to deal with corporate personality issues. Notably, the fact that a specific approach has not been developed does not necessarily mean that the misuse of the corporate personality is allowed. In contemporary cases involving corporate personality issues, the courts have tended to protect the integrity of the corporate personality and justify liability on other grounds. In the cited case of *Chandler v Cape plc*, the court established liability not by disregarding the existence of the corporate veil but by considering the existence of a duty of care towards an affected employee of a subsidiary.

In addition, English authorities have also relied on statutory rules to deal with corporate personality issues. However, statutory rules are not aimed at the corporate personality but instead at the parties responsible for its misuse. In this jurisdiction, the grounds on which an argument to pierce the corporate veil is likely to succeed are limited to cases involving circumstances that affect the interest of the state.

On the other hand, since the early days of the corporate personality, the US has been more open to applying the piercing of the corporate veil; a factor that can be attributed to the plurality of internal jurisdictions that, along with other opinions, feeds the debate over topics such as the piercing of the corporate veil. The doctrines of instrumentality and alter ego, which are in essence the same, have been developed from the corporate veil debate. Both doctrines are aimed at making shareholders liable when it is proven that their excessive control over the corporate entity rendered it a mere instrument for fraudulent purposes.

The US doctrine to pierce the corporate veil has been the subject for criticism because there is not a concrete definition as to what can be considered as control and fraud. Moreover, the application of this doctrine is unpredictable and jurisprudence is full of vagueness. However, despite heavy criticism,

78 *Piercing corporate veil in Anglo-American context*

the doctrines of instrumentality and alter ego are considered as the only systematic approach to deal with corporate veil issues. These doctrines present a set of circumstances that have to occur in order to ignore the corporate personality. The main trigger is the occurrence of wrongful and fraudulent behavior.

In the context of US statutory law, there is no direct exception to the corporate personality. Undoubtedly, US policymakers have gradually introduced exceptions to the corporate entity in areas of law in which public policies have been set in order to protect a public interest but these statutory exceptions are limited to a specific circumstance.

This chapter closes with a brief comparison that gave rise to the metaphors of "sledgehammer" and "backdoor". The purpose of the former was to describe the active American position and of the latter the passive English position, in this context. I decided to briefly analyze that position would be the more appropriate for Panama to adopt because this will gradually introduce the reader to the core of this book. In addition, this chapter contributes to confirm one of the premises of this research; "the piercing of the corporate veil is a remedy that each jurisdiction adapts in accordance with its internal needs". Indeed, although the piercing of the corporate veil can be considered as an Anglo-American occurrence, the development of this subject has taken different paths in both jurisdictions.

III Corporate veil in Latin America; general aspects about Franco-Hispanic civil law that have influenced the development of piercing the corporate veil in Latin America

In order to study the piercing of the corporate veil in Latin America, it is first important to introduce the reader to the framework on which the Latin American countries subject of study have developed their legal system.

The civil law tradition is the legal tradition followed by the countries in this region. Thus, it can be considered as the foundation on which the Latin American countries have supported their legal systems. The legal tradition establishes the basic rules on which a legal system will be developed. Consequently, it is one of the key elements that has born influence over the mechanisms used to deal with the corporate personality. Nonetheless, it has to be pointed out that each legal system is unique despite stemming from the same legal tradition. Moreover, the mechanisms to pierce the corporate veil are developed individually by each jurisdiction. However, in Latin America, the civil law tradition has provided legal concepts and principles that are shared throughout the region. Furthermore, the mechanisms to deal with corporate entity issues have been developed over this shared set of concepts and principles.

In Latin America the piercing of the corporate veil is a subject that has been addressed with a methodology that differs from the Anglo-American doctrine due to the influence of legal tradition. Indeed, the civil law tradition is inclined to strict formalism. Therefore, the Latin American countries that have introduced an exception to the corporate veil have done so through the use of statutory rules, which are based on traditional legal concepts and principles. The objective of this chapter is to address the generalities of the civil law tradition and the legal concepts and principles that have had an influence on the development of the different mechanisms to deal with the corporate personality in Latin America.

This chapter begins with a brief explanation about how the civil law tradition made its way through Latin America. For the reader with no background knowledge regarding Latin American civil law, this chapter will provide a basic introduction and thus leave the reader with a better comprehension of the mechanisms used by Latin American countries to deal with corporate personality issues. Following, two key differences between the

80 *Corporate veil in Latin America*

common law and the civil law tradition (the sources of law and the role of critical thinking) will be addressed as they have had great influence over the piercing of the corporate veil in Latin America. In addition, each of the principles and concepts used by Latin American jurisdictions to deal with corporate veil issues will be explained.

1. The roots of the Latin American civil law tradition

Latin America is a region formed by countries that were predominantly Spanish colonies (from the sixteenth until mid-nineteenth century). During the mid-nineteenth century many colonies had already gained independence and others were fighting for it. By the end of the nineteenth century Spanish political control over the region was almost nonexistent. At the beginning of the twentieth century Latin America was formed by newly independent republics. However, all the institutions introduced by Spain during the colonial period were maintained.

With regards law, the civil law tradition made its way throughout Latin America during the Spanish colonization but it was not sophisticated and organized as we know it today. Civil law in Europe was based on the Roman legacy. Each European kingdom tried to adapt Roman civil law in accordance with its needs and used the Justinian *Corpus Juris Civilis* as a guide.[1] The Spanish attempt to make a compilation of laws was the *Siete Partidas*, which is a code drafted during the medieval period.[2] Although rudimentary, the *Siete Partidas* has been considered one of the most important works of codification since the Justinian *Corpus Juris Civilis*.[3] In addition to the *Siete Partidas*, the *Ordenanzas de Bilbao* was another compilation of law, developed to regulate commerce among colonies. Its necessity lay in the increase of colonies and trade, which in turn demanded a suitable commercial and legal framework.[4] The *Siete partidas* and *Ordenanzas de Bilbao* were the laws applicable in the Spanish colonies. After the Latin American countries became independent, they kept *Siete Partidas* and *Ordenanzas de Bilbao* in force. However, these regulations did not meet the demands of the changing societies and were gradually replaced with the new laws.

The reader may wonder, why does the title of this chapter mention "Franco-Hispanic Civil Law"? It is a fair question because Latin America

---

1 Ozcoide & Falcon (1998) *Historia del Derecho Civil Español*. Madrid: Arazadi.
2 Mirow, M. (2004) *Latin America Law: A History of Private Law and Institutions in Spanish America*. Texas: University of Texas Press. At page 75.
3 *Ibid.*
4 Hernandez, A. (1998) *Curso de Derecho Mercantil*. Madrid: Geminis. Page 40.

has a strong connection with Spain. Therefore, what does France have to do with this?

During the Napoleonic wars in the early nineteenth century, France had occupied many regions of the continent, including Spain. During the French occupation, the French exported their culture and advances, including an innovation, the "Napoleonic Civil Code". Napoleonic Code was considered the most complete work of codification since the *Corpus Juris Civilis*.[5] After Napoleon was defeated French troops left occupied territories, but the Napoleonic Code was left behind. European countries took the Napoleonic Code and used it as a model to develop their own work of codification.[6] This started a "trend" of codification in Latin American countries. Although they had separated from Spain, they kept an interest in the innovations produced in Europe. The codification trend, a result of the Napoleonic Code, was not ignored by Latin American countries, which also developed their own works of codification.

In this brief section, it can be appreciated that the roots of the Latin American civil law tradition have a Franco-Hispanic essence. On the one hand, the Spanish provided the foundations and materials. On the other hand, the French provided the tool to work these materials. The two elements are an important pillar of the Latin American legal systems subject of study in this book.

2. The corporate personality in the Latin American civil law tradition

The civil law tradition made its way to Latin America through the Spanish conquerors and French developments. However, did the contemporary corporate personality arrive with Franco-Hispanic civil law?

The contemporary corporate personality is a relatively new invention. Roman civil law did recognize the legal entity. However, it did not recognize the limited liability of the individuals behind the legal entity.[7] Throughout the years the attribute of limited liability was not part of the European framework for corporate entities. Moreover, even the French Civil Code of 1802, which did recognize what we know today as a corporate entity, did not recognize the limited liability of the individuals behind the corporate entity.[8] In Latin America, the situation was no different because it was a region heavily influenced by the advances and changes in European civil law. It was not until the late nineteenth century, when the English pioneered the use of the

---

5 Serrano, F. (2005) *El Codigo de Napoleon*. Argentina: Porrua. Page 15.
6 *Idem.*
7 Serrano, A. (2013) *Las Ficciones del Derecho*. Colombia: Editorial Temis. Page 50.
8 Orallo, P. (1975) *Persona juridical y Ficcion*. Pamplona: Ariza. Page 120.

82 *Corporate veil in Latin America*

corporate personality together with limited liability due to the need of a means to gather capital to face the challenges of the industrial era. The English initiative was not just a success in England, but also in Continental Europe. European countries decided to copy the English initiative and develop their own type of business association that conferred limited liability to its members. Some examples are the French *Société Anonyme* (SA),[9] the German *Gesellschaft mit beschränkter Haftung* (GmBH)[10] and the Spanish *Sociedad Anónima* (SA).[11]

Once continental Europe introduced the business association that included the attributes of legal personality and limited liability, Latin America started to introduce the contemporary legal entity in their legal framework, based on the European advances on the subject. As can be imagined, contemporary corporate personality issues gradually started to manifest and a remedy became a necessity.

3. Contrast between the common law and the civil law tradition; the influence of legal tradition over the piercing of the corporate veil

The legal tradition followed by a country is an influential factor regarding the development of an approach to deal with corporate personality issues. The concept of legal tradition makes reference to a set of customs and practices used by society to deal with issues among its citizens.[12] In modern civilization, the common law and the civil law are the most influential legal traditions due to historical factors.[13] The legal tradition establishes the basic

---

9 The French *Société Anonyme* was introduced in the French Code of Commerce enacted in 1807. However, the attributes of legal personality and limited liability in addition to capital requirements were established in the *loi de mai de* 1863 and the reforms in 1867.

10 The German *Gesellschaft mit beschränkter Haftung* or limited liability company was introduced in Germany in 1892.

11 In Spain the use of business associations became common during the colonial expansion (from the sixteenth until seventeenth century). However, the concept of corporate personality and limited liability became subject of interest in 1869 and 1885 when reforms to the Spanish code of commerce were made.

12 The author, Patrick Glenn, in his work *Legal Traditions of the World* explores the concept of tradition and its influence on current legal practice. He focuses on aspects such as customs, religion and regional practices as the basis of current legal traditions. See, Glenn, P. (2010) *Legal Traditions of the World*. 4th Edition. New York: Oxford University Press.

13 There are other legal traditions such as Islamic legal tradition and Hindu legal tradition. However, the civil and common law traditions are currently the prevalent legal traditions due to factors such as colonial expansion of European empires. Powerful European countries, such as the UK, Spain and France, exported the common law and the civil law tradition to different regions of the world. After the colonies gained independence, they kept the legal traditions introduced by the colonizing countries. As a result we have common and civil law as the most relevant legal traditions. See, *idem.* At page 361.

Corporate veil in Latin America 83

rules and principles that the judiciary will follow when dealing with legal issues. However, each society has different legal needs, thus each will use the rules and principles of the legal tradition in accordance with these internal needs. A legal system is molded from a legal tradition and this in turn creates the environment in which concepts such as piercing the corporate veil are going to be developed.

Based on the individuality of each legal system, in this book it is argued that Latin American countries have developed their own approaches to pierce the corporate veil, rather than borrowing the US doctrine. This statement derives from the fact that there is a misconception regarding the piercing of the corporate veil. Indeed, some Latin American academics consider that the American doctrine of piercing the corporate veil has made its way to Latin America.[14] It cannot be denied that the American doctrine of piercing the corporate veil has been a subject of interest for Latin American academics and judiciary.[15] However, the Latin American countries that have introduced an exception to the corporate personality have structured this in accordance with the principles and internal beliefs of the civil law tradition.[16]

The piercing of the corporate veil is developed in accordance with the principles established by the legal tradition followed by the legal system dealing with this legal phenomenon. Certainly, common law and civil law are two different legal traditions. However, in this book are considered two aspects as the main influence on the contrast between piercing the corporate veil in Latin America and Anglo-American countries: these are the sources of law and the role of equity.

14 The author, Jose M. Bello, in his paper regarding the piercing of the corporate veil in Latin America, considers the piercing of the corporate veil as a concept loaned to Latin American jurisdictions. He states that "the doctrine of piercing the corporate veil has been trying to make its way through Latin America". This is a statement that is not shared in this thesis, due to the fact that the corporate personality is a universal concept – a point addressed later in greater detail.

See, Bello, J. (2008) 'An Overview of the Doctrine of the Piercing of the Corporate Veil as Applied By Latin American Countries: A U.S. Legal Creation Exported to Civil Law Jurisdictions' [Argentina/Mexico/United States/Venezuela]. *ILSA Journal of International & Comparative Law.* Volume 14, Issue 3. At page 628.

15 The authors Perez and Diaz are some of the Latina American academics who have developed an interest in the study of the American doctrine of piercing the corporate veil. Perez, R. (2008) 'Una Vision Dual de la Doctrina del Levantamiento del Velo de la Persona Juridica' *Revista del Instituto de la Judicatura Federal No. 25.* See also Diaz Olivo, C. (2004) 'Mitos y Leyendas Acerca de la Doctrina de Descorrer el Velo Corporativo' *Revista Juridica de la Universidad de Puerto Rico* (Volume 73: No. 2). Pages 311–91.

16 The civil law tradition is characterized for its formalist nature, which contrasts with the flexibility of common law.

84 *Corporate veil in Latin America*

3.1 *Sources of law*

The sources of law are technically the same in both legal traditions:

- Positive law
- Customs
- Case law
- Principles
- Doctrine

The relevant difference lies in the main source of law. On the one hand, common law has case law as the main source of law; on the other hand, the civil law has positive law as the main source of law.[17]

In the eyes of the lawyer educated under the civil law system, case law is the result of the practice; the judge interprets the legal text and applies it to the circumstances, a process that gives birth to case law. Under common law, on the other hand, case law is not only the result of the application of law, but also the main source of law.[18] In the common law tradition, each legal decision not only establishes the parameter that should be followed in future cases, but also binds the judge. A court decision creates a precedent, which feeds over posterior decisions that follow the same reasoning of the original precedent. The reaffirmation of the original decision over a legal matter binds future judges to follow the same line of reasoning. Certainly, a legal precedent can be challenged because of circumstances that made a legal precedent obsolete or inadequate. However, case law is a binding force in the common law tradition. Case law's binding nature can be attributed to the status of a main source of law, giving by the common law tradition. Positive law, on the other hand, is a secondary source in this legal tradition. Positive law presents the grounds on which humans have to coexist. If an individual(s) acts in a way that negatively affects other individuals, the sanction for their behavior has to be determined according to what has been established in positive law. Certainly, the fact that positive law establishes the grounds to deal with a specific behavior makes it a relevant source of law. However, in the common law tradition, positive law is open to interpretation by the judge. The judge will determine the scope of positive law and his decision over the matter will become the line of opinion to follow. In summary, in the common law tradition, the judge interprets and establishes the grounds on which positive law is applied, the judge can be regarded as an integral part of the law-making process.

---

17 Perdomo, R. & Marryman, J. (2007) *The Civil Law Tradition: An Introduction to the Legal Systems of Europe and Latin America* 3rd Edition. California: Stanford University Press. Page 48.

18 Glenn, P. *Supra Note 12.* Page 237.

Corporate veil in Latin America 85

In contrast, positive law is the main source of law in the civil law tradition. As previously mentioned, it can be defined as the set of rules created by humans with the objective to harmonize human interaction. The codes and statutes are the materialization of these rules. Contrary to the common law tradition, in the civil law tradition positive law is not open to interpretation by judges. The judge has to follow the parameters established by the positive law. In other words, under civil law there is strict adherence to what has been established in the codes. Certainly, this statement is a bit extreme because some principles allow the civil law judge room to interpret the law and thus prevent an unfair administration of justice.[19] However, the interpretation of the rules cannot go against the nature or true meaning of positive law. In the civil law tradition, case law is a secondary source of law and only aids the administration of justice. Case law presents the position of the courts, which helps to clarify confusing texts or concepts. Nonetheless, in the civil law tradition the judge is just a means to apply the law; the legislator or policymaker has in their hands the creation of law.

This is most definitely a complex subject that cannot be addressed in just a few lines. The different appreciation each legal tradition has over sources of law is deeper. However, the objective of this section has not been to determine which tradition has a better approach, but to point out the contrast between both legal traditions on this subject. In the following chapters, it can be appreciated how a different primary source of law has influenced the way the piercing of the corporate veil has been applied in Latin American countries.

3.2 Role of critical thinking or judicial creativity

The role of critical thinking is considerably different between the legal traditions. On the one hand, the common law tradition has case law as the main source of law, which is a source of law whose development depends on judges. In order to develop case law, it is necessary to allow a judge a high degree of critical thinking. They simply cannot be constrained by positive law as doing so would make it difficult to provide consistent case

---

19 For example, civil procedural law is founded in 21 principles. Some of these principles are *igualdad de las partes* (equity among the parties), *principio de economia procesal* (procedural eficiency), *Principio de cosa juzgada* (principle of no retrial). These are some of the principles that aids on the administration of justice and interpretation of law. The purpose of this footnote is not to engage in explaining each principle because these are not part of my research. However, to point out the existence of these principles in Ibero-American civil procedural law gives an insight to the reader who is not familiar with this subject. For further information see, Chiovenda G. (2005) *Instituciones de Derecho Procesal Civil.* Volume 2. Argentina: Valleta Editions.

law. Under the common law tradition, the judge is provided the freedom to use critical thinking and has the function of law maker. On the other hand, the civil law tradition is more limiting in relation to the use of judicial creativity. In the civil law tradition positive law is the main source of law and the judge is only a means to apply the law. The civil law judge has a passive role as they are not allowed to go beyond the boundaries of positive law. Certainly, civil law permits a degree of critical thinking through legal principles because the strict application of positive law may produce an unfair decision. However, the judge cannot go against the spirit of the positive law.

It has to be pointed out that the use of critical thinking should not be confused with acts against the law. In this book critical thinking is regarded as a means to soften the strict application of positive law. In the early days of the common and civil law tradition, positive law was applied in a strict manner. Consequently, unfair decisions were issued. For that reason principles appeared to soften the rigid legal traditions. Certainly, the common and civil law traditions have taken different paths regarding the use of critical thinking. However, critical thinking exists in both legal traditions. Indeed, it can be presumed that critical thinking gives room for personal biases, but the use of critical thinking is controlled through legal principles and doctrine.

In this book, piercing the corporate veil is considered a remedy that has its foundation in critical thinking. This is one of the premises on which the concept of piercing the corporate veil has been constructed. This reasoning is based on the relevant position the corporate personality has in the modern economy. Since its early days, the corporate personality has gained strength to the point its existence is unquestionable. In common law and civil law tradition countries, the primary sources of law (case law and positive law) recognize and reaffirm the existence of the corporate entity and exceptions to this fiction are not common. Therefore, when corporate personality issues have arisen, the authorities have had to find a means to provide a remedy and prevent injustice. On the one hand, the use of critical thinking to decide equity has been used in Anglo-American countries in order to mitigate the negative effects the existence of the corporate veil may produce. As a result, the Anglo-American doctrine of piercing the corporate veil has been developed, an approach based on case law. On the other hand, Latin American judges have implemented critical thinking differently to the Anglo-American jurisdictions, a factor that can be attributed to legal tradition. In the civil law tradition, the judge's ability to assess and develop a critical perspective of the circumstances of the case and the applicable law tends to be constrained. Therefore, critical thinking has been applied through traditional legal concepts and principles. In the civil law tradition there are some legal principles that have been developed to allow the use of critical thinking in certain circumstances. This has been employed to deal with corporate personality issues.

3.3 Role of legal concepts and principles

The use of traditional legal concepts has been one of the most common reactions against the misuse of the corporate veil in Latin American civil law jurisdictions. A civil law judge does not always have the faculty to use judicial creativity, as has the common law judge.[20] Therefore, in deciding early cases that involved a misuse of the corporate veil, civil law judges sought principles and legal concepts contained in positive law in order to support a decision to pierce the corporate veil. It is important to add that although Argentina, Colombia, Mexico and Brazil are different legal systems they have been built on similar legal principles and concepts. Consequently, the legal concepts cited to deal with corporate veil issues are the same. The most used traditional legal concepts in corporate entity issues are:

- *Fraude a la ley* (fraud on the law): the use of alternative legal means to achieve a result intended by another law or laws to be prohibited.[21] For example, an individual who is restricted from contracting with the state due to administrative faults avoids this restriction by using a legally incorporated company to contract with the state. Later, in the chapters in which are studied the Latin American jurisdictions subject of study, it can be appreciated that the concept of fraud on the law has been widely used to deal with corporate personality issues.
- *Simulación*: this is a concept based on the use of legal means to avoid obligations. In civil law there are two types of simulated acts, *simulación absoluta* and *simulación relativa*. *Simulación absoluta* makes reference to an act, which assumes an appearance not corresponding to reality, and is usually the result of two or more persons who attempt to accomplish an unlawful purpose. For example X transfers his property to Y. In reality X continues to own the property but by simulating the transfer, X avoids the enforcement of Z's credit over X's property. *Simulación relativa* refers to an act that is made to conceal the true character of the purpose sought by the parties and therefore once discovered the true act or transaction is made retroactively effective for all purposes.[22] For example, X sells his property to Y for £100,000, but in the contract it is stated that the price is £50,000. The purpose in concealing the original price is to avoid taxation. The remedy provided by *simulación* consists that the business will receive the effects the parties tried to hide.
- *Abuso del derecho* (abuse of rights): intentional exercise of rights by a person that causes harm to another with no benefit to the person, and

---

20 See, Perdomo, R. & Marryman, J. *Supra note* 17. At pages 48–9.
21 Becerra, F. (1999) *Diccionario de Terminología Jurídica Mexicana (español- Inglés)*. Mexico: Escuela Libre de Derecho.
22 *Idem.*

88 *Corporate veil in Latin America*

which entails an indemnity obligation, provided it is proven that such right was exercised for the sole purpose of causing damage or harming the other person.[23] For example, individuals have the right to associate and use the benefits of the corporate personality. However, if the right to use and benefit from the use of the corporate form is used to defraud third parties, there is an abuse.

Besides *fraude a la ley, simulación* and *abuso del derecho* there are also legal devices such as the *acción pauliana*, which has been used to deal with corporate veil issues. The *acción pauliana* is a legal remedy to enforce contractual obligations. This remedy is applied when one of the contracting parties performs other legal acts in order to avoid his obligations to the other party. The affected party may request this remedy in order to nullify the acts made by the other party.[24] Thus, to enforce the contract.

These concepts and principles have been present in civil law tradition and have been an auxiliary means to deal with corporate veil issues. Moreover, some of these concepts have become the basis of current exceptions to the corporate personality in some civil law jurisdictions. Based on this fact it cannot be asserted that the American doctrine of piercing the corporate veil has been adopted or copied by Hispano-American jurisdictions. Indeed, it can be argued that the Hispano-American approach to deal with corporate veil issues has a degree of originality.

The ways in which legal concepts and legal devices have been used to deal with corporate veil issues vary among civil law jurisdictions. As has been stated in previous chapters, piercing the corporate veil is a subject developed individually by each jurisdiction.

Personal observation

Latin America definitely presents a peculiar case study about piercing the corporate veil. The Franco-Hispanic civil law has created the foundations on which the legal systems of the region have been developed. The marked differences between the civil law tradition and the common law tradition have certainly had an impact on piercing the corporate veil. Piercing the corporate veil is known as a doctrine structured on case law, which has been the way Anglo-American jurisdictions have developed this remedy. However, the Latin-American remedy follows a different method; statutory exceptions build on traditional concepts and principles.

---

23 *Idem.*
24 De la Cuesta. (1984) *La Accion Pauliana.* Madrid.

IV The piercing of the corporate veil in Mexico

The piercing of the corporate veil in Mexico is an interesting case study because it is a "paradox". On the one hand, the piercing of the corporate veil is a remedy present in Mexican positive law. Moreover, Mexican policymakers have developed a draft law to allow the systematic application of this remedy. However, this remedy has not been widely applied and the draft law proposal has been frozen since the year 2002.[1] Certainly, the inclusion of such a remedy in positive law is evidence of a degree of willingness to disregard the corporate personality. However, the behavior of the Mexican judiciary towards this remedy creates a contradiction.

The objective of this chapter is to study the Mexican mechanism to deal with corporate personality issues. The early manifestations of this remedy in Mexican positive law will be addressed. This remedy was firstly introduced to the Mexican regulation for publicly held companies. This is of upmost interest since it contrasts with one of the cental pillar of this book: the piercing of the corporate veil as a remedy aimed at privately owned companies. Secondly, the development of the Mexican mechanism to pierce the corporate veil into a law will be studied. Although the Mexican regulation to pierce the corporate veil is just a law project, it is relevant to our study because it presents the position of the Mexican policymaker. Moreover, it feeds our comparative study.

1. The early manifestation of *"la develación de la sociedad anónima"*

The piercing of the corporate veil in Mexico is addressed as *la develacion de la sociedad anonima,* which is a term introduced by the Mexican author Walter Frisch Philipp in 1972.[2] However, *la develacion de la sociedad anonima* did not have its early manifestation in the 1970s; rather, it goes further back.

---

1 *Iniciativa presentada por los senadores del partido de acción nacional* (PAN), D. Jesus Galvan Muños y D. Rafael Gilberto Morgan Alvares.
2 See, Philipp, W. (1982) *La Sociedad Anonima Mejicana.* Mexico: Porrua.

90 *Piercing the corporate veil in Mexico*

The use of an exception to the corporate personality in Mexico was present in the 1940s.[3] It has to be pointed out that this exception is peculiar because not only was it formally established in positive law, but it was also aimed at publicly held companies (the *Ley que Establece los Requisitos para la Venta al Publico de Acciones de Sociedades Anonimas,* published in the *Diario Oficial de la Federacion, 1 de ferbrero de 1940*).The fact that it was formally established in positive law differentiates Mexico from the other civil law jurisdictions studied in this book. Other jurisdictions have hesitated in the use of this remedy and only after a long debate was it formally introduced in positive law.[4] In regard to the type of corporate entity at which this remedy is aimed, it is peculiar. The first chapter explains the general circumstances on which the piercing of the corporate veil is applied. It is argued that in the context of publicly held companies, it is not common to hear about the piercing of the corporate veil. Publicly held companies are subjected to strict market regulation, intended to prevent fraud and corporate disasters. Cases such as ENRON in the US have triggered a global tendency to regulate the equity markets and market-participating companies. Moreover, shareholders in publicly held companies have a passive role seeing that the administration and decision-making is in the hands of the board of directors. Therefore, in order to prevent and punish a director's negligent or fraudulent administration, regulations have been developed. In summary, the existence of preventive measures, in addition to the passive role of shareholders, has made the piercing of the corporate veil a remedy that is not considered in this context. Other means have been found to prevent and deal with the misuse of the corporate personality. In the case of Mexico, the existence of this exception in a regulation for publicly held companies can be attributed to the circumstances during that period of time. In the 1940s the Mexican equity markets were small. Moreover, requirements such as certified financial statements were not a strict requirement.[5] In other words, there was no prevention policy against corporate fraud, and the exception to the corporate personality appeared as a means to combat corporate fraud.

The regulation for publicly held companies, in Article 13, established:

"The personal and unlimited liability of any person who controlled the operation of a *sociedad anonima,* if this has been used for any

---

3 See, Hernandez, R. *Rasgado del Velo Corporativo en Mexico.* Available at http://www. hmh-law.com/Textos/PDF%27s/RasgandoelVeloCorporativoenMexico.pdf (last visit 4 April 2015).
4 Robles, J. *¿En que Consiste el Velo Corporativo?* Available at http://www.hacienda.go.cr/centro/datos/Articulo/En%20que%20consiste%20el%20velo%20corporativo.pdf (last visit 4 April 2015).
5 Coronado, I. (1998) *Derecho Mercantil.* Mexico: Porrua.

Piercing the corporate veil in Mexico 91

wrongdoing. Regardless, if such a person was the owner or not of the majority of shares of stock."[6]

The formal introduction of this remedy gives the impression that Mexican policymakers have been willing to ignore the corporate personality. However, this article was not actively used while it existed. This can be attributed to factors such as poor economic dynamism, which rendered the use of the corporate personality as something casual. Additionally, other means to deal with corporate personality issues in the context of publicly held companies were gradually developed. Furthermore, the reforms made to equity market regulations in 1988 included the derogation of the cited article due to its inactivity.[7] Nonetheless, although the exception to the corporate personality in the context of publicly held companies was an inactive rule, it created the foundations on which the "potential" Mexican mechanism to deal with corporate personality issues have been developed.

The cited article presents "control over the corporate entity" as the point of reference to determine the relationship between the shareholder and the wrongdoing committed by the corporate entity. The article can be considered as vague, but these two concepts were later taken by Mexican policymakers and more extensively developed through the law project *la Desestimación de la Persona Jurídica Societaria.*

1.1 Other early Mexican statutory exceptions to the corporate entity

Besides the regulation for publicly held companies, the disregard of the corporate entity was a remedy present in other areas of Mexican positive law. An example is the Mexican Regulation for Foreign Investment.[8] The Regulation for Foreign Investment contains, in its Article 6, a rule regarding the limits for foreigners in certain industries and activities limited to Mexican nationals. The rationale of this rule is to protect Mexican nationals and to enforce this restriction the law allows the disregard of the corporate entity. In this legislation there is no specific requirement of control and fraud. However, the affected party that summons the exception to the corporate entity in this context has to support their argument on grounds of control and intention to defraud the law. If a corporate entity is used as a means to defeat this restriction, the claimant party has to establish solid grounds for

---

6 *Articulo* 13: "Las personas que controlen el funcionamiento de una Sociedad Anónima, ya sea que posean o no la mayoría de las acciones, tendrán obligacion subsidiaria ilimitada frente a terceros por los actos ilícitos imputables a la compañía."

7 Reforms were made to the Mexican regulation for equity markets through the *Ley que establece los Requisitos para la Venta al Público de Acciones de Sociedades Anónimas de enero 14 de 1988.*

8 *Ley de Inversión Extranjera.*

92 Piercing the corporate veil in Mexico

this exception to be allowed. An example is the case of Pepsi-Cola Mexicana: *S de RL* v *Grupo Coca-Cola*.[9] In this case, Pepsi-Cola Mexicana argued that the Coca Cola group had engaged in monopolistic practices, which are against Mexican positive regulation. The authorities found that, indeed, the companies' part of the group had such a unity that they could be regarded as monopolistic practices. Therefore, a sanction was given to the defendant. The decision over the case can be considered as part of a policy to protect a public interest on the prevention of monopolistic practices.

Mexican positive law has considered the disregard of the corporate personality to prevent wrongdoers from defrauding the law. However, statutory means to deal with corporate personality issues have been limited to specific circumstances.

2 The *ley de la desestimación de la persona jurídica societaria*

In the year 2002, in the Mexican parliament a law project was proposed to establish the guidelines to pierce the corporate veil. In other words, Mexican policymakers took a step that no jurisdiction in common law or civil law systems has ever taken; to make a statute in order to regulate the application of piercing the corporate veil. The law project provided a systematic application of this remedy. The objective of a systematic method was aimed at bringing certainty to this subject because it would prevent any random application of this remedy, which can be damaging for the corporate personality. However, there was strong opposition to this law project by different sectors of the Mexican economy. It was consequently "frozen" for further debate. As this book goes to print, there has not been any development about this law project – it remains frozen.

Although it is not in force, for the purposes of this comparative study it is important to take a look at the basic aspects of the law, because it presents the position of the Mexican policymaker on this subject. To review this law, three aspects must be addressed: first, the elements that have to be present for the application of this remedy; second, in what type of circumstances is this remedy applied; and third, the effects of this remedy.

2.1 The elements required for the application of this remedy

In the previously cited statutory rule aimed at publicly held companies, Mexican policymakers required the occurrence of two elements: control and fraudulent intention. However, in the statutory rule these elements were used in a vague manner. The policymaker did not specify what could be considered as controlling behavior and did not describe what could be considered as fraud.

---

9 *Resolucion de 30 de Junio de 2005 dictada en el Expediente Numero DE-06–2000 por la Comision Fedderal de Competencia.*

Piercing the corporate veil in Mexico 93

Therefore, Mexican policymakers, when working on the *Ley de la Desestimación de la Persona Jurídica Societaria*, focused on the development of the concept of control and fraud, which are the cornerstone of this law.

In the Mexican law regarding piercing the corporate veil, policymakers structured the required elements in the following scheme:

- The objective element, which consists of the controlling behavior of the shareholder(s). In order to consider the occurrence of control, the claimant has to prove that the ownership of the majority of shares gave the shareholder(s) influence over the board of directors (in other words, influence over the decision-making process).[10]
- The subjective element, which consists of the occurrence of fraud. For the authorities to consider the occurrence of fraud, the claimant has to prove that the control over the company allowed the shareholder(s) to circumvent a public policy or statute; or that the control of the company allowed the shareholder(s) to defeat the interests of the creditors.[11]
- Resulting element, which is the effect regarding the occurrence of the objective and subjective elements.[12]

The law provides certainty by establishing the grounds to determine the circumstances that have to occur in order to consider the existence of each of the mentioned elements, and therefore allow *la Desestimación de la Persona Jurídica Societaria*.

2.2 *Circumstances in which* la desestimación de la persona jurídica societaria *is applied; and the entities subject to this regulation*

The Mexican policymaker would apply this remedy when the elements of control and fraud are present. As mentioned in the previous point, it is required that the claimant proves that the controlling behavior allowed the

---

10 In article 10 of the Law Project it is established: "Se considera elemento objetivo, al control efectivo por parte de uno o mas de los integrantes de la persona moral o por terceros a esta, que impongan en ella una influencia dominante."
11 In article 14 of the Law Project it is established: "El elemento subjetivo se acreditara cuando la autoridad considere suficientemente provado que, la conducta del integrante o tercero se ha orientado a abusar de la personalidad jurídica independiente de la persona moral en fraude de acreedores, en fraude de la ley o en general, para violar normar imperativas mediante la utilización de aquella."
12 In article 15 of the Law Project it is established: "El elemento resultante se acreditara cuando la autoridad considere suficientemente probado que, de no desestimar la personalidad jurídica de la persona moral, y extender de modo subsidiario e ilimitado la responsabilidad civil de esta hacia el integrante e o el tercero, ocurrirán daños y perjuicios en contra de un tercero de buena fe, se producirán fraudes de l ley o en general, se generaran violaciones a normas imperativas mediante utilización de la persona moral."

94 *Piercing the corporate veil in Mexico*

wrongdoer to achieve a fraudulent result. This fraudulent behavior has been described as the intention to use the corporate personality to avoid regulations; or the intention to defraud third parties by misusing company assets, commingling of assets, and getting loans from the company funds without providing a guarantee.

Besides establishing certainty about the circumstances required to pierce the corporate veil, the law would also establish the types of entities to which the law is applied. Article 2 establishes that the law would apply to business entities with legal personality whilst Article 3 establishes it would apply to entities that do not have legal personality yet act as if they had. In Article 4, it establishes that this law would not apply to governmental entities and Article 5 establishes which authorities are competent to apply this remedy.[13] The description of the types of legal entities to which this law would apply can be considered one of its biggest contributions because it contributes to the creation of certainty for the application of this remedy.

2.3 *Effects of* la desestimación de la persona jurídica societaria

Article 7 establishes the effects of *la desestimación de la persona jurídica societaria*. These are the enforcement of the law and the extension of liability to the individuals behind a legal entity. This is another aspect of the law that contributes to legal certainty because it prevents vagueness and erroneous use of this remedy.

Personal observation

The *desestimación de la persona jurídica societaria* has most definitely been a complicated subject in Mexico. I use the word complicated because of the contradictions among Mexican policymakers, the Mexican judiciary and

---

13 In article 2 of the Law Project it is established: "Para efectos de esta ley, se entiende por persona moral toda entidad colectiva a la cual, la legislación le reconozco personalidad jurídica independiente a la de sus integrantes"; in article 3 of the Law Project it is established: "Las entidades colectivas que sin tener reconocida por la legislación personalidad jurídica independiente a la de sus integrantes, se exterioricen como tales, quedaran sujetas a los dispuesto por esta ley"; in article 4 of the Law Project it is established: "quedaran excluidas del ámbito de aplicación de esta ley, la federación, las entidades federativas, los municipios, los órganos constitucionales de los poderes federales, estatales y municipales, los órganos autónomos constitucionales, las entidades colectivas reguladas por la legislación electoral, y aquellas reguladas por la legislación de la administración publica, salvo las empresas de participación estatal de cualquier ámbito de gobierno"; In article 5 of the Law Project it is established: "Seran autoridades competentes para la aplicación de esta ley, las judiciales o administrativas que tengan a su cargo la facultad de resolver las cuestiones de responsabilidad de las persona morales, según la legislación aplicable a la naturaleza de cada una de estas".

Piercing the corporate veil in Mexico 95

different sectors of the Mexican judiciary. On the one hand, Mexican policymakers have developed an exception to the corporate personality, aimed at preventing fraudulent use. Moreover, from a statutory rule, the exception to the corporate personality develops into a law. Unarguably, the willingness of the policymaker to create certainty on this subject can be appreciated. However, the Mexican judiciary and different sectors of the Mexican economy have not welcomed the "systematization of this remedy" and this reaction can be attributed to the fear of undermining the corporate entity (as in any other economy dependent on the corporate personality); Mexico cannot afford to undermine its corporate entity. However, in the opinion of the author, the reluctance to accept a systematic method to deal with corporate personality issues can be attributed to ignorance of the subject. I support my criticism based on the lack of study on the subject. In the law proposal, which it should not be forgotten has been frozen, it can be appreciated that Mexican policymakers detailed different aspects of piercing the corporate veil; for example, the concept, the elements necessary to apply this remedy, the effects, among other details, have been developed. Moreover, this law has established the type of legal entities at which it is aimed. The decision to freeze this law can be attributed to a quick reaction against it, rather than a deep reflection.

V The piercing of the corporate veil in Colombia

In Colombia, corporate personality issues have been present since the corporate entity became of common use. However, piercing the corporate veil is a relatively recent subject. Like in other Latin American countries, the creation of an equivalent remedy to piercing of the corporate veil in Colombia has been the result of the country's recent economic dynamism. Certainly, remedies such as the *accion pauliana* and exceptions to the corporate personality in insolvency law have been used in the past. However, the express use of an exception to the corporate personality is relatively recent, a fact that can be attributed to the need of a more effective remedy. Colombia is a particularly interesting case study because it has developed an exception to the corporate personality in order to deal with specific types of business entities. Moreover, the exceptions have been developed in a way there is not a direct attack to the business entity, but to the acts made through it.

The business entities subjects of this remedy derive from the need of business entities with a light regulation. This need is the result of the tight regulation over the Colombian Joint Stock Corporation, known as *sociedad anonima*. This type of business association is popular because of the attributes of legal personality and limited liability. However, its tight regulation presents a burden for small entrepreneurs rather than an advantage. For that reason, Colombian policymakers created the one-man company (*sociedad unipersonal*) and the *sociedad por acciones simplificadas* as an alternative for small entrepreneurs. These legal entities have flexible regulation, which makes them susceptible to be used for fraudulent or illicit purposes. Therefore, exceptions equivalent to the piercing of the corporate veil were included in the regulation of these legal entities.

It should be noted that in Colombia other means have been employed in order to deal with corporate personality issues; for example, bankruptcy law and labour law contain regulations that have, as an indirect effect, the disregard of the legal entity. However, this chapter is aimed at the one-man company and *sociedad por acciones simplificadas* because of the objective of this book; i.e., the study of the Latin American mechanisms equivalent to piercing the corporate veil.

Piercing the corporate veil in Colombia   97

In this chapter, the exceptions contained in the regulation for a one-man company and the *sociedad por acciones simplificadas* will be addressed. However, before addressing the exceptions contained in these regulations, the Colombian *Estatuto Anticorrupcion*, which is the first Colombian regulation that directly allowed the piercing of the corporate veil, will be analysed. The *Estatuto Anticorrupcion* is a public law regulation, which means it has the strength to override the corporate personality. Therefore, there is not a true dilemma about whether or not to pierce the corporate veil. However, it is addressed in this chapter because this regulation directly attacks the corporate personality. The *Estatuto Anticorrupcion*, due to its public law nature, can be considered as more aggressive towards the corporate personality. In this chapter, the approach used in a public law context will be contrasted with the approach used in a private law context.

In addition, the "core" of the Colombian exceptions to the corporate personality will be pointed out. The core of the Colombian mechanism to deal with corporate personality issues is the concept of *abuso del derecho*. The exceptions to the corporate personality contained in the mentioned regulations have been structured around this concept. Moreover, other regulations that have indirectly dealt with corporate personality issues have employed this concept as a point of reference.

This chapter looks at the rationale behind the use of this concept and the issues between the Colombian piercing of the corporate veil and constitutional rules.

1.   Colombian statutory approach to corporate entity issues

This section will focus on the Colombian statutory rules that contain an exception to the corporate personality. The objective is to point out the specific areas where Colombian policymakers have focused their efforts to combat the misuse of the corporate entity.

1.1   *The* Ley 190 de 1995, Estatuto Anticorrupción

This statute provides the judge with the competence required to apply remedies such as the disregard of the legal entity in order to punish wrongdoers. In Article 44 of this statute, it is established that:

> "The authorities can lift the veil of incorporation when it is necessary to determine the individuals behind the corporate entity."[1]

---

1 *Ley 190 de 1995*, article 44: "Las autoridades judiciales podrán levantar el velo corporativo de las personas jurídicas cuando fuera necesario determinar el verdadero beneficiario de las actividades adelantadas por esta."

98 Piercing the corporate veil in Colombia

This exception to the corporate personality derives from the need for legal devices to combat money laundering and organized crime.[2] Certainly, this regulation caused an impact because it provided Colombian authorities enough power to ignore the corporate personality. However, the development of such a rule was not crafted in the blink of an eye. Before the enactment of this rule, the Colombian judiciary was already aware of the potential of the corporation's legal personality to be a device to practise illicit acts. Moreover, the Colombian judiciary had engaged in determining to what extent the corporation's legal personality should be preserved. In 1993, the Colombian *Corte Suprema de Justicia* (Supreme Court of Justice) had to face the dilemma between the preservation of the corporate personality and the punishment of wrongdoers. Their decision established, through creating a legal precedent, that the separate corporate personality only has effect in commercial and civil acts and not in penal law.[3] The court ruled that separate corporate personality has no validity if used as a device to obstruct the administration of justice and practise fraudulent acts against the state.[4] This statement by the Colombian judiciary feeds the proposition established in the first chapter of this book, which is based on the prevalence of a public interest over the fiction of the corporate personality.

It has to be pointed out that the exception contained in the *estatuto anticorrupcion* directly attacks the corporate personality. It completely overrides its existence in order to hold wrongdoers liable and it nullifies all the illicit acts performed through the corporate personality.

1.2 *The* Ley 222 de 1995

This law modified the Code of Commerce and the regulation of Companies. One of the most relevant aspects was the creation of the *empresa unipersonal* (one-man company). Small businessmen have been interested in acquiring the benefits of the corporate entity for individual enterprises. However, the creation of a joint stock corporation or a limited liability

---

2 Martínez, J. (2010) 'Marco General del Levantamiento del Velo Corporativo en Colombia' in Franco, A. *El Levantamiento del Velo Corporativo, panorama y perspectivas. El caso colombiano*. Colombia: Editorial Universidad del Rosario. Page24.

3 "El que para efectos comerciales y civiles la persona juridical sea un ente distinto de sus socios, es una verdad que no trasciende el ambito penal." See, *Corte Suprema de Justicia, Sala Penal, auto 7183 del 20 de enero de 1993*.

4 See, Arrubla, J. '*El Levantamiento del Velo Corporativo en Colombia*' Gil, M. & others. *Supra note 2.* At page 70.

company requires compliance with a series of formalities, which are a burden rather than an advantage, for small entrepreneurs. Therefore, the Colombian legislator made a breakthrough with the introduction of the *empresa unipersonal*, a device for commerce that provides the advantages of the corporate entity to a sole entrepreneur. Traditional company law requires a company to have at least a minimum of two members; the lack of the required membership may produce the voidance of the company. However, the *empresa unipersonal* is not subject to this membership requirement because it is an entity designed to function with a sole member, with the benefits of the attributes of limited liability and legal personality.

The objective of the *empresa unipersonal* is to allow a natural or legal person to develop a personal business and enjoy the benefits of separate legal personality and limited liability.[5] This is certainly a device that encourages entrepreneurs. However, when drafting this law, the potential of this device to be used for practising illicit and fraudulent purposes was also considered. Therefore, in the same artcile that creates this entity (article 71), the policymakers included an exception;

> "if this form of enterprise is used for fraudulent purposes or to affect third parties, the entrepreneur shall answer together with the entity for its debts".[6]

The exception to the one-man company was a proposal made by the Colombian *Superintendencia de Sociedades*.[7] However, the proposal was not only aimed at the one-man company, but to every type of business entity

---

5 *Ley 222 de 1995*, article 71: "Mediante la empresa unipersonal una persona natural o juridical que reúna las cualidades requeridas para ejercer el comercio, podrá destinar parte de sus activos para la realización de una o varias actividades de carácter mercantil. La empresa unipersonal, una vez inscrita en el registro mercantile, forma una persona juridical."

6 *Idem*, article 71, *Paragrafo:* "Cuando se utilice la empresa unipersonal en fraude a la ley o en perjuicio de terceros el titular de las cuotas de capital y los administradores que hubieren realizado, participado o facilitado los actos defraudatorios responderan solidariamente por las obligaciones nacidas de tales actos y por los perjuicios causados."

7 The *Superintendencia de Sociedades* (Superintendence of Corporations) is a technical body, ascribed to the Ministry of Commerce, Industry (in some jurisdictions to the ministry of Tourism). This legal entity has juridical personhood, administrative autonomy and its own assets through which the President of the Republic exercises the inspection, surveillance and control of commercial companies, as well the faculties appointed by law in relation to other entities, legal persons and natural persons. See, http://www.supersociedades.gov.co/English/OurOrganization/WhoWeAre/Pages/default.aspx (last visit, 12 May 2015).

100   *Piercing the corporate veil in Colombia*

recognized by the Colombian legal framework for companies. The policy-makers evaluated the proposal but decided to limit the exception to the one-man company. This decision of the Colombian policymakers can be attributed to two factors. First, to disregard the corporate personality is a delicate subject and to allow its free application can undermine the concept of corporate personality. Second, this remedy was not needed to deal with other business entities due to the strict regulations other business entities are subjected to. However, although the exception included in the regulation to the one-man company was considered an equivalent to piercing the corporate veil, this exception has a different effect. As can be read in the cited article, the remedy does not establish the disregard of the legal entity; rather it makes the wrongdoer liable by nullifying all the fraudulent acts made through the business entity. Accordingly, the business entity is kept alive to safeguard the interest of third parties. Other parties may have contracted in good faith with the business entity and, should it be dissolved, these other parties may be affected.

Besides the exception to the *empresa unipersonal* legal personality, this law also included a rule that addressed the disregard of the corporate entity in the context of corporate groups. In article 148 (derogated by the Ley 1116 de 2006),[8] the law established that a parent company may be held liable for the subsidiary's insolvency if the situation of the latter is the result of the excessive control of the former and if there are decisions made against the interest of the subsidiary.[9] This rule is founded on the dominance of the parent over the subsidiaries, which in some cases is so strong that it leaves the subsidiary with some sort of dependence. However, an argument against a parent company on grounds of this rule may be refuted if the parent proves that the subsidiary's insolvency is a product of other circumstances. The

---

8 The *Ley 1116 de 2006* established the Entrepreneurial Insolvency Regimen in Colombia. Article 61 of the *Ley 1116 de 2006* addressed some aspects that were not covered by the article 148. First, article 61 more extensively developed the concept of parent company. It established that a parent company could be a holding company or could be a group of companies controlling the subsidiary. Additionally, article 62 established the expiration of the action, which is four years. This was not addressed in the *Ley 222 de 1995*. The *Ley 1116 de 2006* also established that the *Superintendencia de Sociedades* is the competent authority to address liquidation proceedings in this context.

9 *Idem*, article 140, *Paragrafo*: "Cuando la situación de concordato o de liquidación obliga-toria haya sido producida por causa o con ocasión de las actuaciones que haya realizado la sociedad matriz o controlante en virtud de la subordinación y en interés de ésta o de cualquiera de sus subordinadas y en contra del beneficio de la sociedad en concordato, la matriz o controlante responderá en forma subsidiaria por las obligaciones de aquélla. Se presumirá que la sociedad se encuentra en esa situación concursal, por las actuaciones derivadas del control, a menos que la matriz o controlante o sus vinculadas, según el caso, demuestren que ésta fue ocasionada por una causa diferente."

Piercing the corporate veil in Colombia 101

Corte Constitucional (Constitutional Court)[10] held in the judgement in *C-510/97*: ". . . if the defendant can prove that its decisions and management was not the cause for the subsidiary's insolvency, the separation of personality and liabilities will be held".[11]

The reforms introduced in the *Ley 222 de 1995* definitely supplemented Colombian commercial legislation and brought innovation. First, a legal entity that encourages entrepreneurship was introduced. Additionally, an exception to deter its misuse was established. Second, a parent company's liability in a case of insolvency was addressed. The Colombian judiciary, based on the concept of control, developed an exception to separate corporate personality; something of a breakthrough during that period.

1.3 *The* Ley 1258 de 2008

This law creates the *sociedad por acciones simplificada*. The *sociedad anónima* (Colombian joint stock company) is subject to regulations that make its creation a burdensome process for small entrepreneurs. Consequently, the *sociedad por acciones simplificada* was created as an alternative. The law that regulates this business entity is flexible in terms of the requirements for its constitution. Moreover, this form of business association has the attributes of legal personality and limited liability. This business entity has the potential to be used for fraudulent purposes, due to its flexible regulation. Therefore, policymakers developed an exception to the legal personality of this form of business association. In article 42 the following is established:

> "If the *Sociedad por Acciones Simplificadas* has been used for fraudulent purposes and against third parties, the shareholders and directors that participated in the fraud shall be held liable."[12]

---

10 The *Corte Constitucional de Colombia* is the highest entity in the judicial branch of government in the Republic of Colombia in charge of safeguarding the integrity and supremacy of the Colombian Constitution of 1991 within the Constitutional laws. However it is not the highest court of criminal appeal, civil appeal, administrative law disputes, and the administration of justice. The Supreme Court of Colombia, the Council of State of Colombia and the Superior Council of the Judiciary are the highest courts of appeal for their respective areas of law. http://www.corteconstitucional.gov.co/ (last visit 10 September 2013).

11 "Se trata, entonces, de una presunción Iuris Tantum, que puede ser desvirtuada por la matriz controlante, o por sus vinculadas, demostrando que sus decisiones no han causado la desestabilización económica de la filial o subsidiaria, sino que esta procede de motivos distintos." *Corte Constitucional, Sentencia C-510 del 9 de octubre de 1997.* MP Jose Gregorio Hernandez Galindo.

12 *Ley 1258 de 2008*, article 42: "Cuando se utilice la sociedad por acciones simplificada en fraude a la ley o en perjuicio de terceros, los accionistas y los administradores que hubieren realizado, participado o facilitado los actos defraudatorios, responderán solidariamente por las obligaciones nacidas de tales actos y por los perjuicios causados.

102 *Piercing the corporate veil in Colombia*

The exception to the *sociedad por acciones simplificadas* personality seems to be a tool against the corporate entity. However, this remedy does not dissolve this business entity and rather it nullifies the fraudulent or illicit acts made through this business entity. It renders the fraudulent shareholder(s) liable without affecting the interests of innocent shareholders and third parties.

The exception to the corporate personality contained in this regulation did not cause an impact because a direct mechanism against the corporate personality already existed in a commercial law context, in the regulation for the one-man company. However, the remarkable aspect of the exception to the *sociedad por acciones simplificadas* personality is in its result. This exception was drafted in a way so as not undermine the concept of corporate personality. Like its predecessor, the exception to the *sociedad por acciones simplificadas* was crafted to punish wrongdoers on grounds of abusive behavior. Certainly, if both statutory rules are observed, these are short and do not give details regarding what can be considered as fraud and the circumstances that must occur to trigger the exception. However, it has to be pointed out that these exceptions have their foundation in a basic civil law tradition concept. This allows the judiciary to apply these exceptions free of vague arguments. This concept is *abuso del derecho*.

2. The foundation of the Colombian approach to corporate personality issues

The Colombian equivalent to the piercing of the corporate veil has been developed on solid grounds. Indeed, as a country of civil law tradition, this remedy cannot be structured on vague principles or doctrines. As with the Argentinean jurisprudence, in Colombia the corporate entity is considered to be the product of a contract. As an entity born from the agreement between two or more parties, the corporate entity is subjected to the principles and concepts governing the contractual relationship.[13] Consequently,

---

La declaratoria de nulidad de los actos defraudatorios se adelantará ante la Superintendencia de Sociedades, mediante el procedimiento verbal sumario.

La acción indemnizatoria a que haya lugar por los posibles perjuicios que se deriven de los actos defraudatorios será de competencia, a prevención, de la Superintendencia de Sociedades o de los jueces civiles del circuito especializados, y a falta de estos, por los civiles del circuito del domicilio del demandante, mediante el trámite del proceso verbal sumario.

13 "El abuso del derecho está plenamente consagrado en la teoría general de los contratos y las obligaciones mercantiles, cuando el artículo 830 del Código de Comercio advierte: El que abuse de sus derechos estará obligado a indemnizar los perjuicios que cause." See, Paucar, J. (2010) '*El Levantamiento del Velo Corporativo en Colombia*'; in Franco, A. *El Levantamiento del Velo Corporativo, panorama y perspectivas. El caso colombiano.* Colombia: Editorial Universidad del Rosario. Page 72.

to deal with corporate personality issues the Colombian authorities have relied on the concept of "*abuso del derecho*".

The *abuso del derecho* makes reference to abuses committed under the exercise of a right; for example, the corporation is based on the right to associate and thus also based on this right the corporate entity is developed to boost commerce and limit shareholders liability. It is not to cover abusive or fraudulent conduct and consequently the exception to the corporate personality will be triggered if the parties that benefit from this right to associate have been used in an abusive way such as to defraud other parties.

The concept of *abuso del derecho* is contained in Article 830 of the Colombian Code of Commerce. This concept is not aimed at the corporate personality. Nonetheless, authorities can rely on it due to the contractual nature of the corporate personality. Moreover, the judiciary has relied on *abuso del derecho* to the extent that statutory exceptions to the corporate personality are based on this concept.

In addition to *abuso del derecho*, in the exception to the *sociedad por acciones simplificadas* the concept of *fraude a la ley* is summoned. The concept of *fraude a la ley* differs from the concept of *abuso del derecho*, but both concepts are triggered by the same circumstance; i.e., the harm to third parties through the commission of an illicit act. The concept of *fraude a la ley* can be considered supplementary to the exception to the corporate entity because it expands the exception to circumstances were the corporate entity has been used to defraud the law. It can be considered that *abuso del derecho* can also cover this type of inappropriate use of the corporate entity. Nonetheless, the concept of *fraude a la ley* frees *abuso del derecho* from this burden and brings more certainty by providing specific grounds for the application of the remedy. Consequently, it can be regarded as the Colombian equivalent to the piercing of the corporate veil and has its foundations on the concepts of *abuso del derecho* and *fraude a la ley*.

3. Controversy between statutory exceptions to the corporate personality and the Colombian constitution

The piercing of the corporate veil has been a controversial subject in every jurisdiction and has been challenged on different grounds. In the case of Colombia, the Colombian statutory exceptions to corporate personality have been challenged at a constitutional level. In Colombia, the case law concerning the piercing of the corporate veil is mainly based on decisions from the Colombian *Corte Constitucional*[14] rather than decisions from

---

14 The *Corte Constitucional* is part of the Colombian judiciary. It is the final appellate court for matters involving interpretation of the Constitution. The *Corte Constitucional* has the power to determine the constitutionality of laws, acts, and statutes. The court was first

104 *Piercing the corporate veil in Colombia*

regular courts.[15] The exception to the corporate entity has clashed with rights such as the preservation of the economic order (article 2)[16] as well as the freedom to associate for any legal purpose (article 38).[17] Freedom of association and the preservation of the economic order are key to the existence of steady economic development and thus for the existence of the corporate personality. On the one hand, the right to associate allows people to join and achieve a common objective, which could be commercial. The use of this right for commercial purposes gave rise to the business entity. Consequently, this right is a factor that contributes to the creation of wealth in contemporary capitalist society; moreover, it aids the development of the country. On the other hand, the state has the duty to create stability for its citizens; for example, citizens have the right to a steady environment for the exchange of goods and services. In other words, they have the right to the existence of an economic order. These rights are at a constitutional level yet in the constitution there are no exceptions to these rights. Consequently, can the statutory exceptions to the corporate personality undermine constitutional rights? If so, to what extent can Congressional legislation override constitutional rights and duties?

The *Sentencia C-865 de 2004* is a relevant precedent in which the Constitutional Court reflected on this controversy.[18] In this precedent, the Constitutional Court emphasised that the rationale for ignoring the corporate personality is the prevention and punishment of fraud. The court established that "the shareholders will be liable when the good faith is affected and limited liability is used to achieve an objective that is against

---

established by the Constitution of 1991, and its first session began in March 1992. The *Corte Constitucional* consists of nine magistrates who are elected by the Senate of Colombia from ternary lists drawn up by the President, the Supreme Court of Justice, and the Council of State. The magistrates serve for a term of eight years. The court is headed by a President and Vice President. See, http://www.corteconstitucional.gov.co/ (last visit 30 November 2014).

15 See, Garnica, C & others (2007) *Corte Constitucional Linea Jurisprudencial 1997–2007, Levantamiento del Velo Corporativo*. Universidad Sergio Arboleda. Available at http://www.usergioarboleda.edu.co/derecho_comercial/jurisprudencias/linea_jurisprudencial.pdf (last visit 30 November 2014). At page 193.

16 Article 2. "Son fines esenciales del Estado: servir a la comunidad, promover la prosperidad general y garantizar la efectividad de los principios, derechos y deberes consagrados en la Constitución; facilitar la participación de todos en las decisiones que los afectan y en la vida económica, política, administrativa y cultural de la Nación; defender la independencia nacional, mantener la integridad territorial y asegurar la convivencia pacífica y la vigencia de un orden justo."

17 Article 38. "Se garantiza el derecho de libre asociación para el desarrollo de las distintas actividades que las personas realizan en sociedad." *Constitución Política de Colombia 1991. Título II, de los derechos, las garantías y los deberes.*

18 *Corte Constitucional. Sentencia C-865 del 7 de septiembre de 2004.* Available at http://www.corteconstitucional.gov.co/relatoria/2004/C-865–04.htm (last visit 30 May 2013).

Piercing the corporate veil in Colombia   105

the purpose of constitutional rights and defrauds third parties". Indeed, the Constitutional Court approached this dilemma taking into account the concept of *abuso del derecho* (abuse of rights). According to this concept, a right cannot be preserved if it is used to affect other parties' rights. It was established that an exception to the constitutional right of association is to be granted when it is used for an illegal purpose. Additionally, in this precedent the fact that the Congress has the authority to regulate the use and limitations of the corporate personality was clarified. In regard of this last point, part of the dilemma over the exceptions to the corporate personality was the power of the Congress to enact a law that challenged constitutional rights. The final decision did not nullify the statutory exceptions to the corporate personality. Although the Congress cannot challenge a constitutional right such as the right of association, it can be considered that the Constitutional Court is inclined to maintain the exception to the corporate personality because it is part of the mechanisms to deter and control the misuse of constitutional rights. This inclination can be attributed to the fact that an introduction of an exception to constitutional rights in the constitution involves a controversial and long process. Therefore, the creation of a law by the Congress can be regarded as more "practical". It also has to be pointed out that the Constitutional Court clarified that the exception to the corporate entity only applies if it has been used to commit wrongdoings and under extraordinary circumstances. In summary, the Constitutional Court can be seen to be following the trend regarding the development of a mechanism to deal with corporate personality issues. However, the Colombian authorities have done it in accordance with their framework for companies.

Personal observation

The Colombian equivalent to the piercing of the corporate veil is considered by this author as not being aimed at the business entity itself; rather, it is aimed at the acts committed through the business entity. This opinion is supported by the rationale for the development of this approach, which lies in the tendency to protect the corporate entity. Certainly, the existence of exceptions to the business entity in Colombian positive law shows a willingness to deal with corporate entity issues. However, this does not mean the Colombian authorities do not protect the business entity. Colombia, as any other emerging economy, depends on the business entity. Consequently, this cannot be undermined. For that reason, the exceptions contained in the regulation for one-man company and *sociedades por acciones simplificadas* do not attack the business entity. Moreover, they are applied in exceptional circumstances.

An exception to the tendency to protect the corporate entity is the *estatuto anticorrupcion*, which directly attacks the corporate personality. Indeed, the exception to corporate personality in the *estatuto anticorrupcion* yields the

106 *Piercing the corporate veil in Colombia*

dissolution of the corporate entity; an effect that can be attributed to the public law nature of this regulation. The difference between the Colombian private law approach and the public law approach unquestionably supports one of the premises presented in this book: public law overrides the corporate personality. Therefore, there is not a real dilemma about piercing the corporate veil in a public law context.

VI The piercing of the corporate veil in Brazil

The piercing of the corporate veil in Brazil is an interesting subject of study. This is so because the corporate personality is often ignored in this jurisdiction due to "pro-social" policies. Whilst in Brazil the corporate personality is a pillar of the economy, since the 1940s Brazilian authorities have adopted a labour law policy to punish the wrong use of the corporate personality.[1] In this area of law there has been a tendency to protect workers' rights because the corporate structure provides ample opportunity to avoid obligations. In the context of labour, the corporate personality tends to be used for example as a means to hide assets, which can be transferred from one company to another and thus be hidden. Therefore, the lack of assets to fulfill obligations to employees is considered by authorities to be the main trigger to disregard the corporate personality; for example, if the company does not have capital, the shareholders automatically answer for the debts. In the context of labour law, there is no reflection over the existence of the corporate personality owing to the importance placed upon workers' rights. For this reason it is not possible to talk about a real dilemma regarding piercing the corporate veil. Nonetheless, it has to be pointed out that this harsh approach to the corporate entity within labour law influenced formal methods developed to disregard the corporate personality.

For approximately 20 years from the 1970s, the Brazilian authorities considered the development of a formal mechanism that could be widely applied to ignore the corporate personality. It was not until the 1990s that these considerations were implemented in Brazilian positive law. At the beginning, the exception to the corporate personality was introduced in specific statutes aimed at dealing with specific circumstances, but gradually its scope of application expanded and was introduced to a core regulation, the Brazilian Civil Code.

---

1 Saloma, B. *The End of Limited Liability in Brazil.* Available at http//works.69bpress.com/ Bruno_mayerhof_Salama/69 (last visit 12 May 2015). At page 6.

108   *Piercing the corporate veil in Brazil*

The Brazilian author Bruno M. Saloma considers that the position of Brazilian authorities towards the corporate personality has given room to a "regime of unlimited liability".[2] The opinion of the author Saloma is strong but he has grounds on which to support his argument; i.e., the policies aimed at preventing and punishing the misuse of the corporate personality in Brazil. First, the labour law policy against the corporate personality and second the gradual development of an exception that can be applied in any area of law are both examples of such policies. However, it has to be pointed out that the strength of an exception to the corporate personality is not the same in all branches of law. Moreover, although there is a "pro-social" policy on this subject the Brazilian authorities keep this remedy as something exceptional that will only be applied as a last resort.

The objective of this chapter is to study the Brazilian mechanism to pierce the corporate veil, the origins of the Brazilian tendency to ignore the corporate personality and the rationale on which the Brazilian mechanism to deal with the corporate personality has been developed.

1.   The origins of the Brazilian exception to the corporate personality

The exception to the corporate personality in Brazil can be traced back to the 1940s, when the country was subject to major social and legal reform.[3] Reforms in the context of labour law can be considered a breakthrough regarding corporate personality matters. These reforms established that shareholders and companies were both liable regarding labour obligations. Nowadays, academics and practitioners may regard such policies as something dangerous. However, they are limited to labour issues and honorably created to prevent and punish the abuses of employers towards employees. It has to be pointed out that in the labour context the existing inequalities between employers and employees were a relevant issue swaying the policies.

In early Brazilian labour law policy against the corporate entity, there was no mention of disregarding the corporate personality or piercing the corporate veil. However, the establishment of joint liability created the precedent for later exceptions to the corporate entity. Indeed, it gave room for reflection about the extent the corporate personality should be preserved.

---

2 *Idem.*
3 One of the key factors on the development of the Brazilian policy towards the corporate personality was the 1930s revolution. This revolution, together with the rise to power of the leader Getulio Vargas, brought a political shift in Brazil. The changes were aimed at developing laws in accord with the needs of the poor and individuals who are susceptible to abuse. The introduction of an exception to the corporate personality in Brazilian labour law is evidence of these changes.

Piercing the corporate veil in Brazil 109

It was not until the 1970s that the metaphor of piercing the corporate veil started to be used among Brazilian academia and judiciary. It has to be pointed out that Brazil only imported the metaphor and not the American doctrine. Policymakers developed their own mechanism to deal with corporate personality issues in accordance with Brazil's own legal framework and needs. However, although the piercing of the corporate veil became a subject of interest in Brazil, the early formal exceptions to the corporate personality were limited to specific circumstances, in specific statutes: Brazilian Consumers Protection Law and regulation for the protection of the economic order and environmental law. Certainly, the use of this remedy was limited, but it was used in accord with Brazilian "pro-social policies". In this book the concept of "pro-social policies" refers to the policies implemented to protect public interest, such as the one protected by the Brazilian Labour Law enacted during the 1940s. Brazilian authorities adopted a position against the use of the corporate entity to defeat regulations aimed at the protection of workers' rights, which are of course *a public interest*. The mentioned statutes clearly have a public interest: consumer's rights, economic order and the preservation of the environment. Indeed, the development of an exception in these three areas shows the Brazilian tendency for a pro-social policy rather than a capitalist policy. This is a factor that influenced the later introduction of an exception to the corporate personality in the Brazilian Civil Code.

The Brazilian authorities did not introduce an equivalent to the piercing of the corporate veil until 2002 with the reforms to the Brazilian Civil Code (a subject we will address later in this chapter). The introduction of an exception in a core regulation such as the Civil Code created a uniform approach to deal with corporate personality issues. The Civil Code is the pillar of the corporate personality concept. Consequently, the rules contained in this Code have an impact on any area of law where the corporate personality has been challenged.

Brazilian statutory exceptions can be considered a breakthrough. However, it should be noted that the piercing of the corporate veil has been present in Brazilian case law since the 1970s.[4] Family, labour[5] and tax law are

---

4 See, Reali, R. (2003) *Desconsideração da Personalidade Jurídica no Direito Positivo Brasileiro*. Universidad Regional de Blumenau. Available at http://www.boletimjuridico. com.br/doutrina/texto.asp?id=327 (last visit 30 May 2013). At page 55.

5 In labour law, the entity doctrine is not a doctrinal issue when workers' rights are affected. The judiciary established that it for the occurrence of fraud or abuse of the corporate form is not necessary. The fact that the company does not have enough assets to comply with its obligation to its workers is enough justification to disregard the corporation's personality and extend liability to the shareholders. The lack of validity in this context has been based on the protection of workers against the abuse of the employer. Clt, Article 2.º, caput. Proceso trt/2 SP, 02429200703102003. Sentence cited by,

110 *Piercing the corporate veil in Brazil*

some of the areas where case law has catalysed a debate regarding to what extent the corporate personality should be preserved.[6] Some statutes, like the Labour Law, had already extended companies' liabilities to shareholders.[7] However, these statutes did not explicitly prescribe the piercing of the corporate veil.[8] Therefore, Brazilian courts were not legally authorized to apply this remedy.[9]

In this book it is considered that the origins of the current Brazilian approach took place in the early 1990s with the enactment of the consumer protection law and the subsequent regulations. Thus, it was at this point of Brazilian legal history that authorities received express authorization to disregard the corporate personality. Certainly, the previous statutory exception and reflections contained in Brazilian case law had an influence on the current mechanism. However, it is only since 1990s that Brazilian authorities have formalized the subject.

1.1 Lei No 8.078 de 11 de septembro de 1990

The *Lei No 8.078 de 11 de septembro de 1990* (Consumers' Protection Code) was the first Brazilian statutory regulation that directly addressed the piercing of the corporate veil.[10] In its article 28, it is established that a judge can disregard the corporation's legal personality if it has been used to the detriment of a consumer's rights.[11] The enactment of this rule is derived

---

Andrade, F. and Pasqualotto, A. in the paper "El Levantamiento de la Personalidad Juridica en el Derecho Privado Brazileño". 2010. Available at dialnet.unirioja.es/descarga/articulo/3696745.pdf (last visit 30 May 2013). At page 98.

6 See, Reali, R. *Supra note* 378. At page 54.

7 The *Lei No 4.137 de setembro de (1962)*, article 9 established that directors and managers will be personally liable for company's debts if they have carried out illegal acts during the course of their administrative duties. Available at http://www.planalto.gov.br/ccivil_03/decreto/1950–1969/D52025.htm (last visit 30 May 2013). Also, the *Lei 4.729* (1965), in Article1 established that courts were allowed to impose criminal sanctions on directors and members of corporations that dishonestly concealed taxes. Available at http://www.planalto.gov.br/ccivil_03/leis/1950–1969/L4729.htm (last visit 30 May 2013).

8 See, Camargo, A. (2003) 'Three Essential Aspects of Corporate Law: A Brief Overview of Brazilian and American Approaches' *Southwestern Journal of Law & Trade in the Americas* (Volume 9). At page 105.

9 *Ibid.*

10 The *Lei No 8.078 de 11 de setembro de 1990* "Dispõe sobre a proteção do consumidor e dá outras providências." Available at http://www3.dataprev.gov.br/sislex/paginas/13/1990/8078.htm (last visit 30 May 2013).

11 Article 28: "O juiz poderá desconsiderar a personalidade jurídica da sociedade quando, em detrimento do consumidor, houver abuso de direito, excesso de poder, infração da lei, fato ou ato ilícito ou violação dos estatutos ou contrato social. A desconsideração também será efetivada quando houver falência, estado de insolvência, encerramento ou inatividade da pessoa jurídica provocados por má administração.

Piercing the corporate veil in Brazil   111

from a constitutional initiative. The *Constituição Federal de 1988* in its articles 5, 48 and 170 establish the defence of the consumer as one of the commitments of the state.[12] Indeed, the authorities considered that the corporate personality had the potential to affect consumers' rights. Therefore, in the law enacted to deal with this subject a means to combat the misuse of the corporate personality was included. The constitution not only motivated the inclusion of an exception to the corporate personality, but also gave weight to this remedy due to the superior status of the constitution of the Brazilian legal framework.

It has to be pointed out that the constitutional rule regarding consumers' protection was not a legislative whim; rather, it was a matter of principle. The judiciary and academia considered that the consumer could be at a disadvantage when coming up against the fraudulent acts performed by a merchant. Moreover, the potential of the corporate entity to affect consumers was not ignored. Therefore, the rationale for giving the judge the authority to disregard the legal entity has been the protection of the weaker party (the consumer) against the abuses of a stronger party (the enterprise). Definitely, the pro-social tendency of the Brazilian authorities can be seen in the enactment of this rule.

It has to be mentioned that although article 28 addresses the issue only in a consumer–merchant relationship, this rule established the template on which later statutory exceptions to the corporate personality were drafted.

1.2   Lei No 8.884 de 11 de junho de 1994

From the consumers' protection statute, Brazilian policymakers gradually expanded the application of piercing the corporate veil to the protection of the economic order. The *Lei No 8.884 de 11 de junho de 1994* aimed at the protection of the economic order, and included in its article 18 (derogated by the *Lei No 12. 529 de 30 de novembro de 2011*) an exception to

---

§ 1° (Vetado).

§ 2° As sociedades integrantes dos grupos societários e as sociedades controladas, são subsidiariamente responsáveis pelas obrigações decorrentes deste código.

§ 3° As sociedades consorciadas são solidariamente responsáveis pelas obrigações decorrentes deste código.

§ 4° As sociedades coligadas só responderão por culpa.

§ 5° Também poderá ser desconsiderada a pessoa jurídica sempre que sua personalidade for, de alguma forma, obstáculo ao ressarcimento de prejuízos causados aos consumidores."

12 "A constituição Federal de 1988 no seu artigo 5.° inciso XXXII, determina que o Estado promoverá, na forma da lei, a defesa do consumidor. No artigo 170 inciso V, preceitua que um dos princípios da ordem econômica, fundada na valorização do trabalho humano e na livre iniciativa, é a defesa do consumidor. E finalmente, no artigo 48 no Ato das Disposições Constitucionais Transitórias, determina que seja elaborado o Código de Defesa do Consumidor."

112 *Piercing the corporate veil in Brazil*

the corporate personality. This article established that the corporate entity would be disregarded if it had been used in a fraudulent way, beyond its commercial objective or in a negligent manner.[13]

The exception contained in this article included the concept of fraud and in addition brought the concept of *ultra vires* into the Brazilian mechanism to ignore the corporate personality. It can be considered that this law expanded the scope of application of the Brazilian exception to the corporate personality. Moreover, the inclusion of *ultra vires* helped to create a more certain concept of fraud in this context. Based on this article, the use of the corporate entity "beyond its commercial objective" is an element that feeds the presumption of fraudulent behavior. Although this article was later derogated, it was part of the foundations of the current Brazilian mechanism to deal with corporate personality issues.

1.3 Lei No 9.605 de 12 de fevereiro de 1998

The *Lei No 9.605 de 12 de fevereiro de 1998* (environmental law), in section 4 established that the corporation's legal personality will be disregarded when the environment has been damaged and the corporation frustrates any efforts to recover any damage to the environment.[14] This exception to the corporate personality has its foundation on a policy aimed at the protection of the environment, which is a policy based on the public interest that exists in this area of law. Indeed, environmental law has gradually gained strength to such a point that it overrides the economic policy that supports the corporate personality. In addition to the public interest contained in environmental law, the Brazilian pro-social tendency also gives strength to the environmental law exception to the corporate personality.

It should be acknowledged that this exception to the corporate personality is limited to circumstances were the activities of the corporate personality have damaged the environment. Therefore, the disregard of the corporate personality in this context should not raise a dramatic concern. The corporate personality does not aim to aid investors to avoid liability derived from environmental damages; rather, it aims to stimulate economic growth by the limitation of liability in a commercial context. This statement is subject to

---

13 Article 18: "O juiz poderá desconsiderar a personalidade jurídica da sociedade quando, em detrimento do consumidor, houver abuso de direito, excesso de poder, infração da lei, fato ou ato ilícito ou violação dos estatutos ou contrato social. A desconsideração também será efetivada quando houver falência, estado de insolvência, encerramento ou inatividade da pessoa jurídica provocados por má administração."

14 Article 4: "Poderá ser desconsiderada a pessoa jurídica sempre que sua personalidade for obstáculo ao ressarcimento de prejuízos causados à qualidade do meio ambiente. Lei No 9.605 de 12 de fevereiro de 1998 Dispõe sobre as sanções penais e administrativas derivadas de condutas e atividades lesivas ao meio ambiente, e dá outras providências."

Piercing the corporate veil in Brazil 113

discussion because some academics may consider that the limitation of liability should extend to environmental disasters. However, I personally consider that limitation of liability should not be allowed on grounds of environmental matters. If limited liability allows shareholders to override environmental regulation, it is likely that due to the lack of a sanction entrepreneurs will not take the necessary steps to prevent environmental damages. The Brazilian exception to the corporate personality in environmental law regulation can be regarded as an initiative to push entrepreneurs to take the necessary measures to prevent environmental disasters.

2. Brazilian Civil Code

The limitation of the power to disregard a corporation's legal personality to specific circumstances can be considered as a gradual introduction of a formal mechanism to deal with corporate personality issues in the Brazilian legal framework. In 2002, the enactment of the new Brazilian Civil Code included a rule that allows the disregard of the legal entity when used for fraudulent purposes. Most notably, this remedy steadily expanded from specific laws to a whole body of law such as the Civil Code.

The exception contained in the Brazilian Civil Code empowers the judge to consider the disregard of the legal entity throughout any area of Brazilian private law. Article 50 of this code establishes that:

> "In the case of abuse of the corporate form characterized by acts against a company's purpose or commingling of assets, a judge may decide, at the petition of the plaintiff or the State Department, if it has the right to intervene, that liability for certain obligations be extended to the personal property or assets of the managers or partners of an entity."[15]

The phrase "In the case of abuse . . ." clearly allows an exception to the corporate personality based on the concept of abuse but what can be considered *abuse* in this context? The use of the word "abuse" by itself is not positive because it is vague; for example, the mere action to incorporate a business to reduce liability may be considered, by a creditor, an abuse. Therefore, Brazilian authorities have structured this exception to the corporate personality with the concept of *abuso del derecho* (abuse of rights). As previously addressed, the concept of *abuso del derecho* establishes that a right is

---

15 Article 50: "Em caso de abuso da personalidade juridica, caracterizado pelo desvio de finalidade, ou pela conflisio patrimonial, pode o juiz decidir, a requerimento da parte, ou do Ministrrio Publico quando the couber intervir no processo, que os efeitos de certas e determinadas relagoes de obrigagdes sejam estendidos aos bens particulares dos administradores ou socios da pessoa juridica."

114 *Piercing the corporate veil in Brazil*

a benefit that is conferred by the law and this benefit can be confiscated if used improperly. In the context of the corporate personality, Brazilian law regards corporate personality and limited liability as rights and as such they must be exercised without affecting other parties' rights. *Abuso del derecho* is the core concept of this exception because it established the misuse of a right as the foundation of an argument based on the concept of abuse. Moreover, in order to contribute to certainty, the cited article has also determined the type of behavior that can be considered as *abuso del derecho* in this context:

- the use of the company against its original purpose
- and commingling of assets

To point out these two circumstances contributes to certainty because it prevents the occurrence of vague arguments. To determine whether the company has been used against its originally intended purpose, or whether there has been commingling of assets, is not a simple process. Evidence and reflection over the claim are required in order to decide the disregard of the corporate personality. However, the existence of this rule gives guidance for applying this remedy.

It has to be noted that Article 50 does not mention fraud. Certainly, fraud is the rationale to pierce the corporate veil. However, it can be considered that Brazilian authorities have not limited this remedy to the occurrence of fraud. Most definitely, the commingling of assets and the inadequate use of the corporate entity are situations that may not necessarily involve fraudulent behavior but are likely to affect third parties. The fact that this exception can be applied in circumstances that may not involve fraudulent behavior shows the "pro-social policy" followed by the authorities in the context of piercing the corporate veil. Indeed, Brazilian authorities have introduced a remedy that compensates the inequalities produced by the corporate entity.

Personal observation

The judiciary and academia have gradually introduced a mechanism to deal with corporate personality issues into the Brazilian legal system. It can be considered that this remedy has had a wide acceptance due to its enactment in a core regulation (the Civil Code). However, its application is not common. Indeed, the judiciary has emphasized the exceptional application of this remedy. In a 1997 judgement, the Brazilian judiciary held: "The legal existence of a corporation may, in certain cases, be disregarded. However, substantial evidence of abuse of rights has to be produced."[16] Although

---

16 TAPR-2 Ap. No. 77.829–4 Relator: Juiz Eraclés Messias, 29.08.1997, J. 29.08.1997.

the piercing of the corporate veil was introduced as a measure to counter the abuse of the entity doctrine, the Brazilian judiciary has been aware of the vital role the corporate personality has had in the development of the national economy. Consequently, jurisprudence has emphasized the fact that the corporate veil may be pierced only when the abuse of the corporate form has been proven.[17] The civil law principle of *abuso del derecho* can be considered as a way to reach the degree of certainty demanded by Brazilian jurisprudence on this subject. Like other Latin American jurisdictions studied in this chapter, Brazilian authorities have relied on the tools already provided by the civil law tradition.

In Brazil, as in other jurisdictions, the piercing of the corporate veil has been the result of a legal need. However, besides the need of a law to deal with corporate personality issues, it can be considered there was a need for equity. The corporate personality tends to produce inequalities in situations where, for example, the environment has been damaged because of negligence and those responsible try to evade liability. The consumers' protection law and environmental law are an example of the Brazilian attempt to combat the inequalities produced by the corporate personality. As has been maintained many times throughout this chapter, the Brazilian mechanism to deal with corporate personality issues has its foundations in a pro-social policy.

---

17 "a jurisprudência da Corte, em regra, dispensa ação autônoma para se levantar o véu da pessoa jurídica, mas somente em casos de abuso de direito". See RESP 6932235/mT, Relator: min. Luis Felipe Salomão, 4.o grupo, j. 17.11.2009.

VII The piercing of the corporate veil in Argentina

With the implementation of a statutory rule that directly addresses the disregard of the legal entity, Argentina is most definitely the jurisdiction that has pioneered the piercing of the corporate veil in Latin America.[1] In 1983, Law 22.903 modified the *Ley de Sociedades Comerciales de 1972-Ley No 19,550*,[2] by adding article 54. That article provides that:

> "The liabilities of a corporation used to seek a purpose *beyond the corporate goals*, as a mere instrument to defraud the law, the public policy or the good faith, or to frustrate rights of third persons, will be imputed directly to its shareholders or to the controlling persons who facilitated such activities."[3]

The Argentinean academia and judiciary have addressed the rule contained in article 54 as *"Inoponibilidad de la Persona Jurídica"*;[4] and the

---

1 The principle of *inoponibilidad de la persona jurídical* is an initiative that is still considered a breakthrough. No other jurisdiction in the region has established a principle or regulation that directly addresses the disregard of the legal entity. See, Hurtado, J. (2008) *La Doctrina del Levantamiento del Velo Societario en España e Hispanoamerica*. España: Atelier. At page 75.

2 The *Ley de Sociedades Comerciales de 1972 (Ley No 19,550)* is the current regulation of the different forms of business associations in Argentina. Moreover, this law includes the regulation of corporate groups, which is a subject not previously addressed in the regulation contained in the *"Codigo de Commercio Argentino de 1890"*.

3 Article 54: "El daño ocurrido a la sociedad por dolo o culpa de los socios o de quienes no siéndolo la controlen, constituye a sus autores en la obligación solidaria de indemnizar, sin que puedan alegar compensación con el lucro que su actuación haya proporcionado en otros negocios.

   El socio contratante que aplicare los fondos a efectos de la sociedad a uso o negocio de cuenta propia o de tercero está obligado a traer a la sociedad las ganancias resultantes, siendo perdida de su cuenta exclusiva.

   La actuación de la sociedad que encubra la consecución de fines extrasocietarios, constituya un mero recurso para violar la ley, el orden publico o la buena fe o para frustrar derecho de terceros, se imputará directamente a los socios o a los controlantes que la hicieron posible, quienes responderan solidaria e ilimitadamente por los perjucios causados."

4 The concept of *inoponibilidad* refers to the infectiveness of an act. In this context, the corporation's legal personality is used as a shield against creditors and third parties.

Piercing the corporate veil in Argentina 117

trigger for this remedy is based on acts beyond the corporation's goals, combined with a fraudulent intention. In the context of corporate personality, the concept of *inoponibilidad* has been used as part of a mechanism to hinder the effectiveness of illicit acts performed through a corporate entity.[5]

It can be regarded that the *inoponibilidad de la persona jurídica,* besides creating a formal parameter to address the misuse of the corporate entity, embodies the ideals that had been introduced in precedents prior to the rule of *inoponibilidad de la persona jurídica.*

1. *Inoponibilidad de la persona jurídica*

As in other jurisdictions, the corporate personality is sometimes used, when considered necessary, in order to achieve an objective; for example, the creation of a computer manufacturing company that requires a considerable amount of capital. In order to gather the necessary capital two or more investors would associate and protect their investment using the corporate personality. In this example the corporate entity would be conceived as a manufacturer of computers, which would receive finance, contract workforce and be held liable for its acts. However, if the investors deviated from the original goal, i.e. the manufacture of computers, then the existence of that corporate entity would be in jeopardy. Certainly, this last statement is a little extreme because in modern economies the corporate entity may be used for an objective different from the one stated in the memorandum of association. Nonetheless, there are circumstances were the deviation from the original corporate goal may affect third parties. Therefore, in some jurisdictions measures have to be taken.

Argentina is a jurisdiction that has developed its approach based on the deviation from the corporate goals. Moreover, it has focused on the essence of the Argentinean corporate entity. The Argentinean judiciary and academia consider that the corporate personality has its essence in a contractual relationship.[6] In other words, it is the product of a contract. This is supported by the fact that the corporate personality originates from the agreement between two or more (natural or juridical) persons, which in turn generates obligations among the parties. Certainly, this is arguable. However, this is the general position in regard to the nature of the corporate personality in this jurisdiction.[7] Consequently, it is the basis on which a remedy such as

---

The rule contained in the Argentinean LSC is aimed at neutralising the shield created by the legal personality.

5 Crispo, D. *Inoponibilidad de la Persona Juridica*. Available at http://www.iprofesional. com/adjuntos/documentos/09/0000929.pdf (last visit 12 April 2015).

6 Bomchil, M. *La Inoponibilidad de la Persona Juridica Societaria y el art. 54, Tercer Párrafo, de la Ley 19.550 de Sociedades Comerciales*. Available at www.bomchil.com.ar (last visit 15 April 2015). Pages 6–8.

7 See, Olivera, N. & Rodriguez, C. *Inoponibilidad de la Persona Juridica*. http://www. derechocomercial.edu.uy/RespInop.htm (last visit 15 April 2015).

118   *Piercing the corporate veil in Argentina*

inoponibilidad de la persona jurídica has been developed. The contractual essence of the corporate personality definitely gives room for the application of the *inoponibilidad de la persona jurídica* due to the degree of similarity between the corporate entity and an ordinary contract. For example, a contract needs to have a legal objective; if the objective is not legal, the contract is considered as *"viciado"* (not legal). Consequently, it would be *inoponible* (it will not have an effect) among the parties and the third parties affected by the contract. In the case of the corporate personality, the *inoponibilidad* works as a means to render the acts of the corporate personality ineffective, as long as the corporate personality has been used against the objective established in the original contract. Coming back to the example; if the computer manufacturing company was used as a means to lure investors and accordingly gather capital that was not used to manufacture computers but was actually used for other purposes that were against the interest of the investors, *inoponibilidad* would hold the shareholders and not the company liable.

2.   Sanction derived from the *inoponibilidad de la persona jurídica*

The *inoponibilidad de la persona jurídica* can be applied to any type of business association. This is an interesting characteristic of this remedy because in other jurisdictions the piercing of the corporate veil is limited only to a specific type of business association. The *inoponibilidad de la persona jurídica* has a wide scope of application. Furthermore, it is contained in the Argentinean core regulation regarding company law, the *Ley de Sociedades Mercantiles de 1972*, a regulation that establishes the parameters that have to be followed for the creation, management and dissolution of the different types of business associations recognized by the Argentinean framework for companies.[8]

Like the piercing of the corporate veil, the *inoponibilidad de la persona jurídica* addresses the wrongdoers behind the corporate entity. First, it renders ineffective the acts carried out by the corporate personality that have affected the claimant party. Second, the wrongdoers must answer for any damage resulting from the acts. It is of upmost importance to observe that the corporate personality will not cease to exist and only the illegal acts will become invalid and the shareholder will be therefore held liable. This has to be attributed to the fact that the *inoponibilidad de la persona jurídica* was not developed as a means to eradicate the corporate personality; rather, it simply renders the illegal acts made through the corporate entity ineffective

---

8 See, Kerr, I. 'La Teoria de Inoponibilidad de la Personalidady su Aplicación al Arbitraje. Posibilidad de Extenderla Clausula Arbitral a Partes no Signatarias' *Revista Argentina de Derecho Empresario*. Available at http://ijeditores.com.ar/articulos.php?idarticulo=65067 &print=2#indice_4 (last visit 15 April 2015).

Piercing the corporate veil in Argentina 119

and holds wrongdoers liable. Accordingly, the rights of innocent shareholders and the interest of good faith creditors are protected.

A sector from the Argentinean academia argues that *inoponibilidad de la persona jurídica* is different from piercing the corporate veil.[9] They support their view by arguing that the effect this remedy has over the corporate personality is the annulment of the acts performed by the entity to achieve the wrong-
doers' fraudulent objective, and not the annulment of the corporate entity. However, this argument is debateable. In this book, the *inoponibilidad de la persona jurídica* is not regarded as different to piercing the corporate veil. As is pointed out in the first chapter, the piercing of the corporate veil is a remedy applied according to the particular needs of each jurisdiction. Therefore, the remedy should not be addressed as a remedy that has simply been borrowed from the US but should be seen as unique to each jurisdiction. The piercing of the corporate veil is not a subject that has been developed in uniformity. Each jurisdiction has developed a "personalized version" that differs to the original US doctrine yet still achieves the same result. Thus, in this book the different means to deal with corporate personality issues have been addressed under the term "mechanism". In turn, the *inoponibilidad de la persona jurídica* must be regarded as the Argentinean mechanism to deal with corporate personality issues. Additionally, it must be noted that it has been created not only in accord with the needs of the Argentinean framework for companies, but also in accord with the essence of the Argentinean corporate personality.

Certainly, the following question may arise: if this remedy does not affect the corporate personality, why does it need a parameter for its application? In my opinion, any remedy or legal phenomena that affects the structure of the corporate entity in any way should be applied in a systematic manner. Should it not be applied in such manner, the foundations of the concept of corporate entity and its attributes of legal personality and limited liability could be undermined.

3. Parameter to apply the *inoponibilidad de la persona jurídica*

The *inoponibilidad de la persona jurídica* cannot be considered as some-
thing limited to one statutory rule contained in the Argentinean regulation for companies. A statutory rule requires certain elements in order to boost its application. For this reason, the Argentinean judiciary has supplemented this statutory exception with a parameter for its application. Indeed, in

---

9 Alonso, J. & Giatti, G. *Aspectos Procesales de la Aplicacion de la Teoria de la Inponibi-
lidad de la Personalidad Juridica*. Available at http://www.rivera.com.ar/sites/default/files/
alonsogiatti_aspectos_procesales_de_la_aplicacion_de_la_teoria_de_la_inoponibilidad_
de_la_personalidad_juridica2.pdf (last visit 2 April 2015). Page 7.

120 *Piercing the corporate veil in Argentina*

order to apply the *inoponibilidad de la persona jurídica*, Argentinean jurisprudence has considered necessary the occurrence of two elements:[10]

- the existence of *vicio* or illegal act
- the occurrence of circumstances such as the *simulación, realización del negocio en fraude a terceros, abuso de derechos, actos en contra de la moral y las buenas costumbres*

The first point, "the existence of an illegal act", is a key factor because it is the rationale on which this remedy has been developed (the prevention and punishment of the misuse of the corporate entity). The circumstances mentioned in the second point are the means through which the illegal act is going to be identified. Definitely, the concept of illegal act cannot be left on its own because it will give room for vague arguments. Consequently, the occurrence of the above circumstances were established as part of the criteria for the application of this remedy. It has to be mentioned that these circumstances were not created by Argentinean authorities. These circumstances are established in the Argentinean Civil Code as circumstances that may produce the nullity of a contract. As has been previously pointed out, the corporate personality in Argentina is considered as the product of a contract. Therefore, the Argentinean authorities have adapted elements of contractual law as a supplement to the *inoponibilidad de la persona jurídica*. The rationale behind this addition is to establish a parameter for the application of this remedy. The corporate entity is important for the Argentinean economy and thus a remedy that upsets its structure cannot be applied in an uncontrolled manner.

Indeed, the aforementioned circumstances are certainly key in determining the application of this remedy. However, there are cases where a public interest may be affected. Thus, it is likely that the corporate personality will be disregarded should there not be an occurrence of the mentioned circumstances. Moreover, it may be disregarded without depending on the *inoponibilidad de la persona jurídica*. As explained in the first chapter, it is likely that public interest will prevail over the corporate personality if the former is affected by the latter. Later in this chapter, the way the Argentinean authorities have reasoned over controversies involving a public interest will be addressed.

4. Who can summon this remedy?

The *inoponibilidad de la persona jurídica* represents an Argentinean willingness to deal with corporate personality issues. However, it is not a remedy that can be easily summoned. Not only does this remedy require the

---

10 Crispo, J. *Supra note 5*. Page 12.

occurrence of special circumstances, but it can only be summoned by specific parties. As a means of controlling the application of this remedy, the Argentinean judiciary has demanded that only specific parties be able to summon the *inoponibilidad de la persona jurídica*. They are as follows:

- **Third parties:** a person (natural or juridical) who has been affected by the corporate entity can summon this remedy. However, the party that has been affected has to prove that the damage is the result of an illegal act performed through the corporate personality. Additionally, the argument under one of the circumstances that triggers the application of this remedy has to be developed.
- **Shareholders:** A shareholder (or group of shareholders) can summon the *inoponibilidad de la persona jurídica* if the actions of the shareholders who have majority control over the company threaten the existence of the corporate entity and the interests of minority shareholders and stakeholders.[11]

It has to be added that in the area of corporate groups this remedy can be summoned by the subsidiary controlled and abused by the parent company, or by a shareholder (or group of shareholders) that has been affected by the actions of the controlling company.[12]

It must be emphasized that the rationale to have the application of this remedy restricted to these parties can give rise to the controversial nature of this remedy. Indeed, the disregard of the corporate personality has been subject of criticism because of the instability and uncertainty it can create in an economy that depends on the corporate personality. For that reason, authorities have decided to take measures such as the one mentioned in this section in order to mitigate any damage that the uncontrolled application of this remedy may produce.

5. The occurrence of *ultra vires*

From article 54, it can be seen that Argentinean policymakers used the concept of *ultra vires* as a basis for their approach to deal with corporate personality issues.[13] Certainly, there is no direct mention of the *ultra vires* doctrine but the phrase "an act beyond the corporate goals" can be

---

11 See, Olivera, N. & Rodriguez, C. *Inoponibilidad de la Persona Juridica*. Available at http://www.derechocomercial.edu.uy/RespInop.htm (last visit 20 April 2015).
12 See, Manovil, R. (1998) *Grupos de Sociedades*. Argentina: Abeledo-Perrot. Page 65.
13 An act carried out by a public authority, a company or a fiduciary person is *ultra vires* when it is not within the scope of the powers entrusted to such authority, company or person. See, Greenberg, D. (2012) *Stroud's Judicial Dictionary of Words and Phrases*. 8th Edition. London: Sweet & Maxwell.

122 *Piercing the corporate veil in Argentina*

interpreted as an act that is made against the objective of the corporate entity presented in the memorandum of association.[14] Through the registration of the memorandum of association, the corporate entity comes into existence. In this document, one of the requirements is to state the objective of the company. This is one of the conditions that should be met in order for the law to recognize the existence of the corporate entity. If a company acts against this objective, it should be considered as having acted beyond that which was authorized by the law. Certainly, in practice, companies may be allowed to act beyond their original objective since changing the objective may involve a burdensome process. However, this omission of formalities goes with a tacit condition, "as long as it is not against the public order". Therefore, an act beyond the corporate goals in this context should be interpreted as the use of the company as a tool for achieving fraud.

6. Corporate personality issues in Argentina before the rule of *inoponibilidad de la persona jurídica*

Prior to the reform that introduced the rule of *inoponibilidad de la persona jurídica,* the Argentinean judiciary had already ignored the corporation's legal personality. However, the areas of Argentinean law where the corporate veil was ignored (bankruptcy law, labour law, family law and tax law) were areas in which there was an interest that had to be protected by the state. Consequently, the corporate personality may have lost relevance when there was a higher interest at risk. One of the most relevant precedents in this context is the *Swift-Deltec* case.[15] *Cia Swift de la Plata SA* was a subsidiary of Deltec International, a holding company incorporated in the US. In this case, the *Corte Suprema de Justicia de la Nación* (Supreme Court of Justice)[16] decided to disregard the legal personality of Cia Swift de la Plata in order to extend bankruptcy proceedings to other companies in the group and to the parent. The judiciary justified the decision to disregard

---

14 The academia has addressed this circumstance under the concept of *"fines- extrasocietarios"*, a concept that refers to the use of the corporate entity for a purpose different to that established in the articles of incorporation. See, Hurtado, J. *Supra note* 1. At page 76.

15 Sentencia de la Corte Suprema de Justicia de la Nacion, de fecha 4 de septiembre de 1973. *Case Cia. Swift de la Plata Sa S/ Quiebra C/ Deltec Arg. Y Deltec Internacional.*

16 The *Corte Suprema de Justicia de la Nación* is the highest court of law of the Argentinean Republic. The Supreme Court functions as a last resort tribunal. Its rulings cannot be appealed. It also decides on cases dealing with the interpretation of the constitution (for example, it can overturn a law passed by Congress if it deems it unconstitutional). The members of the Supreme Court are appointed by the President with the agreement of at least two-thirds of the Senate members present in a session convened for that purpose, and can only be removed by an impeachment process called *juicio político* ("political trial"), initiated by the Chamber of Deputies and carried out by the Senate, exclusively on grounds of improper behavior. See, http://www.csjn.gov.ar/ (last visit 10 September 2013).

Piercing the corporate veil in Argentina 123

the corporate entity on the basis that the holding company controlled the personality of Cia Swift de la Plata and used its influence over the company against the interest of society and third parties. The Argentinean authorities requested the American authorities to enforce judgment against Deltec International. However, the North American courts refused to carry out the Argentinean judgment because it was against the North American internal legal order.

The case *Cia Swift de la Plata* case was not only one dealing with a corporate group subject to insolvency proceedings, but also included an international factor. This has unarguably made an impact on Argentinean company law. Certainly, multinationals may have hesitated when establishing subsidiaries in Argentina due to the existence of a legal precedent in which a parent company is held liable for the acts of its subsidiary. However, the precedent established in the case *Swift-Deltec* can also be regarded as a stand by Argentinean authorities against the inappropriate or reckless use of the group structure. Argentina is a country with natural resources and thus attracts multinationals. Consequently, authorities have to establish the grounds on which the multinationals can operate. The principle established in this precedent has been shared in other areas of Argentinean law. The prevalence of public interest over the corporate personality has been established. Moreover, this precedent can be regarded as one of the factors motivating the later development of the *inoponibilidad de la persona jurídica*.

In the context of labour law, the *Aybar, Ruben E. y otros v Pizzeria Viturro SRL y otros* case is an example of an abuse of the corporate entity. In this case, the defendant company unjustly fired the claimants and the assets were transferred to another company. Therefore, the employing company was left without enough assets to comply with obligations towards its employees. The court regarded that the transfer of assets was made with no connection to the activities of the employing company. Furthermore, the transference of assets was made after the employees were fired. Consequently, the court considered that the new corporate entity was used as a tool to defeat workers' rights. This presumption followed from the conclusion of the Argentinean authorities that if the transfer of assets was made as part of a business strategy, this could be considered as legitimate; but in this case the transfer of assets was not made with adequate justification. Therefore, this strengthened the claimants' argument and contributed to a decision in their favor. This precedent had an impact on Argentinean labour law as it led the Argentinean judiciary to establish that the use of the corporate entity as a tool for hiding assets in order to defraud employees' rights would trigger the disregard of the corporate personality.[17] It has to be pointed out that the Labour

---

17 *Sentencia de la Sala Segunda de la Corte Nacional de Trabajo de 9 de Mayo de 1973 dictada en el caso Aybar, Ruben E. y otros v. Pizzeria Viturro SRL y otros D.T 1974–67.*

124 *Piercing the corporate veil in Argentina*

Court supported its reasoning in the concept of *ultra vires*. It believed the company created had a commercial objective that was not to hide assets to defeat workers' rights and to support the entity would have fed the thought that the corporate personality can be used for illegitimate objectives. Indeed, the concept of *ultra vires* has played a relevant role when dealing with corporate veil issues in Argentina. However, this decision was based on the public interest that exists in the context of workers' rights.

In the context of family law, the judiciary has established that the use of the corporate entity as a tool to defeat hereditary rights triggers the disregard of the corporate personality. In the case *Astesiano Monica C/Gianina Soc. Com. Acciones*, the defendant created two shell companies to transfer assets that were part of a succession process. The claimants argued that the companies holding the assets were part of a "simulation" aimed at defeating their rights. The Argentinean Court of Appeal evaluated the facts of the case and decided, "the corporate entity cannot be used to deprive heirs of their rights; if the corporate entity is balanced against a hereditary right the latter will prevail";[18] therefore, the transfer of assets was declared null by the court.

Family law is not limited to hereditary issues and there are other issues such as the use of the corporate entity to hide assets subjected to a partition due to a divorce process. Another issue may be the use of the corporate entity as a means to hide assets in order for a parent to avoid paying *child allowance*. Although limited to an issue over a will, the cited Argentinian case provides a precedent for the Argentinean courts to act against the corporate personality in a family context. Indeed, it feeds the presumption that elements of family law prevail over the corporate personality if the latter affects the former.

In the context of tax law, the corporate personality is likely to lose relevance if it is used for illicit purposes such as tax evasion. It must be noted that the corporate group structure is more likely to be used for this purpose. In order to deal with this issue, a group of companies may be regarded as an economic unit (for tax purposes) due to the suitability of this structure for schemes of tax evasion. The *Parke Davis y Cia de Argentina, SAIC* case is a prime example.[19] In this case an Argentinean company, Park Davies, paid dividends to its parent company domiciled in the US. Park Davies wanted to deduct the payment of dividends to the parent company from its taxes.

---

18 La C.N.Com-Sala A 27.2.78 Astesiano Mónica c/ Gianina Soc.Com.Acciones. "en este fallo se sostuvo frente a un derecho de familia y sucesorio, que la personalidad societaria no es una realidad sustancial sino más bien accidental y que como tal no puede servir de sostén a una exclusión de herederos legítimos y en consecuencia se desestimó la personalidad jurídica."

19 *Sentencia de la Corte Suprema de la Nación de fecha 31 de Julio de 1973, Case Parke Davis y Cia de Argentina, SAIC.*

Piercing the corporate veil in Argentina   125

Argentinean tax authorities recognized the individuality of each corporate entity. However, in this particular case the parent company owned 99 per cent of the shares in the Argentinean company. Consequently, tax authorities questioned the individuality of both companies. The fact that the parent company owned 99 per cent of the shares made authorities consider the dividend payment a "self-payment". Authorities emphasized that each corporate entity is recognized as an individual taxpayer but in circumstances like the case at hand, the preservation of the corporate entity supports an evident tax evasion. In this case, the parent company and the subsidiary were regarded as a single unit and the request for tax deduction was denied. It can be appreciated that the Argentinean authorities are inclined to follow a single economic unit approach to deal with the corporate group structure in cases involving tax evasion.

The examples presented in this section evidence the Argentinean authorities´ intention to protect public interest against wrongdoers hiding behind the corporate entity. The arguments on which Argentinean authorities support the disregard of the corporate personality were based on public interest, supplemented in some circumstances by the concept of *ultra vires*. The *inoponibilidad de la persona jurídica* appeared later as a formal method to deal with corporate personality issues. Moreover, part of its development can be attributed to the precedents already mentioned. Certainly, the *inoponibilidad de la persona jurídica* has a wide scope of application. However, in the realm of public law, public interest has such strength that the disregard of the corporate personality can immediately be carried out, without the need of a methodical questioning whether or not to preserve the corporate entity. Therefore, it can be considered that the *inoponibilidad de la persona jurídica* does not have relevance in these areas of law; rather, it is a remedy limited to the realm of private law.

Personal observation

The *inoponibilidad de la persona jurídica* is not something improvised by Argentinean policymakers. Previous to the legal reforms that introduced this rule, Argentinean authorities established the foundations for this rule in case law. Although most of the case law was in a public law context, the authorities reflected over the use of corporate entities for purposes against its original objective. Therefore, *inoponibilidad de la persona jurídica* appears as a means to prevent and punish the inequalities produced by the corporate entity. Indeed, the *inoponibilidad de la persona jurídica* undeniably evidences the originality of the Argentinean method to deal with corporate personality issues.

The *inoponibilidad de la persona jurídica* is a breakthrough. However, it must not be forgotten that this rule has loopholes. Among many criticisms of this rule is the fact that it is not certain whether minority shareholders may use it against dominant shareholders. The text in the article provides

126 *Piercing the corporate veil in Argentina*

this remedy in cases where "the rights of third parties are affected".[20] The rule does not expressly exclude minority shareholders, yet in some cases the Argentinean judiciary has maintained that this rule is, nonetheless, not aimed at protecting minority shareholders.[21]

It is important to emphasize that the existence of a statutory rule, in addition to the willingness of the Argentinean judiciary to apply this remedy, does not make the disregard of the legal entity a frequent practice in this jurisdiction. The Argentinean judiciary emphasizes the exceptional application of the rule contained in Article 54 based on the premise that the uncontrolled application of this remedy may affect legal certainty and undermine the benefits of the corporate personality. In the case of *Pardini v Fredel, SRL y otros*,[22] the Argentinean judiciary reiterated this position and drew attention to the fact that a remedy such as *inoponibilidad de la persona jurídica* "must be applied when it is proved that there has been a fraudulent use of the corporate entity and there is no other remedy available".

---

20 See, Grispo, J. 'Inoponibilidad de la Persona Societaria' *Revista de las Sociedade y Concursos,* available at http://www.iprofesional.com/adjuntos/documentos/09/0000929.pdf (last visit 30 May 2013). At page 15.
21 Simancas, Maria Angelica C/ Crosby, Ronald S/ Sum. – Ref. Norm.: L. 19550: 54–22/12/ 1997. Cited by Crispo J. *Idem*. At page 15.
22 *Sentencia de la Camara Nacional de Apelaciones en lo Comercial, Sala C, de fecha 15 de agosto de 2006, Caso Pardini v. Fredel, SRL y otros.*

VIII Comparative study between the Anglo-American and Latin American piercing of the corporate veil

This book has been developed on the following premise; each jurisdiction develops its mechanism to pierce the corporate veil in accord with its own needs. This creates many different approaches and the piercing of the corporate veil is therefore developed in a unique way by each jurisdiction. This premise has been proved throughout the development of this book. However, this book is not a mere description of the different approaches created in Latin American jurisdictions. One of the core objectives of this book is to engage in a comparative study about this subject in Anglo-American and Latin American jurisdictions. The comparative study of the different means used to deal with the corporate entity helps us to understand the reasons behind the development of different mechanisms to deal with corporate personality issues in each jurisdiction.

1. Methodology

In order to make a comparative study, the method on which this study is going to be developed has first to be determined. The author Karen Vandekerckhove uses the functional comparative method in her work about piercing the corporate veil.[1] This method allows comparison of the function that an institution or rule fulfills in one legal system with the same in another legal system. This book shall follow suit. The comparative functional approach will lead to the conclusion that the American doctrine has not been transplanted to Latin American countries but has acted as a template from which other jurisdictions have gained inspiration for the development of their own mechanisms to deal with corporate personality issues.

Vandekerckhove focused her study on the European Union and corporate personality issues in the context of corporate groups. She chose specific legal

---

1 Vandekerckhove, K. (2007) *Piercing the Corporate Veil*. The Netherlands: Kluwer Law International.

128 *Anglo-American/Latin American comparative study*

systems, which in some cases have different legal traditions, and studied the mechanisms used in each of the chosen legal systems. Although this book is similar, its originality lies in the fact that it focuses on Latin America and the mechanisms developed by specific jurisdictions to deal with corporate personality issues. Moreover, this book has not been limited to this legal phenomenon in the context of corporate groups.

The functional comparative method requires a template; in other words, a jurisdiction on which a comparison can be formed. Regarding the piercing of the corporate veil, the US leads the subject and shall therefore act as template. England shall also be considered due to its role in the development of the corporate personality. It is also relevant because it feeds the premise of the individuality of each legal system. Although the US and England share the same legal tradition and the former has adopted the corporate personality from the latter, the piercing of the corporate veil has been developed differently in both jurisdictions. Whilst this book is about Latin American mechanisms to deal with corporate personality issues, the jurisdictions that pioneered the contemporary concept of corporate personality cannot be ignored as Anglo-American company law provided the foundations of Latin American company law.

2. Rationale to pierce the corporate veil

The piercing of the corporate veil is a remedy that has its rationale in fraud. Indeed, the reason behind the creation of this remedy was to create a mechanism to deal with the fraudulent use of the corporate personality. However, what can be considered as a fraudulent use of the corporate personality? The simple creation of a company as a means to reduce liability gives room for creditors to argue fraud if they do not get paid. However, if each jurisdiction molds the piercing of the corporate veil to meet its own needs, so does it define fraud.

Although the concept of fraud is certainly a reason to pierce the corporate veil, the application of this remedy has not been limited only to the occurrence of fraud. The development of the corporate personality as a device for commerce has produced circumstances that have had hazardous effects on third parties yet are not necessarily based on fraudulent behavior. An example of this could be the environmental damages due to negligent management of a factory. The damage may not be intentional but came about due to the lack of supervision. Moreover, third parties may have been heavily affected and compensation may be required. Therefore, the contemporary mechanisms to deal with corporate personality issues have not only been developed on grounds of fraud but also on the protection of a public interest.

This section shall study the justifications given by jurisdictions when piercing the corporate veil and also the application of the remedy in cases that do not involve fraud.

Anglo-American/Latin American comparative study   129

2.1   US

The core approaches, instrumentality and alter ego, stem from the concept of fraud. If the essence of both doctrines is taken into account, the authorities cannot do anything but emphasize the concurrence of fraud and inequitable conduct. However, the alter ego doctrine can be considered to go beyond this as it does not establish fraud as the exclusive cause. The alter ego doctrine merely requires that the excessive control of the corporate entity produces a harm or inequitable result. There have been controversial opinions among the American judiciary about whether non-fraudulent conduct can trigger the application of this remedy[2] but the predominant position demands the occurrence of fraud. However, this does not mean that public interest is not protected by US regulations. In areas such as environmental law, tax law and labour law, there are specific US statutory exceptions to the corporate personality. However, when discussing the piercing of the corporate veil there is no dilemma about the corporate personality in cases involving a public interest because if the corporate personality is used in a way that affects the public interest, it is disregarded. Although this may seem sweeping, the situation is extreme as regulations have not been developed at state level but at a federal level. A case has to be extreme in order to reach federal courts.

Seeing that most US regulation aiming at the protection of the public interest has been developed at a federal level, it could be presumed that states do not want to enact controversial "anti-corporate entity" regulations and therefore leave such controversy to federal authorities. Circumstances that do not involve fraud are treated according to federal law, which deals with subjects that contain elements that are incompatible with the essence of the corporate entity.

2.2   England

In contrast to the US, England has not developed a formal mechanism to deal with corporate personality issues. Certainly, corporate personality issues have arisen and fraud has been a strong argument with regard to the

---

2 Tort damages do not involve fraud. Therefore, it is unlikely that the US authorities will pierce the corporate veil in order to provide adequate compensation to the affected parties. Academics like Davis Hansman and Henry Kraakman argued that the corporate veil should be eliminated in the context of tort. Certainly, the corporate personality is used also to limit liability in the context of tort. However, there are circumstances where damages have been produced because of negligence of the operators of the company; and furthermore parties are unable to access adequate compensation. For that reason there have been opinions regarding setting aside the corporate veil in the context of tort damage. However, there is an intense academic debate on the subject. In order to learn more about this subject see, Hansman & Kraakman (1991) 'Towards Unlimited Liability for Corporate Torts' *Yale Law Journal* (Volume 100).

130   Anglo-American/Latin American comparative study

English attempts to pierce the corporate veil. However, attempts on grounds of fraud have not been successful. As mentioned earlier, in the case of *Salomon* the House of Lords established a precedent on which it concluded that fraud cannot be argued every time the corporate personality cannot comply with its creditors. If it were otherwise, there would be no reason to use the concept of the corporate entity. The precedent in the case of *Salomon* has been one of the main factors that has hindered using the concept of fraud when dealing with corporate entity issues. Therefore, English authorities have adopted a "backdoor approach". This term is used to address the means to establish liability without directly attacking the corporate personality. In my opinion, the protection of public interest can be regarded as the rationale that English authorities have used in order to develop the mechanism required to handle corporate entity issues. The exceptional cases where shareholders' liabilities have been established have been based on the protection of a public interest. An example is the case *Chandler v Cape*,[3] in which public health prevails over the layers of limited liability produced by the corporate group structure. In addition, the exceptions to the corporate entity contained in English statutes are backed up by a public interest.

2.3 Argentina

The Argentinean mechanism, *inoponibilidad de la persona jurídica,* is triggered by the use of the corporate entity to defraud the interest of third parties. The Argentinean authorities have certainly used fraud as the rationale for their approach. However, the concept of fraud is wide and can give room to vague arguments. Therefore, Argentinean policymakers encapsulated fraud in the use of the corporate personality against its original purpose, a behavior included under the doctrine of *ultra vires*. As an approach based on the concept of *ultra vires* it has to have a specific ground on which to be applied. If not, it would be employed in an uncontrolled manner. Policymakers also established the criteria to determine the use of the corporate entity against its original purpose.

The concept of public interest has also played a role on the development of the Argentinean mechanism to deal with corporate personality issues. Although the rationale is the occurrence of fraud, early case law regarding corporate personality issues demonstrated that Argentinean authorities based their decisions on the protection of a public interest rather than in the concept of fraud. This can be attributed to the fact that in the early days of corporate personality issues, authorities found more consistency in the arguments based on the protection of a public interest. However, the protection of a public interest can face some difficulties in the realm of private law.

---

3 *Chandler v Cape plc* [2012] EWCA Civ 525.

Anglo-American/Latin American comparative study   131

Therefore, on the development of a formal mechanism the Argentinean authorities have focused on the occurrence of fraud as the main trigger of this remedy.

In summary, Argentinean authorities have based their mechanism to deal with corporate personality issues on a double rationale: public interest and fraud in the form of *ultra vires*. However, both rationales are currently implemented in two different areas. On the one hand, the protection of the public interest has relevance in public law areas where a statutory rule contemplates an exception to the corporate personality. On the other hand, the concept of fraud is intended to deal with corporate entity issues at private law level.

2.4   Colombia

The Colombian mechanism to deal with corporate personality issues has its rationale in the concept of fraud. Indeed, the exceptions to the corporate personality have been developed in specific statutes and each contemplates the concept of fraud as the rationale on which this remedy is applied. The notion of public interest has also been considered, but has only been fundamental in the development of the Colombian exception to the corporate entity in a criminal law context.

It can be considered that the main difference between Colombia and the other subjects of study is the reduced scope the application has in this jurisdiction. This statement is based on the fact that Colombia, in contrast with Anglo-American jurisdictions and the other Latin American jurisdictions studied in this book, has strict company law regulation. Moreover, it has an institution known as the *Superintendencia de Sociedades*, which oversees all matters related to the creation, administration and dissolution of business entities. Therefore a general exception to the corporate entity has not been a need. However, small entrepreneurs wanted access to the benefits of the corporate personality. For that reason the Colombian one-man company and the *sociedad por acciones simplificadas* were created. These types of business entities are subject to light regulation rather than strict supervision. For that reason, policymakers regarded these entities as potential tools for fraud. Thus, Colombian policymakers have opted to include an exception, which has the occurrence of fraud as a trigger.

The rationale on which Colombia has developed its exception to the corporate personality has been the prevention and punishment of fraud. It has to be pointed out that the concept of fraud has not been used in a raw manner. In order to prevent vague arguments, Colombian jurisprudence has relied on the traditional civil law concepts of *abuso del derecho* and *fraude a la ley*. Both concepts supplement the Colombian mechanism and are the means used by Colombian policymakers to strengthen the rationale over which the exception to the corporate personality is justified in this jurisdiction.

132 Anglo-American/Latin American comparative study

2.5 Brazil

Brazil is a jurisdiction that has used the concept of abuse as the rationale on which the statutory rule to ignore the corporate personality has been developed. It has to be pointed out that the concept of abuse has not been used in a vague manner; rather Brazilian policymakers have made reference to the use of the company against its original objective and the misappropriation of the company's assets as the types of abusive behavior that trigger the exception to the corporate entity.

Definitely, the concept of abuse may be different from fraud but at times they are interlinked. The abuse of the benefit produced by the corporate personality can be considered as a means to achieve a fraudulent objective. In other words, the abusive behavior can establish the path to reach a fraudulent ending. However, the occurrence of abuse does not necessarily involve fraud; for example, an abusive use of privileges provided by the corporate personality could be a negligent administration of a business. If the environment is polluted or stakeholders suffer losses because of negligence, those responsible cannot be protected. Indeed, it is not possible to take for granted the protection provided by the attributes of corporate personality and limited liability.

Besides the concept of abuse, the Brazilian authorities have also supported decisions against the corporate personality based on the concept of public interest. Evidence lies in the pro-social policies made in the 1940s regarding labour law and also later statutory exceptions to the corporate personality, which were introduced in consumer protection and environmental laws. These areas of law are relevant due to the strong public interest protected by them. Therefore, Brazilians have had a wider rationale to ignore the corporate personality. Indeed, they have not been limited to the occurrence of fraud. Nonetheless, it has to be pointed out that the Brazilian rationale is not a *carte blanche* for authorities to ignore the corporate personality whenever they please. Brazilian jurisprudence has emphasized the exceptional nature of this remedy.

In summary, it can be considered that the Brazilian mechanism to deal with corporate personality issues is based on the protection of the public interest against the abusive use of the corporate entity.

2.6 Mexico

The concept of fraud is the rationale on which Mexican authorities have supported the application of their mechanism to deal with corporate entity issues. Since the Mexican authorities considered the use of this remedy in the context of public companies, they have supported its use on grounds of fraud. The concept of fraud that has been used has been raw. However, in the law proposal aimed at the systematic application of this remedy, authorities established the criteria to apply this remedy: the excessive control of

Anglo-American/Latin American comparative study 133

the corporate entity by the shareholders and a fraudulent intention. The Mexican authorities have, indeed, used a similar criteria as the American doctrine. However, the difference lies in the fact that the American criteria has been developed through case law, while the Mexican criteria has been introduced through a statutory rule and supplemented with other elements also contained in the statute. Certainly, at first glance it could be considered that the Mexican concept of fraud is too wide. However, the requirement of controlling behavior, in the shape of *abuso del derecho*, created the ground on which to develop an argument of fraudulent use of the corporate entity.

The Mexican mechanism aimed at dealing with corporate personality issues has been based on this systematic method. Although this statute is not in force, it is evidence of the Mexican effort to create certainty and a strong rationale on which piercing of the corporate veil is applied in this jurisdiction.

2.7 Comparison

The concept of fraud can be considered the foundation on which the piercing of the corporate veil has been developed in the jurisdictions subject of study. English authorities include fraudulent behavior in their reflections on the corporate personality. In the case of Brazil, although the concept of abuse differs from fraud, the concepts are close; an abusive behavior may be part of a scheme to achieve fraud. However, England and Brazil have not exclusively relied on fraud; English authorities have ignored the corporate personality when a public interest has been affected. Additionally, Brazil has used the concept *abuse of the corporate personality* in specific circumstances.

The US, Colombia, Argentina and Mexico, in contrast, have expressly used the concept of fraud as the rationale on which the corporate personality has to be disregarded. However, it has to be pointed out that these countries do not use a uniform concept of fraud. The US has a doctrine based on rich jurisprudence in which different positions regarding fraud in the context of corporate personality issues are contained. In the mentioned Latin American countries, on the other hand, the concept of fraud has been introduced in a statutory rule and the grounds to prove its occurrence are based on a traditional legal concept, which is chosen in accord with the circumstances over which the statutory rule have been developed. In the US and the Latin American countries subjects of study, fraud is the rationale but the means used to prove the existence of fraud tend to vary.

In summary, although fraud may not be the only rationale on which a mechanism to deal with corporate personality issues has been developed, fraud is still the core argument when considering the application of this remedy. Moreover, the Anglo-American countries and Latin American countries have a similar objective, which is the punishment and the prevention of the misuse of the corporate entity.

134 *Anglo-American/Latin American comparative study*

3. Legal concepts and principles

Fraud is a broad concept. Indeed, in the context of corporate personality there are many circumstances that give room to the presumption the occurrence of fraud. Therefore, the concept of fraud has been adapted by each jurisdiction in accordance with its internal needs. The legal concepts and principles can be considered as the principal means used by each jurisdiction to adapt the concept of fraud. This section is going to compare the concepts and principles that the jurisdictions subject of study have used as the base on which the mechanisms to deal with corporate personality have been developed.

3.1 US

The US is a jurisdiction that has a mechanism to deal with corporate personality based on case law. The doctrines of instrumentality and alter ego are the manifestations of the US mechanism. However, it has to be observed that the US federal system prevents the uniform development of an American mechanism to pierce the corporate veil. Each state has applied instrumentality and/or alter ego in accord with its own needs and federal law has taken over matters with which state legislation does not want to deal. Consequently, there is not a general concept or principle on which the North American mechanism has been supported. Rather, state and federal legislation have developed the concept of fraud in accord with the circumstances each state system has to face.

The US, as mentioned in the second chapter, is the jurisdiction that has pioneered the use of an approach to deal with corporate personality issues. Consequently, other jurisdictions have used the US mechanism as a template in order to develop their own. However, the US concept of fraud could not be adopted by other jurisdictions because of the two facts that have been presented throughout this book; first, there is no uniform concept of fraud in this context; second, each jurisdiction develops the concept of fraud, in the context of corporate personality issues, in accord with its internal needs. Therefore, the traditional legal concepts can be regarded as the means that have been used by Latin American jurisdictions to develop a mechanism that produces a similar effect to that produced by the US remedy.

3.2 *England*

England has only borrowed the US metaphor/title of piercing the corporate veil. Instead, it has adopted a "back door approach", where authorities rely on the concepts of sham, agency and single economic unit. First, the concept of sham makes reference to the use of legal means with the objective of defeating a restriction. An example of this is the cited case *Gilford Motors v Horne*, in which the defendant is accused of using a corporate

Anglo-American/Latin American comparative study 135

entity in order to defeat the restrictions established in a covenant. Second, the concept of agency has been used in circumstances that involve corporate groups. Under the concept of "implied agency" it is argued that the subsidiary can be regarded as an agent of the parent company if a series of circumstances concur. The cited case *Smith, Stone and Knight v Birmingham Corporation* establishes the parameter for the use of implied agency. However, English authorities have not embraced this approach. The third, single economic unit, is also a concept used to deal with corporate groups, but it is based on regarding the group as a unit. The case that introduced this concept in the English system was the cited case of *DHN Food Distributors v Tower Hamlets London Borough Council.*

Sham and agency were concepts that already existed in the English legal framework, and were adapted to deal with corporate entity issues. Single economic unit, on the other hand, is a concept born from a judicial initiative to deal with complications of the group structure. These three concepts were introduced with the objective of piercing the corporate veil, but the result achieved has been a degree of liability without the need of ignoring the corporate entity. Although these concepts have not created a parameter to pierce the corporate veil, they represent the grounds on which the English authorities reflect over the different issues created by the corporate structure.

3.3 Latin America

The Latin American jurisdictions, like England, have also borrowed the US metaphor of piercing the corporate veil. However, differing from England, the Latin American jurisdictions subject of study have dared to challenge the existence of the corporate personality. Moreover, as has been demonstrated in this book, Latin American countries have developed their own mechanisms to deal with corporate personality issues.

In the chapters where the Latin American countries have been reviewed, the presence of civil law tradition concepts and principles can be appreciated. As previously commented, the traditional concepts and principles are the foundation of Latin American mechanisms to deal with corporate personality issues. However, it has to be pointed out that the civil law concepts and principles were not originally created to deal with the corporate personality. Certainly, this fact gives room to the following premise: "if civil law concepts and principles are not aimed at the corporate personality, they should not be applied in this context and, by doing so, Latin American countries are at fault".

The above-mentioned premise may be valid. However, throughout this book the mentioned premise has been proven wrong. The use of traditional concepts and principles has not been a random occurrence. Latin American countries have relied on traditional concepts that are not only picked up in accord with the needs of the corporate entity, but also in accord with the essence of the corporate personality in each jurisdiction. This section will

136 Anglo-American/Latin American comparative study

compare the concepts that supplement each mechanism that combats the misuse of the corporate personality in Latin America countries.

3.3.1 Argentina

The concept of *ultra vires* has been the foundation of the Argentinean exception to the corporate entity. *Ultra vires* is a concept that has become outdated in other jurisdictions. However, the Argentinean authorities have demonstrated that the essence of this concept can be useful in the context of corporate personality issues. As mentioned in the chapter regarding Argentina, the Argentinean authorities have been cautious when dealing with the corporate personality. They have not expressly said that if the corporate entity is used against its objective, then the veil will be pierced. Rather, they have emphasized the use of the corporate entity to defraud the law (*fraude a la ley*) as the condition for the *ultra vires* concept to be applicable. Argentinean policymakers have elaborated this approach using these tools provided by the Argentinean legal system. Certainly, it has to be pointed out that to use the corporate entity for an objective beyond the original objective does not necessarily mean an illicit objective; it could be something legal. Therefore, *fraude a la ley* appears as the defining point. *Fraude a la ley* consist in the use of legal means to defeat a legal restriction or third parties' rights. The Argentinean authorities have considered that *fraude a la ley* can be achieved by a wrongdoer the moment they use a legally created corporate personality for a deviated objective, which is to defeat the law or third parties' rights.

The concept of *ultra vires* combined with *fraude a la ley* is, in theory, an ideal approach because it creates certainty about the grounds on which the corporate personality can be disregarded by Argentinean authorities. However, there is no actual and relevant Argentinean case law that can support the application of this statutory exception. Like in other Latin American jurisdictions, the piercing of the corporate veil is rarely applied.

3.3.2 Colombia

The Colombian authorities have been "straightforward" when dealing with corporate personality issues. In the context of criminal law, they have not used an alternative concept to "soften" the application of piercing the corporate veil. As pointed out in the chapter about Colombia, the *estatuto anticorrupcion* allows the judge to ignore the corporate personality whenever considered necessary. Certainly, it is a radical and daring approach. However, this exception is only limited to the context of criminal investigations, an area that contains an interest that can be considered superior to the corporate personality.

In a private law context, the piercing of the corporate veil has been limited to two types of business entities: the one-man company and the *sociedad por acciones simplificadas.* Policymakers have not added a traditional concept or principle in the statutory exception. Thus, the basis on which the fraudulent use of the corporate personality can be determined is not established and the exception only addresses the occurrence of fraudulent behavior as the trigger of an exception to the corporate personality. Although not simple, the statutory exception seems to have a general concept of fraud. The statutory exceptions are supported by the contractual nature of the corporate personality. As mentioned in previous chapters, some Latin American jurisdictions, such as Colombia, regard the corporate personality as the product of a contract. Therefore, certain aspects of contract regulation have been used to deal with the corporate personality. Accordingly, the concept of *abuso del derecho* can be considered as the most relevant.

The concept of *abuso del derecho* refers to the abuse committed under the exercise of a right. This concept was originally included to address issues in a contractual context, but its application has been expanded to supplement the statutory exceptions to corporate personality issues. Therefore, it can be considered that Colombian jurisprudence has elaborated the concept of fraud on grounds of *abuso del derecho*, in order to create a degree of certainty when dealing with corporate personality issues.

3.3.3 Brazil

The Brazilian authorities have introduced an exception to the corporate personality in their Civil Code, the core regulation of the corporate personality and have established *abuso del derecho* as the foundation of their mechanism to deal with corporate personality issues. Instead of using fraud, the Brazilian authorities have established abuse in the form of inappropriate use of the corporate personality and commingling of assets as the trigger to pierce the corporate veil. The concept of abuse is not limited only to fraud, a fact that makes the application of this mechanism wider. It has to be pointed out that before the Brazilian Civil Code, policymakers had introduced exceptions in specific statutory rules, which were already based on the concept of *abuso del derecho* (the consumers protection law and the law regarding the protection of the economic order). This shows that the concept of *abuso del derecho* was not chosen in a random manner. Brazilian policymakers studied the impact of this concept on their framework for companies. The result seems to be positive because it is the means through which the misuse of the Brazilian corporate personality can be deterred and in turn punished.

3.3.4 Mexico

Mexico is the only jurisdiction that has dared to draft a regulation for piercing the corporate veil. However, this regulation is not in force. The foundations of this statute are based on the same elements of the

138 Anglo-American/Latin American comparative study

US doctrine. Nonetheless, the Mexican statute proceeds to develop the concepts of control and fraud. Mexican policymakers have opted for the development of these concepts, rather than rely on traditional legal concepts and principles. It has to be pointed out that Mexico in its law project has not summoned a traditional legal concept or principle. However, if the Mexican law project that regulates the piercing of the corporate veil is enacted, the Mexican judiciary is likely to use legal concepts and principles to supplement the positive law. This hypothesis is supported by the fact that the Mexican judge at some point will need to "frame" the type of behavior of the wrongdoer and develop the jurisprudence that will feed this regulation.

3.4 Comparison

Fraud is a wide concept, especially in the context of the corporate personality. Therefore, the authorities have framed the concept of fraud through traditional legal concepts. Defining fraud yields certainly. Consequently, the use of traditional legal concepts has often been employed in Latin American jurisdictions because they dramatically support the development of a mechanism to deal with corporate personality. As has been pointed out throughout this book, the civil law tradition obliges the Latin America judge to look for alternative means in order to provide an equitable decision in the context of corporate personality issues.

Legal traditions have influence over the development of a mechanism to deal with corporate personality issues. On the one hand, the US doctrine of piercing the corporate veil achieves its objective through the means provided by a legal system based on the common law tradition. Latin America, on the other hand, does not follow the common law tradition and the legal systems of the region have their foundations in civil law. Accordingly, the mechanisms to deal with corporate personality issues had to be developed differently from the US doctrine. The mentioned traditional legal concepts are a fundamental part of the means used by the Latin American jurisdictions to achieve a similar result to that of the US doctrine. The piercing of the corporate veil exists in Latin America but dramatically varies from the US doctrine of piercing the corporate veil.

Similar to Latin America, England has also relied on traditional concepts. However, the English mechanism is not directed to the corporate personality. The English policymaker has adapted traditional legal concepts to attack other aspects of the corporate entity in order to establish a wrongdoer's liability. Although England shares the tendency of using legal concepts, there are some basic differences between England and the Latin American jurisdictions subject of study; for example, the legal tradition followed by each case study and the internal needs unique in each jurisdiction. In addition, it has to be mentioned that England has more experience than Latin American countries regarding the subject of corporate personality issues. Therefore, this jurisdiction has had more room to develop a mechanism to deal with corporate personality issues.

4. The means to achieve the objective of a mechanism to deal with corporate personality issues

The piercing of the corporate veil has its rationale in the concept of fraud, which is a concept that some jurisdictions have framed through traditional legal concepts and principles. As a consequence, different mechanisms have been developed to deal with corporate personality issues. Certainly, in principle the different mechanisms to deal with the corporate personality share the same objective, which is to expose wrongdoers by disregarding the corporate personality. However, in some of the cited jurisdictions the wrongdoers are punished without affecting the corporate entity. As can be observed in previous chapters, some mechanisms do not necessarily disregard the corporate entity; rather, the wrongdoers are punished without affecting the integrity of the corporate personality. In this book, the variation on the means to achieve the objective is addressed as the sledgehammer and the backdoor approach.

4.1 Sledgehammer approach

The sledgehammer approach makes reference to a direct strike on the corporate personality. In other words, it means the disregard of the corporate personality. The US, Colombia, Mexico and Brazil are jurisdictions that fall under the classification of countries with a sledgehammer approach.

4.1.1 US

The US doctrines of instrumentality and alter ego are mechanisms that aim at disregarding the corporate personality as long as the established criteria have been met. Moreover, the metaphor of piercing the corporate veil was developed in this jurisdiction. Therefore, not only the contemporary doctrine, but also the history of this remedy demonstrates the tendency of the US judiciary to deal in a direct, and in other words sledgehammer, manner with the corporate personality.

4.1.2 Colombia

Colombia is a jurisdiction that has adopted a strong position against the use of the corporate personality for fraudulent purposes. In the public law context, Colombian authorities do not hesitate to ignore the corporate personality if this has been used for criminal activities. In the private law context, the Colombian authorities have limited the exception to two types of business entities (the one-man company and *sociedad por acciones simplificada*). This

140 *Anglo-American/Latin American comparative study*

exception is direct (like a sledgehammer); in the statutes that contain these exceptions the policymaker has stated the disregard of the corporate personality if it has been used for fraudulent purposes. Moreover, the Colombian constitutional court has emphasized the strength of the exceptions to the corporate personality.

4.1.3 Mexico

Mexican policymakers went as far as to take the initiative to elaborate a systematic method to deal with corporate personality issues. Although the Mexican statute about the piercing of the corporate veil is not in force, it evidences the Mexican inclination for the sledgehammer approach. In addition, previous to the draft of the Mexican law proposal, the authorities had already considered the piercing of the corporate veil in other areas of the Mexican legal framework.

4.1.4 Brazil

The Brazilian authorities can be considered as willing to ignore the corporate personality. In the early days of the Brazilian mechanism to deal with corporate personality issues, the Brazilian authorities were cautious and exceptions were limited to specific circumstances (consumer protection and environmental law). However, the gradual development and study of corporate personality led Brazilian policymakers to introduce an exception to the corporate personality in the Brazilian Civil Code. The Civil Code is a core regulation regarding the corporate entity. For that reason, in comparison to other Latin American jurisdictions, the Brazilian mechanism can be considered as a direct method to deal with corporate personality issues and thus behaves as a sledgehammer.

4.2 Backdoor approach

The backdoor approach makes reference to a method that does not aim at disregarding the corporate entity; rather, this approach looks for alternative means to hold wrongdoers liable. Some of the countries that have opted for a mild approach are England and Argentina.

4.2.1 England

The English authorities have opted to deal with corporate personality issues by using different methods to deal with the corporate entity. Different from the US, the English authorities have not developed a doctrine. In cases where an exception has been proposed, instead of ignoring the corporate personality, the authorities have provided an alternative solution. An example is the cited case, *Gilford Motors v Horne*. Currently, English jurisprudence recognizes three approaches to deal with corporate personality issues: sham, agency and single economic unit. It has to be pointed out that the single economic unit ignores the legal personality of the entities part of the corporate group in order to address the group as a unit. Certainly it attacks the corporate personality. However, the single economic unit approach has not been welcomed by English jurisprudence. In the opinion of this author, the fact that the single economic unit focuses on the corporate entity makes it incompatible with the English tendency to go for a backdoor approach.

4.2.2 Argentina

Although the Argentinean authorities have introduced a mechanism to deal with the corporate entity in the core regulation for companies, this mechanism does not intend to disregard the corporate personality. The *inoponibilidad de terceros* is a remedy aimed at nullifying the illicit acts performed through the corporate entity. Therefore, the Argentinean mechanism cannot be considered as one that directly "strikes" the structure of the corporate personality. Rather, it frees the corporate personality from any liability of acts that the wrongdoer performed under the name of the corporate entity.

4.3 Overall observation

The objective behind a mechanism to deal with corporate personality issues is to prevent and punish the misuse of the corporate personality. This objective can be achieved without directly striking the corporate personality. Certainly, each country develops its means to piercing the corporate veil in accord with its own framework. Some countries may need a sledgehammer approach, other countries may be better with a backdoor approach. There is not a perfect mechanism to deal with corporate personality issues. No doubt the sledgehammer and backdoor each have their flaws. However, as long as it aids to punish the misuse of the corporate personality, the flaws are a minor worry.

Personal observation

The functional comparative approach is a method that aids the study of piercing the corporate veil. As a personal observation, each jurisdiction that attempts to deal with corporate personality issues follows the same objective, which is the punishment of the wrongdoers who are trying to hide behind the corporate personality. However, in order to achieve that objective there is not a uniform approach. Rather each jurisdiction has developed its mechanism to deal with corporate personality issues in accord with its needs and policy towards the corporate personality.

Conclusion

The contemporary corporate entity is unquestionably a legal marvel. However, this legal marvel has been surrounded by controversy since its conception in the late nineteenth century. An example is the dilemma over the liability of the natural or juridical persons protected and benefited by the corporate entity. This dilemma is better known as the piercing of the corporate veil, a metaphor created in North American courts, which regards the existence of an imaginary veil between the corporate entity and its members, which can be pierced in exceptional circumstances. North American jurisprudence has dealt with corporate personality issues, using this metaphor as its foundation.

The US doctrine of piercing the corporate veil is the core doctrine from which other jurisdictions have crafted their mechanisms to deal with the corporate personality. Certainly, the US doctrine has been subject of interest for researchers in many jurisdictions. However, it is not correct to say that the US doctrine of piercing the corporate veil has made its way through other common and civil law jurisdictions. All of the jurisdictions subject of study have developed a means to deal with corporate personality issues. Furthermore, each jurisdiction has used a different methodology to the one employed by the US doctrine in order to punish wrongdoers. The reasons for this lack of uniformity have been attributed to the uniqueness of each legal system. Although, England and the US follow the same legal tradition, each one has dealt with corporate personality issues differently. The jurisprudence in the US and England demonstrate the need for the different laws that each of these countries have in this context. The same circumstance arises in Latin America, where most of the countries in the region follow the civil law tradition yet each has a unique legal system. Therefore, each country has handled corporate entity issues differently.

Latin American countries as a case study have demonstrated the creativity that each jurisdiction has when it comes to deal with a legal issue or dilemma. Indeed, the use of traditional legal concepts and principles to deal with corporate entity issues are evidence of this creativity. This book has pointed out the concepts and principles that have been the pillar on which the development of a mechanism to deal with corporate personality issues has been built.

The need of traditional concepts is based on the wideness of the concept of fraud. The concept of fraud is the common rationale for the disregard of the corporate personality. However, in the context of corporate personality, to argue fraud is difficult due to the corporate entity attributes of legal personality and limited liability. The fact that the individuals behind the corporate entity are not liable to creditors, if the company run out of assets, definitely gives room for an angry creditor to argue fraud. Therefore, in order to prevent vague arguments based on morals and justice, each jurisdiction has developed its concept of fraud based on a legal concept or principles that are appropriate and fulfill the needs of the law. It has to be pointed out that although the rationale to disregard the corporate personality is fraud, other jurisdictions have preferred to support their exception on other grounds. In this book, Brazil has been highlighted as a jurisdiction that has relied on the abuse concept, rather than on fraud. However, this variation on the rationale to disregard the corporate personality can be attributed to the individuality of each jurisdiction when it comes to deal with corporate personality issues, as has been emphasized throughout this book. Each jurisdiction has developed its own mechanism to deal with corporate personality issues in accord with its internal needs and in harmony with its legal framework.

Another aspect of the mechanism to deal with corporate entity issues that has fed the position of the author regarding the individuality of each jurisdiction is the tendency to adopt a sledgehammer approach or a backdoor approach. The headings *sledgehammer* and *backdoor* are used to address the different tendencies adopted to deal with corporate personality issues. In this book, it can be appreciated that some jurisdictions have been more direct in dealing with corporate personality issues (sledgehammer approach), while others have opted for an approach to punish wrongdoers without undermining the corporate entity (backdoor approach). This book does not advocate a particular preference of approach. It instead comments (with the objective of supporting the premise on which this book has been developed) as part of comparative study. Each jurisdiction has developed the corporate entity in accordance with its economic needs; hence, each jurisdiction has also created a mechanism that does not undermine the corporate personality and the benefits it provides.

To conclude, the corporate entity can be compared with a building designed without an emergency exit, which is vital in case of a disaster. Therefore, it can be concluded that each of the jurisdictions studied in this book has managed to create an emergency exit without affecting the traditional architecture of the building.

Bibliography

Books

Alsina, H. (1956) *Tratato Teorico Practico de Derecho Civil y Comercial*. Ediar S.A.: Buenos Aires.

Arauz, H. (2006) *Fundamentos de la Prueba Judicial* (1st Edition). Universal Books: Panama.

Baker, J. (1990) *An Introduction to English Legal History* (3rd Edition). Butterworths: UK.

Barber, S. (2003) *Company Law* (4th Edition). Old Bailey Press: UK.

Becerra, F. (1999) *Diccionario de Terminología Jurídica Mexicana (español–Inglés)*. Escuela Libre de Derecho: Mexico.

Bertola, L. & Ocampo, J. (2012) *The Economic Development of Latin America Since Independence*. Oxford University Press: UK.

Bevans, N. (2007) *Business Organization and Corporate Law*. Thomson Delmar Learning. US.

Brunetti, A. (2002) *Sociedades Mercantiles. Tomo I*. Editorial Juridica Universitaria: Colombia.

Blumberg, Ph. (2005) *Blumberg on Corporate Groups* (2nd Edition). Aspen Publishers: US.

Blumberg, Ph. (2007) *The Law of Corporate Groups*. Aspen Publisher: US.

Blumberg, Ph. (1987) *The Law of Corporate Groups. Tort, Contract and other Common law Problems in the Substantive Law of the Parent Subsidiary Corporations*. Aspen Publisher: US.

Boeger, N., Murray, R. and Villiers, C. (2008) *Perspectives on Corporate Social Responsibility*. Edward Elgar Publishing Limited: UK.

Boldo, C. (2006) *Levantamiento del Velo Corporativo y Persona Juridica en el Derecho Privado Español* (4th Edition). Editorial Arazandi: Navarra.

Butler, E, & Others (editors) (2011) *Fundations of Comparative Law: Methods and Typologies*. Wildy: Simmonds & Hills.

Caballenas, G. (2009) *Dicctionario Juridico Elemental*. Heliasta: Buenos Aires.

Cachon, J. (2000) *La Sociedad Anonima. Cien Preguntas Claves y sus Respuestas* (3rd Edition). Dykinson S.L.: Panama.

Chong, A. & Lopez de Silanes, F. (2007) *Investors Protection and Corporate Governance; Firm Level Across Latina America*. Stanford University Press: New York.

Chiovenda, G. (2005) *Instituciones de Derecho Procesal Civil, Volumen 2*. Valleta Editions: Argentina.

146 Bibliography

Clarke, T. (2007) *Corporate Governance: Comparative Approach*. Routledge: US.

Cresswell, J. (2008) *Research design: Qualitative, quantitative, and Mixed Methods Approaches* (2nd Edition). Sage Publications Inc: London.

Davis, P. & Worthington, S. (2008) *Gower & Davis Principles of Modern Company Law* (9th Edition). Sweet & Maxwell: London.

Dignam, A. & Lowry, J. (2012) *Company Law* (7th Edition). Oxford University Press: Oxford.

Dine, J. (2009) *Company Law* (7th Edition). Palgrave Macmillan: Basingstoke.

Dongui, T. & others (2002) *Historia Economica de America Latina desde la Independencia hasta nuestros Dias*. Cambridge University Press: Cambridge.

Durling, R. (1986) *La Sociedad Anónima de Panamá*. Editorial Lil. S.A.: Panama.

Enciclopedia Juridica OMEBA § TOMO XVIII. Driskill S.A. Ed. (1979). Mexico.

Espa, L. (2002) *El Juez Como Aplicador de las Normas del Derecho Mercantil*. Escuela Judicial: Panama.

Estribí, H. (2000) *Compendio de Legislación Offshore en Panamá Doctrina, Normas y Glosario*. Sistema Juridico S.A.: Panama.

Fabrega, J. (2010) *Ley Panameña sobre Sociedades de Responsabilidad Limitada*. Sistema Juridico S.A.: Panama.

Fabrega, P. (2004) *Diccionario de Derecho Procesal*. Plaza & Janes Editores: Colombia.

Fabrega, J. (2004) *Instituciones de Derecho Procesal Civil § TOMO I*. Editora Juridica Panameña: Panama.

Fabrega, J. (2008) *Tratado Sobre la Ley de Sociedades Anónimas, Comentada por Articulos*. Sistema Juridicos S.A.: Panama.

Farrar, J. (1998) *Farrar's Company Law* (4th Edition). Butherworths: London.

Fernández, M., (2004) *La sociedad Unipersonal en el Derecho Español*. La Ley: Madrid.

Ferran, E. (2008) *Principles of Corporate Finance Law*. Oxford University Press. Oxford.

Ferreira, F. (1998) *Acción de Amparo, Confidencialidad y Levantamiento del Velo Corporativo*. Editorial Portobelo: Panama.

Figueroa, D. (2011) *Levantamiento del Velo Corporativo LatinoAmericano; Aspectos Comparados con el Derecho Estado Unidense* (1st Edition). Editirial el Jurista: Chile.

Garcia, E. (2003) *Eficacia de la Prueba Ilícita en el Proceso Penal (a la Luz de la STS 81/98 de 2 de Abril)*. Guarda Impresores S.L.: Valencia.

García, M. & Camargo, L. (2002) *El Juez como aplicador de las normas de Derecho Mercantil*. Equipo Nacional de Trabajo *Fondo Mixto Hispano Panameño Consejo General del Poder Judicia. Proyecto de apoyo al Poder Judicial* Escuela Judicial de Panamá. Panamá.

Garriguez, J. (1987) *Curso de Derecho Mercantil* (Tomo II). Editorial Temis: Bogota.

Gil, M. & others. (2010) *Levantamiento del Velo Corporativo*. Universidad del Rosario: Colombia.

Gillooly, M. (1993) *The Law Relating to Corporate Groups*. The Federation Press: Australia.

Glenn, P. (2010) *Legal Traditions of the World* (4th Edition). Oxford University Press. New York.

Granda, F. (2004) *El Rasgado del Velo Societario para Determinar la Competencia Dentro del Arbitraje*. Sistema Juridico S.A.: Panama.

Bibliography 147

Grantham, R. & Rickett, C. (1998) *Corporate Personality in the 20th Century.* Oxford University Press: Oxford.

Greenberg, D. (2012) *Stroud's Judicial Dictionary of Words and Phrases* (8th Edition). Sweet & Maxwell: London.

Griffin, S. (2006) *Company Law Fundamental Principles* (4th Edition). Pearson Education Limited: Essex.

Gutierrez, E. (1988) *Lecciones de Derecho Commercial* (3rd Edition). Biblioteca Juridica Dique: Medillin.

Hannigan, B. (2012) *Company Law* (3rd Edition). Oxford University Press: Oxford.

Henn, H. (1983) *Laws of Corporations and Other Business Enterprises* (3rd Edition). Student Edition. West Pub. Co.: US.

Higgs & Goo's. (2011) *Cases & Materials on Company Law* (7th Edition). Oxford University Press.: Oxford.

Hoffman, C. (2013) *Nociones del Derecho Norteamericano* (2nd Edition). CreateSpace Independent Publishing Platform: US.

Hudson, A. (2012) *Understanding Company Law.* Routledge: Oxon.

Hurtado, J. (2008) *La Doctrina del Levantamiento del Velo Societario en España e Hispanoamerica.* Atelier: España.

Ivamy, H. (1983) *Dictionary of Company Law.* Butterworths: London.

Kraakman, R. & Others (2009) *The Anatomy of Corporate Law; A Comparative and Functional Approach.* Oxford University Press: Oxford.

Konrad, Z. and Kötz, H. (1998) *Introduction to Comparative Law* (3rd Edition). Clarendon Press: Oxford.

Laporta, J. (1992) *Comentarios al Codigo Civil y las Compilaciones Forales.* Tomo I. Editorial Temis: Madrid.

LaRosa, M. & Mejia, G. (2012) *Colombia: a Concise Contemporary.* Rwoman & Littlefield Publishers, Inc.: UK.

Lee, D & Mckenzie, R. (2008) *In Defense of Monopoly, How Market Power Foster Creative Production.* University of Michigan Press: US.

Leet, J., Clarke, J., Nollkamper P., & Whynott P. (2007) *The Limited Liability Company* (Revised Edition). Adkinson: Texas.

Lowry, J. & Reisberg, A. (2012) *Pettet's Company Law and Corporate Finance.* Pearson Education Limited: Essex.

Madriñan, R. (2000) *Principios de Derecho Comercial* (8th Edition). Editorial Temis S.A.: Colombia.

Martin, E. (2006) *A Dictionary of Law* (6th Edition). Oxford University Press: Oxford.

Mayson, French & Ryan (2013) *Company Law.* Oxford University Press: Oxford.

Mellifont, K. (2009) *Fruit of the Poisonous Tree: Evidence Derived from Illegally or Improperly Obtained Evidence.* Federation Press: Australia.

Mevorach, I. (2009) *Insolvency within Multinational Enterprise Groups.* Oxford University Press Inc.: New York.

Micklethwait, J. and Wooldridge, A. (2003) A. *The Company: A Short History of a Revolutionary Idea.* Modern Library: US.

Midon, M. (2007) *Derecho Probatorio, Parte general.* Ediciones Juridicas Cuyo: Argentina.

Mirow, M. (2004) *Latin America Law: A History of Private law and Institutions in Spanish America.* University of Texas Press: Texas.

Moskowitz, J. (1995) *Environmental liability and Real Property Transactions* (2nd Edition). Aspen Law & Business: New York.

148 Bibliography

O'Neal & Thompson. (2004) *Close corporations and LLCs* (3rd Edition). Clark Boardman Callaghan: US.

Perdomo, R. & Marryman, J. (2007) *The Civil Law Tradition: An Introduction to the Legal Systems of Europe and Latin America* (3rd Edition). Stanford University Press: California.

Politis, V. (2004) *Routledge Philosophy Guidebook to Aristotle and Metaphysics.* Routledge: New York.

Rosas, J. (2001) *La Persona Juridica Societaria.* Oxford University Press: Mexico.

Rudorfer, M. (2006) *Piercing the Corporate Veil, A sound Concept.* New York University: New York.

Scheneeman, J. (2012) *The Law of Corporations and other Business Organizations* (6th Edition). Delman. Cengage Learning: US.

Serick, R. *Rechtsform und Realitiit Juristischer Personen.* Translated to Spanish by Brutau, P. (1998) *Aparencia y Realidad en las Sociedades Mercantiles.* Edit. Ariel: Barcelona.

Spitz & Clarke. (2005) *Offshore Service, Introduction: Commentary in Offshore Services.* Butterworths: UK.

Vanasco, C. (2001) *Manual de Sociedades Comerciales* (8th Edition). Astrea: Buenos Aires.

Vandekerckhove, K. (2007) *Piercing the Corporate Veil.* Kluwer Law International: The Netherlands.

Yaguez, A. (1997) *La Doctrina del Levantamiento del Velo en la Jurispridencia* (4th Edition). Civitas: Navarra.

Articles

Amatrudo, A. (2012) 'An Intentional Basis for Corporate Personality' *International Journal of Law in Context.* Available at http://journals.cambridge.org/action/disp layAbstract?fromPage=online&aid=8675441&fulltextType=RA&fileI d=S1744552312000274 (last visit 31 May 2013).

Andrade, F. and Pasqualotto, A. (2010) 'El Levantamiento de la Personalidad Juridica en el Derecho Privado Brazileño'. Available at dialnet.unirioja.es/descarga/articulo/ 3696745.pdf (last visit 30 May 2013).

Bainbridge, S. 'Abolishing LLC Veil Piercing'. SSRN eLibrary. Available at http:// papers.ssrn.com/sol3/papers.cfm?abstract_id=551724 (last visit 30 May 2013).

Bainbridge, S. 'Abolishing Veil Piercing'. SSRN eLibrary Available at http://papers. ssrn.com/sol3/papers.cfm?abstract_id=236967 (last visit 30 May 2013).

Baker, T. 'Doing Business in Panama'. available at http://www.bakertillyinternational. com/media/36926/doing%20business%20in%20panama.pdf (last visit 30 May 2013).

Barber, D. (1981) 'Piercing the Corporate Veil' *Williamette Law Review* (Volume 17).

Barrios, B. *Teoria de la Sana Critica.* Available at http://www.academiadederecho. org/upload/biblio/contenidos/Teoria_de_la_sana_critica_Boris_Barrios.pdf (last visit 30 May 2013).

Barsallo, C. (2007) *Corporate Governance in Emerging Markets.* Corporate governance and enforcement mechanisms in emerging markets. Forum 2. Istanbul, Sabanci University.

Barsallo, P. (1996) 'La Doctrina del Velo Corporativo' *Revista LEX* (Issue 160).

Bibliography 149

Bello, J. (2008) 'An Overview of the Doctrine of the Piercing of the Corporate Veil as Applied By Latin American Countries: A US Legal Creation Exported to Civil Law Jurisdictions [Argentina/Mexico/United States/Venezuela]' *ILSA Journal of International & Comparative Law* (Volume 14, Issue 3).

Bendremer, F. (2004–2005) 'Delaware LLCs and Veil Piercing: Limited Liability has its Limitations' *Fordham Journal of Corporate and Finance Law* (No. 10). Pages 385–496.

Bergkamp, L. (2009) 'Piercing the corporate veil: shareholder liability for corporate torts' *The Journal of Business Law* (Issue 2).

Beekarry, N. & Gup, B. (2009) 'Limited liability companies (LLCs) and financial crimes' *Journal of Money Laundering Control* (Volume 12 Issue 1). Pages 7–18.

Blankernburg, S. Plesh, D. & Wilkinson, F. (2010) 'Limited Liability and the Modern Corporation in Theory and in Practice' *Cambridge Journal of Economics* (Issue 34).

Blumberg, M. and Burnett, R. (1996–1997) 'Piercing the Corporate Veil in Florida: Defining Improper Conduct' *Nova Law Review* (Volume 21).

Blumberg, Ph. (2001) 'Accountability of Multinational Corporations: the Barriers Presented by Concepts of Corporate Juridical Entity' *Hastings International and Comparative Law Review* (Issue 24).

Blumberg, Ph. (1990) 'The Corporate Entity in an Era of Multinational Corporations' *Delaware Journal of Corporate Law* (Volume 15).

Boumer, S. (2000) 'To Pierce or not to pierce the corporate veil – why substantive consolidation is not an issue under English law' *Journal of international banking law* (Issue 15). Pages 193–7.

Boutin, G. (2007) 'Panamanian offshore company law and conflicting laws' *International Business Law Journal* (Issue 7). Pages 171–210.

Castillo, J. (2006) '*La Fundamentación de las Sentencias y la Sana Crítica*' *Revista Chilena de Derecho* (Volume 33).

Camargo, A. (2003) 'Three Essential Aspects of Corporate Law: A Brief Overview of Brazilian and American Approaches' *Southwestern Journal of Law & Trade in the Americas* (Volume 9).

Cary, W. (1973) 'Federalism and Corporate Law: Reflections Upon Delaware' *The Yale Law Journal* (Volume 83).

Cheng, T. (2010) 'Form and Substance of the Doctrine of Piercing the Corporate Veil' *Mississippi Law Journal* (Volume 80).

Cheng, T. 'Piercing the Corporate Veil Across the Atlantic: A Comparative Study of the English and the U.S Corporate Veil Doctrines' Available at:http://works. bepress.com/thomas_cheng/3 (last visit 30 May 2013).

Cihlar, F. (2008) 'The "Delaware LLC Problem" cracking the shell' *Company Lawyer* (Issue 29). Pages 176–8.

Corcoran, J. (2003) 'Aristotle's Prior Analytics and Boole's Laws of Thought' *History and Philosophy of Logic* (Issue 24).

Dewey, J. (1926) 'The Historic Background of Corporate Legal Personality' *Yale Law Journal* (Volume XXXV).

Diaz Olivo, C. (2004) 'Mitos y Leyendas Acerca de la Doctrina de Descorrer el Velo Corporativo' *Revista Juridica de la Universidad de Puerto Rico* (Volume 73: No. 2). Pages 311–91.

Dobson, J. (1983) 'Lifting the Veil in Four Countries: the Law of Argentina, England, France and the United States' *International Law & Comparative Law Quarterly.* (Issue 839).

150 Bibliography

Dorrell, D. (2005) 'Alter Ego Analysis to Find Hidden Assets' *American Journal of Family Law* (Volume 18. No. 4). Pages 213–33.

Droi, J. (2009) 'The Bases for Piercing the Corporate Veil' *Massachusetts Law Review* (Volume 91, No. 4). Pages 193–6.

Durham, R. 'The Functional Method of Comparative Law'. Available at https://www.law.kuleuven.be/ccle/pdf/Michaels%20-%20Functional%20Method%20-%20edited.pdf (last visit 30 May 2013).

Fabrega, J. (2004) 'Panama como centro para la Estructuracion de Transacciones Internacionales o Extraterritoriales y su diferencia con los Paraisos Tribiutarios o Tax Havens'. Available at JP Fábrega – fabamm.com (last visit 30 May 2013).

Fernández, C. (2003) 'Que clase de objeto es la persona juridical?' *Gazeta Juridica, Lima* (Tomo 112). Pages 9–25.

Fischel, D. (1985) 'Limited Liability and the Corporation' *U. Chi. L. Rev.* (Volume 52, No. 89). Pages 89–116.

Flannigan, R. (1986) 'Corporations Controlled by Shareholders: Principals, Agents or Servants' *Sask Law Review* (Volume 51).

Flynn, L. (2007) 'Piercing the Corporate Veil: Caper industries and Multinational Corporate Liability for a Toxic Hazard, 1950–2004'. Published by Oxford University Press on behalf of the Business History Conference. http://es.oxfordjournals.org/content/8/2/268.short (last visit 30 May 2013).

Fox, E. (1993–1994) 'Piercing the veil of limited liability companies' *George Washington Law Review* (No. 62). Pages 1143–78.

Fuentes, C. (2009) '*Acercamiento al Concepto de Grupos Empresariales: Concurrencia de Elementos para su Existencia*' Revist@ e-Mercatoria (Volume 8, No. 1). Available at SSRN: http://ssrn.com/abstract=1493764 (last visit 30 May 2013).

Gaertner, M. (1989) 'Reverse Piercing the Corporate Veil: Should Corporation Owners have it Both Ways?' *William and Mary Law Review* (Volume 30).

Garnica, C & others (2007) '*Corte Constitucional Linea Jurisprudencial 1997–2007, Levantamiento del Velo Corporativo*' Universidad Sergio Arboleda. Available at http://www.usergioarboleda.edu.co/derecho_comercial/jurisprudencias/linea_jurisprudencial.pdf (last visit 30 May 2013).

Garzon, C. (2005) 'El Mercado y las Bases del Grupo Empresarial' *REVIST@e-Mercatoria, Universidad Externado de Colombia, Revista del Departamento de Derecho Comercial* (Volume 4, No. 1). Available at http//www.emercatoria.edu.co/paguinas/volumen4/01.htmmercado (last visit 1 February 2010).

Gelbh, H. (2009) 'Limited Liability and Veil Piercing' *Wyoming Law Review* (Volume 9 No. 2). Pages 551–73.

Gevurtz, F. 'Piercing, Piercing: An Attempt to Lift the Veil of Confusion Surrounding the Doctrine of Piercing the Corporate Veil'. Available at http://papers.ssrn.com/sol3/papers.cfm?abstract_id=140280 (last visit 30 May 2013).

Grispo, J. 'Inoponibilidad de la Persona Societaria' *Revista de las Sociedade y Concursos*. Available at http://www.iprofesional.com/adjuntos/documentos/09/0000929.pdf (last visit 30 May 2013).

Hamilton & Macey (2005) 'The doctrine of disregarding a corporation's separate and independent existence is commonly referred to as "piercing the corporate veil"' *American Jurist* (No 18) Pages 55–90.

Hansman & Kraakman (1991) 'Towards Unlimited Liability for Corporate Torts' *Yale Law Journal* (Volume 100).

Bibliography 151

Hargovan, A. & Harris, J. 'Piercing the Corporate Veil in Canada: A Comparative Analysis'. Available at http://papers.ssrn.com/sol3/papers.cfm?abstract_id=980366 (last visit 30 May 2013).

Harris, J. (2005) 'Lifting the Corporate Veil on the Basis of an Implied Agency: A Re-Evaluation of Smith Stone & Kingth' *Company and Securities Law Journal* (Volume 23).

Hartman, P. (1982) 'Piercing the Corporate Veil in Federal Courts: Is Circumvention of a Statute Enough' *Pacific Law Journal* (Volume 13).

Hillman, R. (2005) 'Law, Culture, and the Lore of Partnership: Of Entrepreneurs, Accountability, and the Evolving Status of Partners' *Wake Forest Law Review* (No. 40). Pages 793, 815.

Hincapie, E. and Ramirez, J. (2009) *El Sistema de Valoración de la Prueba Denominado la Sana Critica y su Relación con el Estándar mas allá de la Duda Razonable Aplicado al Proceso Penal Colombiano*. Universidad EAFIT. Available at http://repository.eafit.edu.co/bitstream/10784/436/1/Elizabeth_HincapieHincapie_2009.pdf (last visit 30 May 2013).

Huss, R. (2007) 'Revamping Veil Piercing for all Limited Liability Entities: Forcing the Common Law Doctrine into the Statutory Age' *University of Cincinnati Law Review* (Volume 70). Available at http://papers.ssrn.com/sol3/papers.cfm?abstract_id=1014432 (last visit 30 May 2013).

Inguza, B. (2010) '*La Sentencia Arbitraria por Falta de Motivacion en los Hechos y el Derecho*.' Universidad San Martin de Porres. Available at http://www.uigv.edu.pe/facultades/derecho/documentos/biblioteca/Articulo03_BeatrizFranciskovic.pdf (last visit 30 May 2013).

Ireland, P. (2008) 'Limited Liability, Shareholder Rights and the Problem of Corporate Irresponsibility' *Cambridge Journal of Economics* (Volume 32 No. 6). Pages 4–20.

Iwai, K. The Nature of the Business Corporation: Its Legal Structure and Economic Functions. http://iwai-k.com/NatureofBusinessCorporation.pdf (last visit 30 May 2013).

Jordan, T. (1995) 'History of the bankruptcy law in the United States' *American Bankruptcy Institute Law Review* (Issue 8). Pages 5–30.

Keatin, G. (1996–1997) 'The Idea of Fairness in the Law of Enterprise Liability' *Michigan Law Review* (Volume 95).

Krendl, C. (1978) 'Piercing the Corporate Veil: Focusing the Inquire' *Denver Law Journal* (Volume 55).

Lacke, E. (2002) 'Piercing the limited liability in the non-corporate setting' *Arkansas Law Review* (No. 55). Pages 553–62.

Lahm, R. & Geho, P. (2007) 'Holes in the Corporate Veil: Confronting the Myth of Reduced Liability for Small Businesses and Entrepreneurs Under Corporate Forms' *The Entrepreneurial Executive* (Volume 12).

Leonelli, P, & Others. (2004) '*Abuso de la Personalidad Juridia*' Universidad Catolica de Temuco. Thesis.

Linklater, L. (2006) '"Piercing the corporate veil" – the never ending story?' *Company Lawyer* (Issue 27). Pages 65–6.

Magallon, M. 'Como Crecemos el Mercado de Valores Panameño: Propuestas para atraer mas Inversionistas y Emisores'. Available at http://www.supervalores.gob.pa/educacion-al-inversionista/concursos-de-monografia.html (last visit 4 August 2013).

152   Bibliography

Mansor, H. (2011) 'Solvency, Company Director's Duties and the Problem of Process and Enforcement – A Comparative Study' The University of Waikato. Available at http://researchcommons.waikato.ac.nz/handle/10289/5851 (last visit 30 May 2013).

Martorell, R. (2004) 'La Doctriona de la Infracapitalizacion: Aproximacion Conceptual a la Infracapitalizacion de las Sociedades.' *Revista de Derecho Societario.* Available at www.aedssite.com/revista/pdfs/aeds_revista_7_10.doc (last visit 30 May 2013).

Matheson, J. (2009) 'The Modern Law of Corporate Groups: An Empirical Study of Piercing Corporate Veil in the Parent-Subsidiary context' *North Carolina Law Review* (Volume 87: No. 4). Pages 1091–550.

Mcleod, W. (1991–2) 'Shareholder's Liability and Workers' Rights: Piercing the Corporate Veil Under Federal Labor Law' *Hofstra labor law* (Volume 91).

Mcpherson, R. & Raja, N. (2010) 'Corporate Justice' *Wake Forest Law Review* (Volume 45).

Millon, D. (2006) *Piercing the Corporate Veil, Financial Responsibility and the Limits of Limited Liability.* SSRN eLibrary. Available at http://papers.ssrn.com/sol3/papers.cfm?abstract_id=451520 (last visit 30 May 2013).

Morressey, D. (2007) 'Piercing All the Veils: Applying an Established Doctrine to a new Business Order' *The Journal of Corporation Law* (Volume 32, No. 3). Pages 529–63.

Moore, M (2006) 'A temple built on faulty foundations: piercing the corporate veil and the legacy of *Salomon v Salomon*' *Journal of Business Law.* Pages 180–203.

Morris, A. (2009) *Changing the rules of the games: Offshore financial centers, regulatory competition & financial crisis.* U. Illinois Law & Economics, Research Paper No. LE09–031. Available at SSRN: http://ssrn.com/abstract=1501402 (last visit 2 February 2010).

Myfield, V. (2004) 'Limited liabilities companies in Delaware and Tennessee: A comparative approach' *Tenn J. Bus.* (No. 25). Pages 329–60.

Neuman, T. (2006) La Protección Constitucional de la Empresa: La Individualidad Determinada y la 'Teoria del Levantamiento del Velo in Sentencias Destacadas'. Available at http://www.lyd.com/wp-content/files_mf/sentencias/200610.pdf (last visit 30 May 2013).

Nichols, C. (2008) 'Piercing the Corporate Veil and the Pure Form of the Corporation as Financial Innovation' *Canadian Business Law Journal* (Volume 4, No. 2). Pages 233–68.

Noonan, P. (1990) 'Pierce or not to Pierce? When, is the question. Developing a Federal Rule for Piercing the Corporate Veil Under CERCLA' *Washington University Law Quarterly* (Volume 60).

Olthoff, M. (1995) 'Beyond the Form – Should the Corporate Veil be Pierced?' *UMKC Law Review* (Volume 64).

Oh, P. (2010) 'Veil-Piercing' *Texas Law Review* (Volume 89). Page 81. U. of Pittsburgh Legal Studies Research Paper No. 2010–06. Available at SSRN: http://ssrn.com/abstract=1557972 (last visit 8 August 2013).

Perez, R. (2008) 'Una Vision Dual de la Doctrina del Levantamiento del Velo de la Persona Juridica' *Revista del Instituto de la Judicatura Federal* (No. 25).

Presser, S. (2006) 'The Bolgalusa Explosion, "Single Business Enterprise" "Alter Ego" and other error: Academics, Economics, Democracy and Shareholder Limited Liability. Back Towards a Unitary "Abuse" Theory of Piercing the Corporate Veil' *Northwestern University law Review* (Volume 100).

Bibliography 153

Reali, R. (2003) 'Desconsideração da Personalidade Jurídica no Direito Positivo Brasileiro.' Universidad Regional de Blumenau. Available at http://www.boletimjuridico.com.br/doutrina/texto.asp?id=327 (last visit 30 May 2013).

Reyes, F. (2011) 'A new Policy Agenda for Latin America Company Law: Reshaping the Closely-Held Entity Landscape.' University of Tiburg. .

Sacco, R. (1991) 'Legal Formants: A Dynamic Approach to Comparative Law' *The American Journal of Comparative Law* (Volume 39, Issue 1).

Salinas, F. (2004) 'Que es la Sana Critica? La Valoración Judicial del Dictamen Experto.' Available at http://www.juecesdemocracia.es/publicaciones/revista/articulosinteres/ZUBIRI.pdf (last visit 30 May 2013).

Sandoval, C. (2004) 'Apostillas Sobre la Personalidad Juridica Societaria en el Derecho Argentino.' Available at http://www.emercatoria.edu.co/paginas/volumen3/pdf01/apostillas.pdf (last visit 30 May 2013).

Santas, C. 'El Juez, la Prueba y el Delicado Arte de Juzgar' *Revista de Opinión Juridica*. Available at http://dialnet.unirioja.es/servlet/articulo?codigo=2192720 (last visit 30 May 2013).

Schwartz, J. (2008) 'Piercing the Corporate Veil of an Alien Parent for Jurisdictional Purposes: A Proposal for a Standard that Comports with Due Process' *California Law Review* (Volume 96: No. 3). Pages 731–63.

Sesarego, C. (1999) 'Naturaleza Tridemensional de la Persona Juridica' *Revista de la Facultad de Derecho de la Pontificia Universidad Catolica de Peru.*

Sheikh, S. (2008) 'The Corporation: Villain or Victim' *International Company and Commercial Law Review* (Volume 19: No. 11). Pages 348–54.

Shu, E. (2005) 'Piercing the Veil in California LLCs: Adding Surprise to the Venture Capitalist Equation' *Santa Clara L. Rev.* (No. 45). Pages 1009, 1016.

Siems, M. (2007) 'The end of Comparative Law' *The Journal of Comparative Law* (Issue 2).

Slye, R. (2008) 'Corporate Veil and International Criminal Liability' *Brooklyn Journal of International Law* (Volume 33, No. 3) Pages 955–73.

Smith, G. (2008) 'Piercing the Corporate Veil in Regulated Industries' *Brigham Young University Law Review* (Volume 2008, No. 4). George Mason Law & Economics Research Paper No. 08–08. Available at SSRN: http://ssrn.com/abstract=1090027 (last visit 2 February 2010).

Smith, T. *The Use and Abuse of the Corporate Personality.* Available at http://agora.stanford.edu/agora/libArticles/smith/smith.pdf (last visit 30 May 2013).

Strasser, K. (2005) 'Piercing the Veil in Corporate Groups' *Connecticut Law Review* (Issue 37).

Taruffo, B & others. (2007) 'Consideraciones Sobre la Prueba y Motivación.' Fundacion Coloquio Europeo Juridico. Available at http://www.fcje.org.es/wp-content/uploads/file/Libros_Publicados/Cuadernos_Fundacion/CONSIDERACIONES_____.pdf (last visit 30 May 2013).

Tham, C. (2007) 'Piercing the Corporate Veil: Searching for Appropriate Choice of Law Rules' *Lloyd's Maritime and Commercial Quarterly* (Volume 2007, No. 1). Page 22–43.

Thompson, R. (1991) 'Piercing the Corporate Veil: An Empirical Study' *Cornell Law Review* (Issue 76).

Thompson, R. (2005) 'Piercing the veil: is the Common Law the problem?' *Connecticut Law Review* (Volume 37: No. 3). Pages 619–35.

154 Bibliography

Thompson, R. (1994) 'Unpacking Limited Liability: Direct and Vicarious Liability of Corporate Participants for Torts of the Enterprise' *Okla. L. Rev.* (Volume 47 No. 1). Pages 2–43.

Vallejo, A. (1996) 'La Impugnacion de las sociedades anonimas en Panama' *Asociacion Profesionales de la Nueva Generacion Juridica, Revista de derecho.* (No. 1). Pages 59–74.

Vandervoort, J. (2004–2005) 'Piercing the Veil of Limited Liability companies, the need of better standards' *Depaul Business and Commercial Law Journal* (No. 3). Pages 51–104.

Witting, C. (2000) 'Justifying Liability to Third Parties for Negligent Misstatements' *Oxford J. Legal Studies* (Volume 20). Pages 615–43.

Wulf, O. (2009) *A critical examination of the international regulation of offshore financial centres.* Available at SSRN: http://ssrn.com/abstract=1359127 (last visit 2 February 2010).

Youabian, E. (2004) 'Reverse Piercing of the Corporate Veil: the Implications of Bypassing "Ownership" Interest' *Southwestern University Law Review* (Volume 33: No. 4). Pages 573–96.

Zarate, H. (2013) 'Inoponibilidad de la Persona Juridica. Cuestiones Procesales. Su Aplicacion Jurisprudencial en el Derecho Argentino y Derecho Comparado.' Available at http://www.unne.edu.ar/unnevieja/Web/cyt/cyt/2002/01-Sociales/S-038.pdf (last visit 30 May 2013).

Zorsi, N. 'Abuso de la Personalidad Juridica.' Available at revistas.uexternado.edu.co/index.php/derest/ . . . /743 (last visit 30 May 2013).

Cases

UK cases

Adams v Cape Industries [1990] BCC 786

Antonio Gramsci Shipping Corporation and others v Stepanovs [2011] EWHC 333 (Comm)

Bartholomay Brewing Company v Wyatt (surveyor of taxes). [1890–98] 3 TC 224

Broderip v Salomon [1895] 2 Ch 323,

Chandler v Cape plc [2012] EWCA Civ 525

Costello & Anor v Macdonald & ORS [2011] EWCA Civ 930

Creasy v Breachwood Motors Ltd [1992] BCC 639

Daimler v Continental Tyre & Rubber Co [1916] 2 AC 307

DHN Distributors Ltd v Tower Hamlets London Borough Council [1976] 1 WLR 852

Earp & another v Stevenson & another [2011] EWHC 1436 (Ch) (transcript)

ESS Production Ltd v Sully [2005] EWCA Civ 554

First Independent Factors and Finance Ltd v Churchill and another [2006] EWCA Civ 1623

Gilford Motor Co v Horne [1933] Ch 935

Goldfarb v Higgins & Ors [2010] EWHC 1587 (Ch)

H and others (restraint order: realisable property), Re [1996] 2 BCLC 500

Instant Access Properties Ltd; Secretary of State for Business, Innovation and Skills v Gifford and others, Re [2011] EWHC 3022 (Ch)

Bibliography 155

Jones v Lipman [1962] 1 WLR 832
Lightning Electrical Contractors Ltd, Re [1996] 2 BCLC 302
Liquidator of Idessa (UK) Limited) v John Morrison & Christopher Povey [2011]
  EWHC 804 (Ch)
Morphitis v Bernasconi [2003] EWCA Civ 289
Ord v Belhaven Pubs Ltd [1998] BCLC 447
Patrick & Lyon Ltd, Re [1933] Ch 786
Prest v Petrodel Resources Ltd [2013] UKSC 34
R v Terrence Freeman [2011] EWCA Crim 2534
Revlon Inc v Cripps & Lee Ltd [1980] FSR 85
Ricketts v Ad Valorem Factors Ltd [2003] EWCA Civ 1706
Salomon v Salomon & Co [1897] AC 22
*Sepia Logistics Ltd (formerly known as Double Quick Supplyline Ltd) and another
  v Office of Fair Trading* [2007] CAT 13, (Transcript)
Smith, Stone and Knight Ltd v Birmingham Corporation [1939] BCLC 480
Trustor AB v Smallbone [2001] 2 BCLC 436
VTB Capital plc v Nutritek International Corp and others [2013] UKSC 5
Woolfson v Strathclyde Regional Council 1978 SC (HL) 90

US cases

AMW Materials Testing, Inc. v Town Babylon, 584F. 3d 436, Court of Appeals, 2nd
  Circuit (2009)
Angelo Tomasso, Inc. v Armor Construction & Paving, Inc., 187 Conn. 544, 552,
  447 A.2d 406 (1992)
Bank of the United States v Deveaux, 9 US 61 (1809)
Berkey v Third Ave. Ry. Co., 244 N.Y. 602 (1927)
Complete Transportation, LLC v CPM Colchester, et al LLC., 2013 Conn. Super.
  Lexis 342
Cotton v Gaylord Container Corp, 691 So. 2d 760, 763 (La. Ct. App. 1997)
Fantazia International Corp v CPL Furs New York Inc., 67AD 3d 511, NY Appel-
  late Div., 1st (2009)
Higgings v Smith, 308 US 473, 60 S.Ct. 355, 84 L.Ed. 406 (1940)
Jaclinn Pulman v Alpha Media Publishing Inc, 2013 US Dist. Lexis 50697
Joseph Friend, v Remac America Inc., Civil Action No. 3:12-CV-17 (2013)
Lowendahl v Baltimore & Ohio Railroad, 247 A.D. 144, 287 N.Y.S. 62, aff'd, 272
  N.Y. 360, 6 N.E.2d 56 (1936)
Oil Spill of the Amoco Cadiz off the Coast of France, 35 Fed. R. Evid. Serv. 1204
  (1984)
Roofing Ctr. v On Top Roofing, Inc., 807 S.W.2d 545, 547 (Mo. Ct. App. 1991)
Sea-Land Services v Pepper Source, 941 F.2d 519 (CA7, 1991)
Semmaterials, L.P. v Alliance Asphalt, Inc., 2008 WL 161797 at 4 (D. Idaho 2008)
Trustees of Dartmouth College v Woodward, 17 US 518 (1819)
United States v Bestfoods, 524 US 51 (1998)
United States v Cordova Chem Co. of Michigan, 113 F.3d 572, 582 (1997)
Van Dorn Co. v Future Chem. & Oil Corp., 753 F.2d 565, 569–70 (7th Cir. 1985)
Walkovsky v Carlton, 18 N.Y.2d 414 (1966)

156 Bibliography

Argentina

Sentencia de la Cámara Nacioanl de Comercia, Sala A, de fecha 12 de diciembre de 2006, caso Nueva California, S.A v Legona, S.A (expte núm. 29052)

Sentencia de la Cámara Nacional de Apelaciones en lo Comercial, Sala C, de fecha 15 de agosto de 2006, caso Pardini v Fredel, SRL y otros

Sentencia de la Cámara Nacional de Apelaciones en lo Comerciales Sala B, caso Casademont, Paul A. V. Talentum Think Tank Ltd. y otro fecha 30 de junio de 2005

Sentencia de la Camara Nacional de lo Civil, Sala G, de fecha 11 de Abril de 1986 del Derecho Commercial y de las Obligaciones

Sentencia de la Corte Suprema de Justicia de la Nacion, de fecha 4 de septiembre de 1973. case Cia. Swift de la Plata Sa S/ Quiebra C/ Deltec Arg. Y Deltec Internacional

Sentencia de la sala primera de la corte nacional de trabajo de fecha 29 de febrero de 2000, caso "Puente, Graciela A. y otros c. djivelekian, Obannes y otros" (DT, 2000-B, 1594)

Sentencia de la Sala Segunda de la Corte Nacional de Trabajo de 9 de Mayo de 1973 dictada en el caso Aybar, Ruben E. y otros v Pizzeria Viturro SRL y otros

Sentencia de la Sala Segunda de la Corte Nacional de Trabajo, de fecha 30 de Abril de 2004 dictada en el caso "Rodriguez, Carmen Silvina contra Creaciones Manaly y otros"

Simancas, Maria Angelica C/ Crosby, Ronald S/ Sum.,Ref. Norm.: L. 19550: 54–22/12/1997

Colombia

Corte Constitucional, Sentencia C-510/97.

Corte Constitucional, Sentencia SU-1023, 26 de septiembre de 2001.

Corte Constitucional, Sentencia SU-636, 31 de julio de 2003.

Corte Constitucional, Sentencia T-014, 21 de enero de 1999

Corte Constitutional. Sentencia C-865 del 7 de septiembre de 2004

Corte Suprema de Justicia, Sala Penal, auto 7183 del 20 de enero de 1993

Legislation

UK

Companies Act 2006

Income and Corporation Taxes Act 1988

Insolvency Rules 1986

US

Comprehensive Environmental Response, Compensation, and Liability Act (CERCLA) of 1980, 42 USC § 9601 et seq.

Sarbanes–Oxley Act of 2002 (Pub.L. 107–204, 116 Stat. 745, enacted 30 July 2002)

Worker Adjustment and Retraining Notification Act (WARN Act) of 1988 USC §§ 2101–2109 (2000)

Bibliography 157

Argentina

Ley de Sociedades Comerciales de 1972 (Ley No. 19,550)

Colombia

Constitución Politica de Colombia 1991
Estatuto anticorrupcion (Ley 190 de 1995)
Ley 1116 de 2006, Por la cual se establece el Régimen de Insolvencia Empresarial en la República de Colombia y se dictan otras disposiciones.
Ley 222 de 1995, Por la cual se modifica el Libro II del Código de Comercio, se expide un nuevo régimen de procesos concursales y se dictan otras disposiciones.
Ley de sociedades por acciones Simplificadas (Ley 1258 de 2008)

Brazil

Código Civil Brasileiro LEI No. 10.406, de 10 de Janeiro de 2002.
Constituição Federal de 1988
Lei No. 4.137 de setembro de (1962). Regula a repressão ao abuso do Poder Econômico
Lei No. 8.078 de 11 de septembre de 1990. Dispõe sobre a proteção do consumidor e dá outras providências
Lei No. 8.884 de 11 de junho de 1994. (Lei de Defesa da Concorrência), que transforma o Conselho Administrativo de Defesa Econômica (CADE)
Lei No. 9.605 de 12 de fevereiro de 1998 Dispõe sobre as sanções penais e administrativas derivadas de condutas e atividades lesivas ao meio ambiente, e dá outras providências.

Panama

Código Civil de la Republica de Panama. the Ley N° 2 de 22 de agosto de 1916. Publicada en la Gaceta Oficial N° 2.404 de 22 de agosto de 1916
Código de Comercio de Panama. Ley 2 del 22 de agosto de 1916, publicada en la Gazeta Oficial 2418 de 7 de septiembre de 1916
Codigo de Trabajo de Panama Decreto de Gabinet 252(Publicado por la Series Legislativa. 1971- Pan. 1) Modificado por la Ley N° 44 de agosto de 1995)
Código Procesal Penal de Panamá. Asamblea Nacional. República de Panamá
Decreto de Gabinete 247 del de16 de Julio de 1970, por el cual se crea la Comision Nacional de Valores, se Reglamenta la Venta de Acciones en la Republica de Panama y se Adoptan Medidas para los Accionistas Minoritarios
Decreto Ley 1 de 8 de Julio de 1999 (Published in the Gazeta Oficial 23,837 del 10 de Julio de 1999
Ley 32 de 26 de febrero sobre Sociedades Anonimas. Publicada en la Gazeta Oficial 5067 de 16 de marzo de 1927
Ley 4 de 9 de enero 2009 sobre Sociedades de Responsabilidad Limitada. Publicada en Gazeta Oficial 26202-A
Ley de Contratación Pública de 1995

Index

abuse of company name 43–5
abuso del derecho 87–8
action pauliana 88
Adam v Cape Industries 30–8; agency
argument 33–4; corporate veil
point 32–3; facts 31–2; piercing of
corporate veil after 35–8; reception
of decision 34–5; sham argument
32–3; single economic unit 33
agency 26–8, 62
alter ego doctrine 52–6
Argentina 116–26; areas of law where
corporate veil ignored 122; backdoor
approach 141; bankruptcy approach
122–3; deviation from corporate
goals 117–18; existence of illegal act
120; family law 124; *Inoponibilidad
de la Persona Juridica* 116–21;
labour law 123–4; Law 22.903
116; legal concepts and principles
136; *Ley de Sociedas Mercantiles de
1972* 118; parameter of statutory
exception 119–20; personalized
version of US doctrine 119; rationale
to pierce corporate veil 130–1;
shareholders 121; *Swift-Deltec* case
122–3; tax law 124–5; third parties
121; *ultra vires* 121–2; wrongdoers
behind corporate entity 118–19

backdoor approach 75–6, 140–1; 143;
Argentina 141; England 140–1
Brazil 107–15; *abuso del derecho*
113–14; Civil Code 113–14; labour
law 107, 108–13; legal concepts
and principles 137; *Lei No 8.078 de
11 de septembro de 1990* 110–11;
*Lei No 8.884 de 11 de junho de
1994* 111–12; *Lei No 9.605 de

12 de fevereiro de 1998 112–13;
origins of exception to corporate
personality 108–13; pro-social policy
107, 108–13; public interest 109;
rationale to pierce corporate veil 132;
sledgehammer approach 140
business associations 6

capitalist policy 11
civil law tradition 79–88
Colombia 96–106; *abusa del derecho*
97, 103; constitution 103–5;
corporate groups 100–1; *Corte
Constitucional* 104–5; *empresa
unipersonal* 98–9; *Estatuto
Anticorrupcion* 97, 98; foundation
of approach to corporate personality
issues 102–3; *fraude a la ley* 103;
legal concepts and principles 136–7;
Ley 190 de 1995 97–8; Ley 222 de
1995 98–101; Ley 1258 de 2008
101–2; methodology 127–8; money
laundering 98; one-man company
98–9; organised crime 98; rationale to
pierce corporate vail 131; *Sentencia
C-865 de 2004* 104–5; sledgehammer
approach 139–40; *sociedad
anonima* 96; *sociedad por acciones
simplificadas* 96, 97, 101–2; *sociedad
unipersonal* 96, 97; statutory
approach to corporate entity issues
97–102; Supreme Court of Justice 98
colonial companies 4–5
comparative study 127–41
contract and tort cases 59–61
corporate groups 15–19; rationale to
pierce corporate veil 17–18; single
economic unit 18–19
corporate personality: development 1–2

Index 159

England: backdoor approach 140–1; legal concepts and principles 134–5; rationale to pierce corporate veil 129–30
environmental law 68–9

Franco-Hispanic civil law 79–88
fraud, concept of 69–73; importance of concept 143
fraude a la ley 87
fraudulent trading 39–41

instrumentality 52–4, 56–8

joint stock corporation 5–6
Justinian *Corpus Juris Civilis* 80

labour law 67–8
Latin America 79–88; contrast between common law and civil law tradition 82–8; corporate personality in civil law tradition 81–2; creativity of jurisdictions 142; critical thinking, role of 85–6; Franco-Hispanic civil law, and 79–88; influence of legal tradition over piercing of corporate veil 82–8; judicial creativity, role of 85–6; legal concepts and principles, role of 87–8, 135–6; ; sources of law 84–5
legal concepts and principles 134–9; Argentina 136; Brazil 137; Colombia 136–7; comparison 138–9; England 134–5; Latin America 135–6; Mexico 137–8; United States 134
legal personality x

mechanisms to deal with corporate personality 139–41
Mexico 89–95; control 92–3; control over the corporate entity 91; early statutory exceptions to corporate entity 91–2; effects of *la desestimacion de la persona juridical societaria* 94–5; fraudulent intention 92–3; judiciary 89; la develacion de la sociedad anonima 89–91; *ley de la desestimacion de la persona juridica societaria* 92–5; objective element 93; publicly held companies 90–1;rationale to pierce corporate veil 132–3; resulting element 93;

sledgehammer approach 140; subjective element 93

Napoleonic Civil Code 81
negligence, concept of 69–73

Ordenanzas de Bilbao 80

phoenix companies 43–5
piercing corporate veil: Anglo-American context 20–78; backdoor approach 75–6; comparative study x–xiii; concept 2–3; corporate groups, and 15–19; creation of metaphor x; derivations 13–19; disregard of legal entity in context of English statutory law 38–9; England 21–48; general aspects 1–19; Latin American countries xi; origins of doctrine 4–8; private law 8–11; public law 8–11; rationale 2–3; regulation and its critics 14–15; reverse 14–15; sledgehammer approach 75–6; standard 7; sham exception 24–6; terminology 7–8; US 48–78 *see also* US doctrine of piercing corporate veil; US and England compared 74–6; US method x–xi
private law 8–11
pro-social policy 11
public companies 12–13
public law 8–11

rationale to pierce corporate veil 128–33; Argentina 130–1; Brazil 132; Colombia 131; comparison 133; England 129–30; Mexico 132–3; US 129
Roman civil law 80

Saloma, Bruno M 108
Salomon case 21–4; decision 22–3; effects 23–4; facts 21–2
sham, concept of 24–6
Siete Partidas 80
simulacion 87
single economic unit or enterprise liability 62–4
sledgehammer approach 75–6, 139–40, 143; Brazil 140; Colombia 139–40; Mexico 140; US 139
sources of law 84–5

160   *Index*

tax law 66–7; corporate entity, and 45–7

United States: core doctrine 142; legal concepts and principles 134–9; rationale to pierce corporate veil 129; sledgehammer approach 139

US doctrine of piercing corporate veil 48–78; agency 62; agency and enterprise liability 61–6; alter ego doctrine 52–6; American statutory law, and 66; causation 53–4; CERCLA 51–2; conflict of law 51; contract and tort cases 59–61; current position of American courts 64–6; Delaware 49; environmental law 68–9; excessive control/lack of separate existence 52; federal policies 50–1; fraud, concept of 69–73; fraud and inequitable conduct 52–3; instrumentality 52–4, 56–8; labour law 67–8; negligence, concept of 69–73; New York 49–50; reality of 58; single economic unit or enterprise liability 62–4; state and federal law 49–52; tax law 66–7

Wormzer, Maurize 48–9
wrongful trading 41–2